Evidence

CONSULTANT EDITOR: LORD TEMPLEMAN

OLD BAILEY PRESS

OLD BAILEY PRESS
200 Greyhound Road, London W14 9RY

1st edition 1997
Reprinted 1999

© Old Bailey Press Ltd 1997

Previous editions published under The HLT Group Ltd.

ISBN 1 85836 239 3

British Library Cataloguing-in-Publication.

A CIP Catalogue record for this book is available from the British Library.

Printed and bound in Great Britain.

Contents

Acknowledgement

Some questions used are taken or adapted from past University of London LLB (External) Degree examination papers and our thanks are extended to the University of London for their kind permission to use and publish the questions.

Caveat

The answers given are not approved or sanctioned by the University of London and are entirely our responsibility.

They are not intended as 'Model Answers', but rather as Suggested Solutions.

The answers have two fundamental purposes, namely:

a)   To provide a detailed example of a suggested solution to an examination question, and

b)   To assist students with their research into the subject and to further their understanding and appreciation of the subject of Laws.

Introduction

This Revision WorkBook has been designed specifically for those studying Evidence to undergraduate level. Its coverage is not confined to any one syllabus, but embraces all the major evidence topics to be found in university or polytechnic examinations, and will be of utility to students preparing for Bar examinations as the book covers that syllabus also.

However, since it is anticipated that many students will be intending to sit the University of London LLB external examinations, the questions used are primarily from past evidence papers from that course. Each chapter contains in its first few pages, brief notes explaining the scope and overall content of the topic covered in that chapter. There follows, in each case, a list of key points which will assist the student in studying and memorising essential material with which the student should be familiar in order to fully understand the topic.

Additionally in each chapter there will be a question analysis which will list and compare past examination questions on similar topics in evidence papers. The purpose of such a question analysis is to give an appreciation of the potential range of questions possible, and some idea of variations in wording, different formats in questions and alternative modes of combining different issues in one question.

Each chapter will end with several typical examination questions, together with skeleton solutions and suggested solutions. Wherever possible, the questions are drawn from University of London external evidence papers. However it is inevitable that, in compiling a list of questions by topic order rather than chronologically, not only do the same questions crop up over and over again in different guises, but there are gaps where questions have never been set at all. Where a topic has never been covered in an examination question, a specimen question will have been written as an example, together with skeleton answer and suggested solution.

Undoubtedly, the main feature of this Revision WorkBook is the inclusion of as many past examination questions as possible. While the use of past questions as a revision aid is certainly not new, it is hoped that the combination of actual past questions and specially written questions, where there are gaps in examination coverage, will be of assistance to students in achieving a thorough and systematic revision of the subject.

Careful use of the Revision WorkBook should enhance the student's understanding of Evidence and, hopefully, enable him to deal with as wide a range of subject matter as anyone might find in an Evidence law examination, while at the same time allowing him to practise examination techniques while working through the book.

In this new edition the final chapter contains the complete June 1996 University of London LLB (External) Evidence question paper, followed by suggested solutions to each question. Thus the student will have the opportunity to review a recent examination paper in its entirety, and can, if desired, use this chapter as a mock examination – referring to the suggested solutions only after first having attempted questions.

Studying Evidence

The study of Evidence, whether as a first degree subject or for Bar examinations, requires an awareness that topics cannot be learned in isolation. Evidence is very closely integrated, in that very few topics can be compartmentalised; in most instances material studied at any one point will impinge upon and relate to materials studied at other points. Whatever the approach taken by lecturers, or authors of textbooks, on Evidence, there will invariably be cross-referencing.

In the early stages the subject will appear disjointed and difficult to rationalise and therefore understand; only towards the end of a course of study of the subject will the pieces of the jigsaw start to interlock. A recommended approach, therefore, is to read, several times, an introductory book on Evidence *before* beginning study of the subject in depth – thus acquiring a somewhat superficial but usefully coherent and cohesive awareness which will be invaluable when examining specific areas and relating them to others. The same introductory book can also be used to good effect as part of the revision process, to reinforce the 'lateral thinking' needed in Evidence.

Evidence is never taught as a first year undergraduate subject. Whether studying for a law degree or Bar examinations, an Evidence student must have some knowledge of law, especially Criminal Law, and of basic procedure (both criminal and civil) to excel in this adjectival subject. However, in Evidence examinations it is not detailed knowledge of substantive law which is required, but merely a very basic knowledge of substantive law and procedure, and detailed knowledge of the evidentiary issues involved. Evidence 'problem questions' may appear to require the examinees to deal with Criminal, Company, Tort, Contract Law etc, but the examiner is testing knowledge of Evidence – using as a realistic vehicle some criminal or other scenario.

In studying Evidence, therefore, the student must be aware of the integrated nature of the subject, be basically conversant with principles of substantive law; and be wary of concentrating on a few topics – as they might well be covered in only one or two examination questions!

Revision and Examination Technique

(A)   REVISION TECHNIQUE

Planning a revision timetable

In planning your revision timetable make sure you don't finish the syllabus too early. You should avoid leaving revision so late that you have to 'cram' – but constant revision of the same topic leads to stagnation.

Plan ahead, however, and try to make your plans increasingly detailed as you approach the examination date.

Allocate enough time for each topic to be studied. But note that it is better to devise a realistic timetable, to which you have a reasonable chance of keeping, rather than a wildly optimistic schedule which you will probably abandon at the first opportunity!

The syllabus and its topics

One of your first tasks when you began your course was to ensure that you thoroughly understood your syllabus. Check now to see if you can write down the topics it comprises from memory. You will see that the chapters of this WorkBook are each devoted to a syllabus topic. This will help you decide which are the key chapters relative to your revision programme. Though you should allow some time for glancing through the other chapters.

The topic and its key points

Again working from memory, analyse what you consider to be the key points of any topic that you have selected for particular revision. Seeing what you can recall, unaided, will help you to understand and firmly memorise the concepts involved.

Using the WorkBook

Relevant questions are provided for each topic in this book. Naturally, as typical examples of examination questions, they do not normally relate to one topic only. But the questions in each chapter will relate to the subject matter of the chapter to a degree. You can choose your method of consulting the questions and solutions, but here are some suggestions (strategies 1-3). Each of them pre-supposes that you have read through the author's notes on key points and question analysis, and any other preliminary matter, at the beginning of the chapter. Once again, you now need to practise working from *memory*, for that is the challenge you are preparing yourself for. As a rule of procedure constantly test yourself once revision starts, both orally and in writing.

Strategy 1

Strategy 1 is planned for the purpose of *quick revision*. First read your chosen question carefully and then jot down in abbreviated notes what you consider to be the main points at issue. Similarly, note the cases and statutes that occur to you as being relevant for citation purposes. Allow yourself sufficient time to cover what you feel to be relevant. Then study the author's *skeleton solution* and skim-read the *suggested solution* to see how they compare with your notes. When comparing consider carefully what the author has included (and concluded) and see whether that agrees with what you have written. Consider the points of variation also. Have you recognised the key issues? How relevant have you been? It is possible, of course, that you have referred to a recent case that is relevant, but which had not been reported when the WorkBook was prepared.

Strategy 2

Strategy 2 requires a nucleus of *three hours* in which to practise writing a set of examination answers in a limited time-span.

Select a number of questions (as many as are normally set in your subject in the examination you are studying for), each from a different chapter in the WorkBook, without consulting the solutions. Find a place to write where you will not be disturbed and try to arrange not to be interrupted for three hours. Write your solutions in the time allowed, noting any time needed to make up if you *are* interrupted.

After a rest, compare your answers with the *suggested solutions* in the WorkBook. There will be considerable variation in style, of course, but the bare facts should not be too dissimilar. Evaluate your answer critically. Be 'searching', but develop a positive approach to deciding how you would tackle each question on another occasion.

Strategy 3

You are unlikely to be able to do more than one three hour examination, but occasionally set yourself a single question. Vary the 'time allowed' by imagining it to be one of the questions that you must answer in three hours and allow yourself a limited preparation and writing time. Try one question that you feel to be difficult and an easier question on another occasion, for example.

Mis–use of suggested solutions

Don't try to learn by rote. In particular, don't try to reproduce the suggested solutions by heart. Learn to express the basic concepts in your own words.

Keeping up-to-date

Keep up-to-date. While examiners do not require familiarity with changes in the law during the three months prior to the examination, it obviously creates a good impression if you can show you are acquainted with any recent changes. Make a habit of looking through one of the leading journals – Modern Law Review, Law Quarterly Review or the New Law Journal, for example – and cumulative indices to law reports, such as the All England Law Reports or Weekly Law Reports, or indeed the daily law reports in The Times. The Law Society's Gazette and the Legal Executive Journal are helpful sources, plus any specialist journal(s) for the subject you are studying. In particular, for Evidence, the *Criminal Law Review* is the best source of the most recent cases, most of which will be supplied with an excellent summary.

(B)   EXAMINATION SKILLS

Examiners are human too!

The process of answering an examination question involves a communication between you and the person who set it. If you were speaking face to face with the person, you would choose your verbal points and arguments carefully in your reply. When writing, it is all too easy to forget the human being who is awaiting the reply and simply write out what one knows in the area of the subject! Bear in mind it is a person whose question you are responding to, throughout your essay. This will help you to avoid being irrelevant or long-winded.

The essay question

The essay-type of question may be either largely factual, in asking you to explain the meaning of a certain doctrine or principle, or it may ask you to discuss a certain proposition, usually derived from a quotation. In either case, the approach to the answer is the same. A clear programme must be devised to give the examiner the meaning or significance of the doctrine, principle or proposition and its origin in common law, equity or statute, and cases which illustrate its application to the branch of law concerned. Essay questions are a good way to obtain marks if you have thought carefully about a topic since it is up to you to impose the structure (unlike problem questions where the problem imposes its own structure). You are then free to *speculate* and show imagination.

The problem question

The problem-type question requires a slightly different approach. You may well be asked to advise a client or merely discuss the problems raised in the question. In either case, the most important factor is to take great care in reading the question. By its nature, the question will be longer than the essay-type question and you will have a number of facts to digest. Time spent in analysing the question may well save time later, when you are endeavouring to impress on the examiner the considerable extent of your basic legal knowledge. The quantity of knowledge is itself a trap and you *must* always keep within the boundaries of the question in hand. It is very tempting to show the examiner the extent of your knowledge of your subject, but if this is outside the question, it is time lost and no marks earned. It it inevitable that some areas which you have studied and revised will not be the subject of questions, but under no circumstances attempt to adapt a question to a stronger area of knowledge at the expense of relevance.

When you are satisfied that you have grasped the full significance of the problem-type question, set out the fundamental principles involved. You may well be asked to advise one party, but there is no reason why you should not introduce your answer by:

'I would advise A on the following matters ...'

and then continue the answer in a normal impersonal form. This is a much better technique than answering the question as an imaginary conversation.

You will then go on to identify the fundamental problem, or problems posed by the question. This should be followed by a consideration of the law which is relevant to the problem. The source of the law, together with the cases which will be of assistance in solving the problem, must then be considered in detail.

Very good problem questions are quite likely to have alternative answers, and in advising A you should be aware that alternative arguments may be available. Each stage of your answer, in this case, will be based on the argument or arguments considered in the previous stage, forming a conditional sequence. In many cases the facts given in the question will be inherently ambiguous. Don't ignore the problem, and clearly and decisively *disambiguate* the facts showing the legal consequences of each possibility. It is not as difficult as it sounds since usually there are only two possibilities, one of which has no legal consequences at all.

If, however, you only identify one fundamental problem, do not waste time worrying that you cannot think of an alternative – there may very well be only that one answer.

The examiner will then wish to see how you use your legal knowledge to formulate a case and how you apply that formula to the problem which is the subject of the question. It is this positive approach which can make answering a problem question a high mark earner for the student who has fully understood the question and clearly argued his case on the established law.

Examination checklist

1   Read the instructions at the head of the examination carefully. While last-minute changes are unlikely – such as the introduction of a compulsory question or an increase in the number of questions asked – it has been known to happen.

2   Read the questions carefully. Analyse problem questions – work out what the examiner wants.

3   Plan your answer before you start to write.

4   Check that you understand the rubric *before* you start to write. Do not 'discuss', for example, if you are specifically asked to 'compare and contrast'.

5   Answer the correct number of questions. If you fail to answer one out of four questions set you lose 25 per cent of your marks!

Style and structure

Try to be clear and concise. Basically this amounts to using paragraphs to denote the sections of your essay, and writing simple, straightforward sentences as much as possible. The sentence you have just read has 22 words – when a sentence reaches 50 words it becomes difficult for a reader to follow.

Do not be inhibited by the word 'structure' (traditionally defined as giving an essay a beginning, a middle and an end). A good structure will be the natural consequence of setting out your arguments and the supporting evidence in a logical order. Set the scene briefly in your opening paragraph – regard it as your 'impact paragraph'. Provide a clear conclusion in your final paragraph.

Table of Cases

Table of Statutes

1 Introduction to Evidence

1.1 General

1.2 Types of evidence

1.3 Cogency of evidence

1.1 General

Rules of evidence are mainly exclusionary, because many of them developed at a time when trial by jury was the rule rather than the exception, and it was thought that jurors would be unduly influenced by knowledge of previous convictions of the accused; by hearsay evidence; by character evidence; by opinion evidence of a non-expert etc. Despite many recent reforms, it is still generally true to state that the courts in England are not apprised of all the facts, not even of all the relevant facts, but only of those facts which the laws of evidence allow – and even some of these facts may be excluded in the discretion of the judge.

To be capable of admissibility, evidence must be *legally* relevant, ie must have reached a sufficiently high point on the scale of relevance. For example, if D is charged with theft, it is not legally relevant (although it may be logically relevant) that he has several previous convictions for theft. It *is* legally relevant that he was seen in the store at the time and that he had the goods – alleged by the prosecution to have been stolen by him – in his possession.

However, although his being seen in the store is legally relevant, the fact of his being seen is not necessarily admissible – eg the prosecution may wish to inform the court that a customer, or a store detective, not available to give evidence at the trial, saw D in the store. Such evidence would be *hearsay* if it is to be related by a person other than said customer or store detective, and may therefore not be admissible. Thus, the hearsay rule may exclude relevant evidence. Further, relevant evidence may be excluded by other exclusionary rules, such as that giving protection against a person's incriminating himself (self-incrimination privilege); evidence may be in a communication between a person and his legal adviser and therefore protected by legal professional privilege; evidence may be excluded as a matter of public policy on the grounds that disclosure would be injurious to state security or some other protected public interest (public interest immunity). Therefore, it is vital that at the outset one realises that in evidence relevance and admissibility are *not synonymous*. To be admitted in court, evidence *must* be legally relevant – but legally relevant evidence will not necessarily be admitted in court, because of one or more of the exclusionary rules which comprise most of the law of evidence.

1.2 Types of evidence

Admissible evidence may take one of several forms, for example:

a) *Testimony*

This is the oral evidence of a witness. It may be evidence of what that witness perceived, ie 'direct testimony', or alternatively it may be what another person perceived and the witness is reporting that to the court as evidence of its truth, ie 'hearsay'. In civil trials hearsay is now generally admissible, since the passing of the Civil Evidence Act 1968; in criminal trials hearsay is inadmissible unless it falls into one of the recognised categories of admissible hearsay, eg *res gestae* statements, freely made confessions, dying declarations.

b) *Documentary evidence*

Here, a document is adduced in evidence. For the purposes of evidence, there is no all embracing definition of 'document'. It includes not only a document in writing but also photographs, maps, plans, drawings, blue-prints, cassettes, micro-dots etc. The document may be admitted because its content, or its existence, is relevant. As regards content of a document, the 'best evidence' rule would dictate production of the original, but increasingly the law of evidence provides for admissibility of copies of documents. The original document is 'primary' evidence, the copy is 'secondary' evidence.

c) *Real evidence*

Real evidence comprises objects produced for inspection by the court in order that the court may draw inferences from the condition, existence etc of the object. Real evidence would therefore include a document produced purely as evidence of its condition or existence rather than of its contents. In the case of both documentary and real evidence there must be some testimony as to, for example, the authenticity of the documents, the location where the real evidence was discovered, otherwise the documentary or real evidence will have little if any cogency in itself.

d) *Circumstantial evidence*

Circumstantial evidence may be contrasted with 'direct' evidence, in that the latter relates to some fact in issue of which the witness has 'direct' or first-hand knowledge, whereas the former comprises evidence of facts from which an inference may, or may not, be drawn as to the fact in issue. For example, in a murder trial a witness may give testimony which is 'direct' evidence of his seeing the accused stab the victim, or may give circumstantial evidence of the accused's motive, eg that on several occasions he had heard the accused voice his violent disposition toward, hatred of, and/or intention to kill the victim. Circumstantial evidence may be in the form of testimony, documentary or real evidence; examples are evidence of motive, opportunity, identity (eg finger prints of the accused at scene of crime).

1.3 Cogency of evidence

Evidence may be admissible, but mere admissibility does not further the cause of the party adducing the evidence. What must be assessed, and what will be crucial in deciding the case, is the cogency, ie the probative value, or the weight of the admissible evidence. Cogency is a matter of degree, from technical admissibility with little or no probative value at one end of the spectrum to cogency so strong as to be probative to the extent of being conclusive at the other end.

Admissibility of evidence is a question of law to be determined by the judge, often in a *voir dire* ('trial within a trial') in the absence of the jury. Cogency of such admissible evidence is a question of fact, to be determined by the jury; for example, in a criminal trial the jury will evaluate the cogency of prosecution and defence evidence which they have been allowed to hear (ie which the judge has ruled admissible) in deciding whether the prosecution has proved the guilt of the accused beyond reasonable doubt.

However, in deciding on the admissibility of an item of evidence, the judge will be influenced by the degree of relevance of that evidence and thus to some extent by its cogency. Also a judge may withdraw an issue from the jury where a party has failed to discharge an evidential burden, eg if the defence in a criminal trial attempts to run a defence of sane automatism in an effort to secure an acquittal, the judge will withdraw that defence from the jury unless the defence adduce sufficient evidence in support of the alleged automatism. So, although the jury, as the tribunal of fact, is not concerned with the admissibility of evidence, the judge, when deciding the legal question of admissibility, cannot divorce this completely from the cogency, or weight, of the evidence under scrutiny.

Finally, to add to the uncertainty in evidence, the judge in a criminal trial has a discretion to exclude admissible evidence where its probative value is outweighed by its prejudicial effect on the defence; here again the judge is concerned with the cogency of evidence. This overriding discretion is, apparently, in addition to the statutory discretion given by s78, Police and Criminal Evidence Act 1984, to exclude 'unfair evidence'.

All these concepts, all these issues, will be examined in depth in the ensuing chapters, and constitute the major part of the law of evidence.

2 Evidence Illegally or Unfairly Obtained

2.1   Introduction

2.2   Key points

2.3   Recent cases

2.4   Analysis of questions

2.5   Questions

2.1 Introduction

If evidence has been obtained by some criminal or tortious or other unlawful act (eg in breach of contract) or by some unfair or improper means which is not in breach of the law (eg trickery, bribery), then at common law such evidence would usually be admissible if it was relevant to the facts in issue before the court.

2.2 Key points

The first question to be asked is whether the evidence is admissible as a matter of *law*; if that is answered in the affirmative, the question is then whether the judge ought, in his discretion, to exclude it.

a) *Admissibility in law*

The common law position prevails, ie 'It matters not how you get it; if you steal it even, it would be admissible in evidence' (per Crompton J in *R* v *Leatham* (1861) 8 Cox CC 498, 501). There are two exceptions to this:

i)   If evidence consists of a confession which has been obtained in consequence of some inducement, or by oppression (s76 Police and Criminal Evidence Act 1984)

ii) If the evidence of one party is filched in court by the other party – as this would probably amount to a contempt of court (*ITC Film Distributors* v *Video Exchange* [1982] Ch 431).

b) *Discretion to exclude*

i)   Civil cases

There is a paucity of authority, but it would seem that in civil cases there is no discretion to exclude admissible evidence (*Helliwell* v *Piggott-Sims* [1980] FSR 582).

ii) Criminal cases

• Common law discretion

In criminal cases there has been evidence of ambivalence by the courts in the exercise, and control, of discretion to exclude. The conflict is between admitting all relevant, admissible evidence to ensure that those who are guilty of crime are convicted, and the view that to admit such improperly obtained evidence condones and even encourages the improprieties of (usually) the police. This conflict was discussed at length in the House of Lords in *R* v *Sang* [1980] AC 402, but there was still a substantial amount of uncertainty. *R* v *Sang* was authority for the overriding discretion to exclude evidence which is more prejudicial than probative, but apart from that denied the existence of any exclusionary discretion (confessions apart) unless, apparently, the evidence was obtained by oppression, or improperly obtained from the suspect after the commission of the offence.

This uncertainty remained until an attempt was made by Parliament to clarify matters.

- Statutory discretion

Section 78(1) Police and Criminal Evidence Act 1984 provides:

'In any proceedings the court may refuse to allow evidence on which the prosecution proposes to rely to be given if it appears to the court that, having regard to all the circumstances, including the circumstances in which the evidence was obtained, the admission of the evidence would have such an adverse effect on the fairness of the proceedings that the court ought not to admit it.'

It has been held that s78 applies to all evidence including evidence of identification (*R* v *Quinn* [1990] Crim LR 581) and confessions (*R* v *Mason* [1987] 3 All ER 481). The courts have been much more prepared to exercise their exclusionary discretion since s78 became operative in 1986, and have given due weight to breaches by the police of the Codes of Practice issued under s66 of the Act.

Although the discretion to exclude is being more widely exercised, it is not clear for what reason evidence is being excluded under s78 – some cases imply that the rationale is that of discouraging police misconduct (eg *R* v *Mason*, above; *Matto* v *Crown Court at Wolverhampton* [1987] RTR 337; *R* v *Alladice* [1987] NLJR 141), others that it is protecting the civil rights of the suspect in police custody (eg *R* v *Samuel* [1988] 2 WLR 920; *R* v *Smurthwaite* [1994] Crim LR 53). There is, however, some doubt whether s78 affects the so-called defence of entrapment. In *R* v *Sang*, the House of Lords said entrapment is no defence, and that cannot be changed by any evidential discretion. But the case of *Gill and Ranuana* [1989] Crim LR 358 suggests otherwise (see suggested solution to Question 1, below).

If the exclusion is to discipline the police, then only where they wilfully abuse their powers should the discretion be exercised; if the exclusion is to protect the suspects' rights then the *bona fides* of the police are irrelevant. In the case of *R* v *Quinn* [1990] Crim LR 581, the cases of *Walsh* [1989] Crim LR 822 and *Keenan* [1989] Crim LR 720 were approved to suggest that where there is a significant and substantial breach of a Code of Practice, this could result in the exclusion of the evidence obtained, even in absence of bad faith. Also see *R* v *Okafor* [1994] Crim LR 221 and *R* v *Christou and Wright* (1992) 95 Cr App R 264.

- While it is clear that a judge in a criminal trial has a discretion to refuse to admit a piece of otherwise relevant and admissible evidence on which the prosecution intends to rely if he concludes that its prejudicial effect outweighs its probative value. *Lobban* v *R* [1995] 1 WLR 877 established that a judge has no discretion on that basis to exclude at the request of one co-defendant, in a joint trial, evidence tendered by another co-defendant, or to edit a co-defendant's statement on which the co-defendant wanted to rely. A defendant has an absolute right, subject to considerations of relevance, to present his case asserting his innocence as he thinks fit. The court recognised that in joint trials there is a real risk of prejudice to co-defendants where evidence is admitted which is admissible against one defendant but not against the others, and suggested that a possible remedy in such situations was for an application to be made for separate trials. If separate trials are not ordered then it is crucial that the trial judge gives the jury a direction in the terms given on this occasion.

• The accused's right to silence was radically altered by the Criminal Justice and Public Order Act (CJPOA) 1994. Basically, s34 says that from the time the accused is under caution until he is charged failure to answer a question which he reasonably could have been expected to answer is evidence from which a court may draw appropriate conclusions. Section 35 says the same, but the period relates to the court stage and the failure to give evidence there may lead to the court drawing appropriate conclusions. A Practice Direction has been given on the Crown Court satisfying itself that a defendant was aware of the opportunity to give evidence and the effect of his deciding not to do so: *Practice Direction (Crown Court: Evidence: Advice to Defendant)* [1995] 2 All ER 499. In the subsequent case of *R* v *Cowan* [1995] 4 All ER 939, the Court of Appeal highlighted five essential elements of a trial judge's direction to a jury under s35 CJPOA 1994. The trial judge must make it clear to the jury that:

1. the burden of proof remained on the prosecution throughout and what the required standard was;

2. the defendant was entitled to remain silent;

3. an inference from a failure to give evidence could not on its own prove guilt;

4. the jury had to be satisfied that the prosecution had established a case to answer before drawing any inferences from silence;

5. if the jury concluded that the silence could only sensibly be attributed to the defendant having no answer or none that would stand up to cross-examination, they could draw an adverse inference.

Lord Taylor CJ stressed that the right to silence had not been abolished, and that no one could be convicted solely because of their silence. It was also emphasised that s35 applied to all cases and was not (as contended by the defence) restricted to exceptional ones, and that the Court of Appeal would not lightly interfere with a trial judge's exercise of discretion in directing a jury on the issue, provided that the correct formula was followed.

2.3 Recent cases

Lobban v *R* [1995] 1 WLR 877

Practice Direction (Crown Court: Evidence: Advice to Defendant) [1995] 2 All ER 499

R v *Cowan* [1995] 4 All ER 939

2.4 Analysis of questions

Since s78 Police and Criminal Evidence Act 1984 became law in 1986, the tendency has been to set questions on judicial discretion to exclude. Although confessions will be dealt with in Chapter 8, it is at this stage useful to examine the discretion given to the courts to exclude evidence which is otherwise in all respects admissible.

2.5 Questions

QUESTION ONE

Martin, a bank manager, is shot and killed during a robbery of the bank. Inspector Pecksniff arrests and cautions Tom after receiving information that Tom was involved in the robbery. At the police station, Pecksniff refuses Tom's request for a solicitor on the ground that granting the request immediately will lead to the alerting of Tom's accomplice. He then questions Tom for long periods over the next 24 hours. Eventually, Tom agrees to make a statement. He admits that he and Gamp carried out the robbery but claims that the gun was carried by Gamp and that he, Tom, did not know it was loaded.

Pecksniff then goes to Gamp's flat. Because no-one answers the doorbell, he decides to break in. A search of the flat reveals money from the robbery and a gun bearing fingerprints later identified as Tom's. Gamp is arrested later that day. In an interview with Pecksniff, Gamp refuses to answer any questions about the robbery or the presence of the gun and money in his house. The defence have now discovered that Pecksniff's notebook records a statement by Gamp at the end of the interview in which he admits taking part in the robbery. Gamp has never been shown the notebook.

Advise Tom and Gamp.

University of London LLB Examination
(for External Students) Evidence June 1995 Q5

General Comment

The question requires an overview of the law upon improperly obtained evidence and other evidence obtained as a consequence. It is necessary to look briefly at aspects of Police and Criminal Evidence Act (PACE) 1984 and the Codes of Conduct and also at the Criminal Justice and Public Order Act (CJPOA) 1994, and to apply these to the many issues raised.

Skeleton Solution

Treatment of Tom on arrest.

Refusal of access to lawyer – prolonged questioning – breaches of Code C.

Tom's statement – ss76 and 78 PACE 1984.

Use of statement by police.

Methods employed at Gamp's flat.

Gamp's off-the-record statement – Code C and verballing.

Gamp's refusal to answer questions.

Evidence of accomplices.

Suggested Solution

Pecksniff, in arresting and taking Tom into custody, has moved the matter within the scope of Police and Criminal Evidence Act (PACE) 1984 and Code C. Tom is refused a solicitor because Pecksniff believes that this will lead to an accomplice being alerted. Unless Tom has asked for a particular solicitor, whom Pecksniff has good reason to suspect as likely to do such a thing, there may be a breach of Code C6 and Annex B. Section 58 PACE 1984 provides for access to a solicitor, but s58(8) will give Pecksniff the right to delay access in the circumstances of a 'serious arrestable offence', which this is (s116).

In *R* v *Silcott; R* v *Braithwaite; R* v *Raghip* (1991) the Court of Appeal held that, to deny access under s58(8), the officer must reasonably suspect that the particular solicitor, if allowed consultation, would thereafter commit a criminal offence – nothing less suffices because of the fundamental nature of the right. Tom is questioned for prolonged periods over 24 hours before agreeing to make a statement. It sounds as if there have been further breaches of the Codes during this period, and it can be said with some certainty that Tom's statement and confession will have to be considered in the light of ss76 and 78 PACE 1984. Tom may be able to rely upon both limbs of s76 to have his statement excluded: s76(2)(a) in respect of the oppression (*R* v *Beales* (1991)); and s76(2)(b) in consequence of things said or done which would render any confession made by him unreliable. This would require the prosecution to prove, to the criminal standard, that the statement was not so obtained, a considerable problem here.

Tom should also be able to rely upon s78 for the court's discretion to exclude on the grounds of adverse effect upon the fairness of the proceedings caused by significant and substantial breaches of s58 and the Codes (*R* v *Alladice* (1988)). Section 78 expressly requires consideration of the circumstances in which evidence is obtained, and most of the cases under s78 illustrate willingness to exclude statements obtained by serious breaches of the Codes.

Pecksniff then uses the information to go in search of Gamp. Section 76(4)(a) confirms the common law rule from *R* v *Warwickshall* (1783) that the admissibility of evidence as a result of a confession is not affected by the inadmissibility of the confession, provided the the confession is not referred to in evidence (s76(5)). Pecksniff breaks in because no one is there to let him in. This matter is governed by s17 PACE 1984 and Code B and it does sound as if there may have been breaches of both, unless Pecksniff believes Gamp to have been on the premises so that he could claim to enter for the purpose of arrest (s17(2)(a)). It is hard to see what unfairness to the proceedings can follow from this because the same results would follow if the search was under warrant, this seems to be the effect of the judgment in *R* v *Wright* (1994) which concerned s18. The common law position on this was that the evidence would undoubtedly have been admissible (*Kuruma* v *R* (1955), *Jeffery* v *Black* (1978)). There was no trickery practised as in *R* v *Mason* (1987).

When Gamp is arrested and interviewed he refuses to answer questions, but according to Pecksniff made a confession at the end. Gamp has never seen the notebook. In *R* v *Scott* (1991) the Court of Appeal considered the admission of a note made in similar circumstances, which was not signed by the accused or put to him, and it was said that it was 'hard to conceive a clearer breach of Code C'. The philosophy behind the Code, of preventing 'verballing', will either exclude this statement or found an appeal, if admitted. As to Gamp's silence, either outside or inside court, since *R* v *Martinez-Tobon* (1994) it seems that the judge will be positively required to direct the jury as to its significance – in effect not to attach excessive significance to it. The effect of ss35 and 168 Criminal Justice and Public Order Act (CJPOA) 1994 will allow prosecution comment and proper inferences to be drawn, particularly where some explanation would be a reasonable expectation. Section 34 applies this to the silence on interview.

Any evidence given by Tom or Gamp which implicates the other in the same offence will almost certainly require some sort of direction to the effect that the witness may have a purpose of his own to serve as in *R* v *Prater* (1960). The requirement for formal accomplice corroboration warnings has been abrogated by s32 CJPOA 1994, but care is needed as shown by *R* v *Cheema* (1994). This may not be necessary with regard to the shooting incident if it is clear that one or the other, but not both, must have committed the offence (*R* v *Whitaker* (1977)).

QUESTION TWO

'Whether the courts should refuse to entertain evidence because it has been obtained by the party tendering it in an illegal or improper manner is a question principally of policy, to which no answer is to be found in the law of evidence.' (Murphy).

Discuss.

University of London LLB Examination
(for External Students) Evidence June 1991 Q1

General Comment

This question requires the candidate to discuss the principles governing the exercise of discretion, thereby demonstrating the legal (as opposed to policy) basis on which such evidence is excluded. It primarily concerns criminal trials.

Skeleton Solution

• Admissibility of illegally or improperly obtained evidence as a matter of law in criminal and civil trials.
• Role of discretion at common law – *R* v *Sang*; s78 of the Police and Criminal Evidence Act 1984.
• Present status of agent provocateur evidence (*R* v *Harwood*; *R* v *Gill*).
• Interpretation of s78 (*R* v *Mason*; *R* v *Samuel*; *R* v *Alladice*; *R* v *Keenan*).

Suggested Solution

It is fair to say that the principles on which illegally or improperly obtained evidence is excluded are less than clear, particularly in criminal cases. There are, nevertheless, some established ground rules which demonstrate that exclusion of such evidence depends primarily on the exercise of judicial discretion. The manner in which the discretion is exercised is not, however, based simply on policy questions, but rather on rules which form part of the law of evidence.

In order to explore the quotation in the question, it is necessary to examine the way in which the courts have approached the question of excluding such evidence. By that means, it becomes more easy to establish the rules by which courts make decisions.

One proposition is well established, and is authority for limiting the discussion to discretion. The fact that evidence has been illegally or improperly obtained makes no difference to its admissibility as a matter of law in a criminal case – it remains admissible: *Kuruma* v *R* (1955). This is also true for civil cases, and, according to Lord Denning in *Helliwell* v *Piggott-Sims* (1980), no discretion even exists to exclude it.

In criminal cases, the governing authority for the exercise of discretion at common law is *R* v *Sang* (1980). The common law now lies alongside a statutory discretion in s78 of the Police and Criminal Evidence Act 1984 and is preserved by s82(3) of that Act. Under the *Sang* principles:

a) the fact that evidence has been obtained as a result of the activities of an agent provocateur is no reason to exclude such evidence;

b) apart from admissions and confessions and other evidence obtained from the accused after the commission of an offence, there is no discretion to exclude evidence by reason of the manner in which it was obtained; but

c) the court always has a discretion to exclude evidence where necessary to ensure a fair trial.

The common law discretion to exclude improperly obtained evidence where it is not either a confession (which is governed by special rules – now s76 of the Police and Criminal Evidence Act 1984) or unduly prejudicial compared with its probative value, is, however, extremely rarely exercised. One of the few authorities is the driving case of *R* v *Payne* (1963) in which a motorist was duped into providing evidence against himself by false representations as to the purpose of medical examination.

It is therefore apparent that the exercise of discretion to exclude improperly or illegally obtained evidence at common law is governed by ground rules laid down by the law of evidence as developed by case law. It may be said that policy considerations have affected the way the rules have developed but it is the rules which govern admissibility.

The other basis for excluding this sort of evidence is s78 of the Police and Criminal Evidence Act. A discretion arises where, in all the circumstances, including the circumstances in which evidence is obtained, its admission would adversely affect the fairness of the proceedings. Taking this section at face value, it confers a very broad discretion on a judge and, as was made clear in *R* v *Mason* (1987), it is not to be taken as a recitation of the common law.

That said, it is as yet unclear how far the discretion to exclude will be applied in practice. There are conflicting indications in *R* v *Gill* (1963) and *R* v *Harwood* (1989) on the question of whether evidence obtained through the activities of an agent provocateur might be excluded under s78. Likewise, it is unclear how far the circumstances of the obtaining (other than by the agent provocateur) will result in a trigger for exclusion under s78. *R* v *Mason* in which exclusion under s78 arose when the police deliberately misled an accused and his solicitor into thinking there was evidence against the accused, is an example of a deliberate deception which might have been sufficient to trigger the common law discretion comparable with what happened in *R* v *Payne*. In *Kinsella* v *Marshall* (1988), a refusal to exercise the s78 discretion where plain clothes policemen made a test purchase to see if a shopkeeper was selling alcohol unlawfully was explained on the basis that it was not a 'clear deception'. Perhaps rather, it was a recognition of the fact that evidence in such cases would be difficult to secure by any other means.

Cases involving exclusion of confessional evidence have been a rich source of case law under s78, which is not excluded by the operation of s76 – *R* v *Mason*. It is possible to distil some general principles from them. Failure to afford access to legal advice, being a fundamental right under the Police and Criminal Evidence Act, will be a good ground for exclusion: *R* v *Samuel* (1988). Bad faith on the part of the police will, according to the Lord Chief Justice in *R* v *Alladice* (1988), mean that courts will have little difficulty in excluding evidence thereby obtained. This principle was applied in case of a failure to give access to legal advice, but indications are that it is a principle capable of application more broadly.

The Code on Detention and Questioning issued under s66 of the 1984 Act (the third and latest being in 1995) is to be taken into account (s67) in deciding whether to exclude under s78.

According to *R* v *Keenan* (1990) the requirement is that the breach of the Code's provisions is significant and substantial. Failure to give access to legal advice is such a breach, but there are, of course, many others related to the questioning process which can be so described.

Again, what can be said from the above analysis is that whilst the judicial approach to s78 is still developing, it is not simply a matter of policy. The judge is restrained by the terms of s78, the principles developed by the case law and guidance in the Codes of Practice. A judge is not entitled to apply his discretion simply on policy grounds. It is a fair assumption that policy considerations have played their part in developing the principles by which discretion is to be decided and undoubtedly, played a role in the formulation by Parliament of the statutory provision in s78. Such considerations will, no doubt, affect future developments. In particular, one might note the remarks made in the Court of Appeal in *R* v *Bailey and Smith* (1993) in relation to covert police activity: 'We recognise ... that some may well think it odd and even perhaps unsatisfactoy that alongside a rigorously controlled legislative regime governing the detention, treatment and questioning of those in police custody parallel covert investigations can legitimately continue.' What, however, the courts have to be concerned with in any given case is the way the principles which have emerged are to be applied, and it is that rather than the underlying policy concerns which determine the exercise of discretion to exclude evidence.

3 Burdens and Standards of Proof

3.1   Introduction

3.2   Key points

3.3   Analysis of questions

3.4   Questions

3.1 Introduction

The most important distinction is that between the legal burden – the burden of *proof* – and the evidential burden – the burden of adducing evidence. Only when this distinction is clearly understood can a student do justice to the express and implied exceptions in criminal cases where the legal, as opposed to evidential burden, is on the accused. The recent House of Lords decision in *R* v *Hunt* [1987] AC 352 has made this a popular area for examiners.

3.2 Key points

It is vital that students understand the following concepts and issues:

a)   Legal burden is the obligation placed on a party to prove a fact in issue, eg on the prosecution to prove the guilt of the accused and to prove all other issues they raise during the trial.

b)   Evidential burden is the obligation placed on a party to adduce enough evidence about an asserted fact for that fact to become a justiciable issue, eg the prosecution must adduce enough evidence of the guilt of the accused for the court to be satisfied that there is a case for the defence to answer.

c)   Evidential burden is considered at only two points in a trial:

   i)   at the beginning, to decide which party begins;

   ii)   at any time during the trial in deciding whether enough evidence has been adduced in support of an asserted fact for it to become a justiciable issue, ie require the opposing party to adduce evidence in rebuttal.

d)   Which party must prove the issue in dispute, and other issues raised during the trial, ie which party must discharge the legal burden, is decided by rules of law, either statute or case law. This aspect may be further complicated by the impact of various types of presumptions, both of law and of fact. These matters are dealt with in detail in Chapter 14 below and a thorough understanding of the incidence of burdens will require an understanding of presumptions, particularly in civil evidence.

e)   The rule in civil cases is, generally, that the party who asserts must prove, ie he must discharge the legal burden of proof. For example, in a suit in negligence, the plaintiff (as well as having to discharge the evidential burden) has the legal burden of proving duty, breach and consequential damage. The defendant, if the defence is a simple denial, bears no legal burden, *but* if some defence is raised which goes beyond that, eg an assertion that the plaintiff was contributorily negligent, then the defendant has the legal burden of proving that assertion. Thus, generally, the party asserting an affirmative bears the legal burden; there are exceptions to this, where a negative assertion is an essential element of a party's case, eg in a suit in malicious prosecution the plaintiff must prove the absence of reasonable cause for the defendant's institution of proceedings.

f)   The rule in criminal cases is, generally, that where a burden is borne by the accused it is an evidential burden only. There are three types of defences which, exceptionally, will require the accused to discharge a legal burden of proof if they are to succeed:

i)   insanity and unfitness to plead;

ii) express statutory exceptions – ie where a statute expressly stipulates that the accused must prove an issue (eg a defence of diminished responsibility to a charge of murder, per s2(2) Homicide Act 1957);

iii) implied statutory exceptions – s101 Magistrates' Courts Act 1980 in summary trials and *R* v *Edwards* [1975] QB 27 in jury trials provide that if the accused relies for his defence on any 'exception, exemption, proviso, excuse or qualification', then he has the legal burden of proving that defence. In this area of the incidence of the legal burden in criminal trials, the House of Lords decision in *R* v *Hunt* (1987) is important.

g)   The *standard* of proof, which determines how much evidence a party must adduce to discharge a legal burden of proof, varies depending on whether it is a civil or a criminal trial. In civil trials the standard is on balance of probabilities; the more serious the allegation made by a party the more evidence the court will require to be satisfied, but even where the allegation by a party is of the commission of a crime by his opponent the standard remains the civil one, ie he must prove that what he alleges is more likely than not the truth. In criminal trials the prosecution must prove the guilt of the accused to the criminal standard, ie beyond reasonable doubt; additionally, whenever the prosecution bears a legal burden of proving any issues during the course of the trial it must prove beyond reasonable doubt. In the exceptional situations where the accused bears a legal, as opposed to merely evidential, burden (see (f)(i), (ii) and (iii) above) the *standard* of proof is always the civil standard.

3.3 Analysis of questions

Burdens (and standards) had tended to form only part of a question, often merged with presumptions, judicial notice etc, until *R* v *Hunt* was reported in 1987, since when examiners have considered that there is now sufficient controversy for this area to merit a self-contained question. An understanding of the reasoning shown in *R* v *Hunt* is vital to a thorough grasp of the circumstances in which exceptions to the general rule may be seen to be implied.

3.4 Questions

QUESTION ONE

Section 27 of the Financial Services Act 1986 provides that 'subject to s58 below, no person other than an authorised person shall issue ... an investment advertisement in the United Kingdom, unless its contents have been approved by an authorised person'.

Section 58 provides that 'Section 27 does not apply to ... any advertisement which ... consists of ... any document permitted to be published by listing rules ...' of the International Stock Exchange in London.

Evidence

Section 207(3) provides that 'for the purposes of this Act an advertisement issued outside the United Kingdom, shall be treated as issued in the United Kingdom if it is directed to persons in the United Kingdom ...'

Suppose that Makeabuck is charged with contravening s27 in that he had issued such an advertisement in the UK inviting investors to buy shares of Hong Kong companies without obtaining approval of its contents from an authorised person. Suppose that Makeabuck's position is that though some of his advertisements did appear on video screens in the UK, they were issued in Hong Kong and were not directed at persons in the UK; that all documents which were issued in the UK were permitted by the International Stock Exchange's listing rules; and that in any case his advertisements were approved by the Bang-On Bank which was an 'authorised person' under the Act.

Consider the burden and standard of proof in the case under English Law in the context of the following items of evidence:

a) a document produced by a computer containing a register of all persons authorised to carry on investment business in the UK kept under the Financial Services Act, but which does not contain the Bang-On Bank's name;

b) a copy of an authorisation issued to Bang-On Bank under the Act which is in Makeabuck's possession.

Adapted from University of London LLB Examination
(for External Students) Evidence June 1988 Q1

General Comment

No difficulty should be caused by the requirement to state the standard of proof placed on the prosecution and defence in a criminal case. But the placing of the burden is more difficult. There is no authority on the Financial Services Act provisions in question, so general principles must be applied. Necessarily the examiner may disagree with the candidate in his application of the rule in *Hunt*, but provided the principles are stated clearly full credit will be given.

Skeleton Solution

• Elements of the offence – burden and standard in general.

• Burden and standard on each element.

Suggested Solution

In general it is for the prosecution to prove every element of a criminal charge, both actus reus and mens rea, beyond reasonable doubt (*Woolmington* v *DPP* (1935)). But this general principle is subject to exceptions and, in particular, to an exception that where statute expressly or by implication places a burden on the defendant then that is where the burden lies (*R* v *Hunt* (1987)).

The offence under s27 of the Financial Services Act 1986 has five elements: (a) the publication of an investment advertisement; (b) which is not permitted to be published by listing rules of the International Stock Exchange in London; (c) in the UK; (d) by an unauthorised person; and (e) without the approval of an authorised person.

Whether, as regards any element the burden of proof is on the prosecution or defence is a matter of the proper construction of the Act. In *R* v *Hunt* the House of Lords held that the

14

presumption must be that it is for the prosecution to prove everything which needs to be proved. Where an offence is committed by someone who does an act without first obtaining a licence or some other permission from an official body this presumption will be rebutted provided it is simple for the defendant to prove that he had the necessary permission, but very difficult for the prosecution to prove that he did not. Lord Griffiths recognised in his speech that the vast majority of cases in which a burden is placed on the defendant will be cases where he is accused of doing something without the necessary permission. But he also recognised that a careful definition must be made of the act which is prohibited so that it is known whether the defendant really is asserting a defence. For example, in *R* v *Hunt* itself the offence charged was the possession of a certain type of morphine. The Court of Appeal held that once it was established that the defendant had possession of morphine it was for him to prove that it was not of the type alleged, but the House of Lords disagreed. In other words the defendant was not putting forward the defence that the substance was not as alleged, rather it was a necessary ingredient of the prosecution case for the prosecution to prove that it was of the alleged type.

The prosecution will have to call its evidence first and if at the close of its case it has failed to call evidence which could amount to proof beyond reasonable doubt on those issues on which it bears a legal burden, the judge will have no option but to accede to a submission from Makeabuck that there is no case to answer (*R* v *Galbraith* (1981)).

In Makeabuck's case the five elements of the offence must be considered separately because the burden may not be on the same party on each. Undoubtedly it will be for the prosecution to prove that the advertisements about which complaint is made are investment advertisements. This is a matter on which the prosecution is certainly competent as the defence to call evidence. Makeabuck does not raise as his defence that the advertisements were not investment advertisements, but that does not preclude the prosecution from having to prove that they were.

Section 58 of the 1986 Act provides that s27 does not apply to any document permitted to be published by listing rules of the International Stock Exchange in London. The effect of this section depends upon whether it means: (a) it is an offence to publish an investment advertisement unless it is permitted by the rules; or (b) only those advertisements which are not permitted by the rules should not be published. The difference between these meanings is one of substance and not just emphasis in that the first construction means that Makeabuck is putting forward a defence when he says the advertisements are permitted by the rules, whereas the second makes it a necessary part of the prosecution case that the advertisements are not permitted. The case of *Cross* (1990) involved similar wording to the present statute. It concerned s1 of the Company Securities (Insider Dealing) Act 1985 s1(1) which creates the offence and is said to be subject to s3, which allows the dealing where it is not done by the individual for profit, or avoidance of loss. The Court of Appeal held that the burden to prove the applicability of s3 lay with the defendant. However, the court seemed to place emphasis on the fact that the matters in s3 were peculiarly within the defendant's own knowledge. Here, we are concerned with a document permitted to be published by listing rules, and the absence of permission in the rules is something which can be proved just as simply by the prosecution as by the defence. In effect this element of the offence is in the same position as the requirement in *R* v *Hunt* that the morphine was of the prohibited type. Naturally Makeabuck should call what evidence he has if he wishes to allege that the advertisements were authorised by the listings rules, but there would not formally be a burden on him to do so.

The need for the advertisement to be issued in the UK raises a different point. Section 207(3)

15

extends the definition of issuing in the UK from its obvious starting point of advertisements which are issued in the UK for use in the UK to cover also advertisements issued outside the UK but directed to persons in the UK. In the same way the prosecution would have to prove that any advertisement was an investment advertisement so it would be necessary for it to call evidence of the origin of the advertisement. There is no reason in principle why the prosecution should not have to prove that the advertisement was of the prohibited type. It is submitted that the origin of the advertisement is just as much a vital element of the prosecution case as is whether or not it is an investment advertisement. It may be that all the prosecution has to do is prove that the advertisement was received in the UK and then it will be for the defence to bring forward evidence that it was issued outside the UK. But the burden on the defence may be no more than an evidential burden so that it would then be for the prosecution to prove that although it was issued outside the UK it was directed to persons in the UK.

Whether or not Makeabuck is an authorised person is a matter on which he is likely to bear a legal burden, that is a burden to prove authorisation on a balance of probabilities. The position is effectively the same as where someone charged with selling alcohol without a licence claims that he has a licence, in which case the burden is on the defence to establish that a licence has been granted (*R* v *Edwards* (1975)). It appears, in any event, that Makeabuck does not claim that he has is authorised. It if is correct that the burden is on the defence, the prosecution will not have to call evidence with a view to establishing that Makeabuck is not authorised because it will be presumed that he is not unless he raises the issue.

Makeabuck does argue that the Bang-On Bank is authorised and that he issued the advertisements with its approval. It would, it is submitted, be unreasonable to expect the defence to have access to information from which it could prove whether someone who approved an advertisement was authorised to do so. We are told that Makeabuck may be in a position to do so in this case, but where the burden lies under s27 must be the same in every case and not all defendants can expect to be in Makeabuck's position. The prosecution may not know that Makeabuck is going to raise the defence that his advertisement was approved by the Bang-On Bank. Therefore it will be for Makeabuck to raise the issue. He will bear an evidential burden, in other words he must raise some credible evidence that the Bang-On Bank gave approval. But it will then be for the prosecution to prove beyond reasonable doubt that the Bang-On Bank is not authorised.

QUESTION TWO

The decision in *Hunt* [1987] AC 352 'fashions some workable guidelines out of unpromising material and encourages courts to seek out and apply the intentions of Parliament in a consistent way.'
Discuss.

University of London LLB Examination
(for External Students) Evidence June 1989 Q5

General Comment

A mere narrative on the express and implied reversal of the burden of proof in some criminal statutes leading to the decision in *R* v *Hunt* would not be sufficient to achieve high marks. A critical analysis of the law pre-*Hunt* and discussion of the guidelines in that case is imperative for a comprehensive answer.

Skeleton Solution

• Incidence of the legal burden of proof generally in criminal cases – *Woolmington* v *DPP*.

• Exceptions, where defence bears the burden:

  i) at common law;

  ii) examples of express statutory exceptions;

  iii) implied statutory exceptions.

• Discussion, and criticism of *R* v *Hunt*.

Suggested Solution

The general rule in criminal cases is that the prosecution bears the legal burden of proving every element of its case; whether the prosecution assertions be positive or negative is immaterial, thus once the defence discharges the evidential burden in respect of any defence that defence, even if affirmative in its nature, must be disproved beyond reasonable doubt by the prosecution if the accused is to be convicted. Thus, for example the prosecution has the burden of proving absence of consent if that is raised as a defence to a charge of assault (*R* v *Donovan* (1934)) or of rape (*R* v *Horn* (1912)).

This general rule was enunciated by Lord Sankey LC in the celebrated case of *Woolmington* v *DPP* (1935). From his now famous speech, the following passage is notorious:

'Throughout the web of the English criminal law one golden thread is always to be seen, that it is the duty of the prosecution to prove the prisoner's guilt subject to what I have already said as to the defence of insanity and subject also to any statutory exception. No matter what the charge ... the principle that the prosecution must prove the guilt of the prisoner is part of the common law of England and no attempt to whittle it down can be entertained.'

Implicit in Lord Sankey's classic statement are exceptions to the 'golden thread', ie, where the defence of insanity is raised, and where the legal burden is placed by statute on the defence.

In the case of insanity the legal burden is affected by the presumption of sanity – therefore the accused pleading insanity (*M'Naghten's Case* (1843)) or unfitness to plead because of defective intellect (*R* v *Podola* (1960)) bears the burden of proving that assertion; the standard of proof in such cases is merely the civil standard of balance of probabilities (*R* v *Podola*). (Where the prosecution raises the issue of unfitness to plead, or alleges insanity or diminished responsibility under the provisions of s6 Criminal Procedure (Insanity) Act 1964 (which is not changed by the provisions of the Criminal Procedure (Insanity and Unfitness to Plead) Act 1991), then the prosecution bears the burden of proof but to the criminal standard of beyond reasonable doubt: *R* v *Grant* (1960); *R* v *Robertson* (1968)).

Evidentially, insanity causes few problems, and was recognised as a loose strand of the 'golden thread', as were statutory exceptions. Again, in the case of express statutory provisions, Parliament has in those situations decreed that on some issue the defence shall exceptionally bear a burden of proof, although obviously the prosecution still bears the legal burden of proof to the criminal standard on all other issues. For example, s32 Sexual Offences Act 1956 provides that regarding the offence of knowingly living on the earnings of prostitution, a man who lives with a prostitute 'shall be presumed to be knowingly living on the earnings of prostitution, unless he proves the contrary.' Another example is provided by s1(1) Prevention of Crime Act 1953, whereby it is an offence for a person to have an offensive weapon in a public place 'without lawful authority or reasonable excuse, the proof whereof shall lie on him.' (There are other express provisions in s2 Prevention of Corruption Act 1916; s2(2) Homicide Act 1957; s28(2) Misuse of Drugs Act 1971.) The reasons for the reversal of the burden of proof on these specific issues are mainly of public policy, and although purists disagree with these exceptions there is no scope for inconsistency in the courts' applying Parliament's intentions.

The 'unpromising material' where inconsistency abounded was in the area of implied, as opposed to express, statutory provisions. Section 101 Magistrates' Courts Act 1980 (formerly s81 Magistrates' Courts Act 1952 which revised s14 Summary Jurisdiction Act 1848) provides in essence that where a defendant in a summary trial relies for his defence on 'any exception, exemption, proviso, excuse or qualification', the burden of proof shall be on the defence, 'notwithstanding that the information or complaint contains an allegation negativing the exception, exemption, proviso, excuse or qualification.' This provision applies to summary trials, but in 1975 it was held that similar principles applied to trials on indictment (*R* v *Edwards* (1975)); and this was confirmed by the House of Lords in *R* v *Hunt* (1987).

A clear-cut example of a provision to which s101 applies is the offence of driving a motor vehicle on a road without being the holder of a current driving licence. Once the prosecution prove that the defendant was driving a motor vehicle on a road, the defendant will be convicted of the offence unless he proves the qualification on which he must rely for his defence, ie proves that at the relevant time he held a current driving licence for that class of motor vehicle (*John* v *Humphreys* (1955)). Although whether a driver is qualified or not is easily checked by the prosecution, s101 has been held to apply to this, and other 'licence' cases; the reason for the application of s101 is not that the court is dealing with facts peculiarly within the knowledge of the defendant (and thus easier for him to prove the affirmative than the prosecution prove the negative) but that s101 is undoubtedly applicable so the burden of proving the qualification is on the defendant.

A case giving rise to some difficulty was that of *Nimmo* v *Alexander Cowan* (1968). Under s29(1) Factories Act 1961: 'every place at which any person has at any time to work ... shall, so far as is reasonably practicable, be made and kept safe for any person working therein.' An employee alleged that his place of work had not been made and kept safe, and although the case was a civil one, it has substantial relevance in the present context. In the House of Lords it was made clear that where the burden of proof lay would be the same whether the proceedings were criminal or civil. The House of Lords, on their interpretation of the statute, decided that the employee did not have to show that it was reasonably practicable to keep the place safe, but rather the defendant (the employers) had to discharge the legal burden of proving that it was *not* reasonably practicable to keep the place safe. The decision was by a bare majority, which is indicative of the problems of construing statutory provisions which may by implication reverse the burden of proof.

An earlier, and difficult, case concerned a prosecution for the offence of acquiring rationed goods without surrendering the appropriate ration coupons (*R* v *Putland* (1946)). The Court of Criminal Appeal held that the prosecution bore the burden of proving the acquisition of the goods *and* the failure to surrender the coupons.

It was against this background of apparent inconsistency in interpretation that the case of *R* v *Hunt* reached the House of Lords in 1987. Hunt was charged with the unlawful possession of a controlled drug (morphine), contrary to s5 Misuse of Drugs Act 1971. The Misuse of Drugs Regulations 1973 provide that s5 does not apply to any morphine preparation containing no more than 0.2 per cent morphine. The prosecution adduced no evidence of the percentage of morphine in the substance found in Hunt's possession and the defence therefore submitted there was no case to answer. The judge refused to accept the submission and Hunt was convicted, having then changed his plea to guilty. The Court of Appeal dismissed his appeal, holding that the facts were covered by the implication in the statute and regulation that the burden of proving the substance's morphine content was on Hunt.

On appeal to the House of Lords, the decision of the Court of Appeal was reversed. Their Lordships stated that every case must depend on the construction of the particular legislation, and further stated that if there is, on construction, no clear indication as to where the burden of proof should lie, then the court may consider policy, including considerations of practicality such as the ease with which one party or the other could discharge the burden of proof (whether affirmative or negative). They further stated that it can never be readily assumed that Parliament intended a defendant to prove his innocence, so the courts should be reluctant to make such an inference from the wording of any but the clearest of statutory provisions. Especially where the statutory offence was a serious one (as in the case of Hunt's alleged unlawful possession of morphine) any ambiguity must be resolved in favour of the accused person.

The 'guidelines' of their Lordships in *R* v *Hunt* may be workable; if the guidelines are followed then, apart from unambiguous wording in a statute, there is virtually a presumption that the accused shall not bear a burden of proving the issue(s) referred to in the statute, and the more serious the offence charged the stronger the presumption. However, this may be in conflict with the 'policy' guideline, and in any case it pre-supposes that the courts cannot construe the statute to discover a clear indication of where the burden shall lie. Although the courts may have been encouraged to seek out and apply the intentions of Parliament in a consistent way, the courts are prone to overlooking the intention of Parliament in their fervour to construe statutes linguistically. More important was the failure of the House of Lords to adopt the proposal of the 11th Report of the Criminal Law Revision Committee ([1972] Cmnd 4991) that burdens on the defence should be evidential only, both on general principles of criminal law and for the sake of clarity – clarity which will probably become increasingly elusive as conflicting guidelines in *R* v *Hunt* are bent by the courts.

QUESTION THREE

'Throughout the web of the English Criminal Law one golden thread is always seen, that it is the duty of the prosecution to prove the prisoner's guilt ...' (Viscount Sankey in *Woolmington* v *DPP*).

Discuss the contemporary truth of this statement.

University of London Examination
(for External Students) Law of Evidence June 1993 Q4

General Comment

This is another common question and it is easy to put your own 'stamp' upon it (and another one for Jurisprudential analysis). The essay below gives a clear indication as to the writer's feelings; you, too, should develop your own views on these matters. If you think that the presumption of innocence is important, then how can you possibly approve of *Hunt*, in which the House of Lords said clearly that, in criminal statute the judges can 'imply into' the statute, as a matter of statutory construction, a reversal of the onus? It beggars belief, especially in the light of the important principle of statutory interpretation that criminal statutes should be construed *in favour of the defendant*. But everyone has different views, and you may take the view that defendants have been getting away with too much recently and that they shouldn't have the benefit of the doubt! The important thing is to say clearly what you think *and why*.

Skeleton Solution

- General principle.
- Three exceptions.
- Express statutory exceptions.
- Implied statutory exception.
- *Edwards*.
- Section 101 Magistrates Court Act 1980.
- Grammatical distinction and silliness of the section.
- *Hunt* and its relation to *Edwards*.
- Tests in *Hunt*.
- Birch's arguments in *The Hunting of the Snark*.
- Conclusion that *Hunt* a retrograde case.

Suggested Solution

It was stated in *Woolmington* v *DPP* (1935) that the golden thread running through the criminal law was that the burden of proof remained on the prosecution to prove all elements of the offence; it can be seen that this principle embodies the general principle that a man (or woman) is innocent until proved guilty. We are thus supposed to be in a fundamentally different position in this country from the continental legal systems, where the criminal method is inquisitorial in nature.

Nevertheless, there are three exceptions to the *Woolmington* principle. In the common law, the defence must prove insanity on a balance of probabilities. As far as statute is concerned, Parliament can either expressly or, by implication, declare that a statutory enactment has shifted the burden of proof onto the defendant. Parliament has expressly done this in several areas, notably for diminished responsibility (Homicide Act 1957) and for corruption (Prevention of Corruption Act 1916). But it is the implied exception which gives rise to the most grief, mostly arising from the fact that any departure from the presumption of innocence is dangerous. It is possible that the former apparent departure from the rule is less dangerous to the presumption of innocence principle now because of the case of *Hunt* (1987) and, since it is the most important recent and contemporary case, it would be as well to examine it.

Hunt altered the state of law as it existed – up to and including the case of *R* v *Edwards* (1975). In *Edwards*, the Court of Appeal had tried to relieve the courts of any burden of statutory interpretation by declaring the common law for indictable offences to be the same as that within (for summary offences) s101 of the Magistrates' Court Act 1980. This provision states that the accused had the burden of proof if his allegedly offending act came within an exception to a generally prohibited act: such an exception being preceded by words such as 'exemption', 'proviso' and so on. But it was clear (and still is!) that the distinction in the provision was one of grammar only and that legislative draughtsmen did not conform to any sort of practice as to the use of these words, other than economy and elegance).

Further, the Court of Appeal in *Edwards* did not draw a substantial distinction between the element providing the definition of an offence and the element providing a defence to it. As Zuckerman points out, if we do not do so there is no substantial difference between saying 'You are forbidden to drive without a licence' or 'You may not drive unless you have a licence'.

The Court of Appeal in *Hunt* drove this sort of reasoning out the door by simply declaring that the underlying reasoning in *Edwards* was that these grammatical distinctions were only a guide to statutory interpretation, in that case a licensing statute; this made it obvious that grammar was not enough. The court should instead look to what the statute was trying to achieve (in other words, to pay attention to the normal guidelines governing the construction of statutes).

This means that the appearance of the word: 'exemption' or 'exception' and so on, would not be sufficient to shift the burden. Instead, the court would have to take into consideration the fact that Parliament would not lightly have intended to shift the burden, in the light of the presumption of innocence, as well as how difficult the task would be for the defendant to 'prove' his innocence if the burden shifted. Hunt was himself charged with possession of a proscribed drug, with exceptions as to amounts being detailed in a schedule to the Act. The House of Lords held that he did not have to provide rebutting proof of the chemical composition of the particular drug.

Why? It would have been impossible for Hunt to provide proof because the drug had been taken out of his possession by the police and had already been the subject of chemical analysis by them. The prosecution had failed to bring evidence concerning the amount of morphine present and the House of Lords therefore took the view, in the light of these factors, that the relevant provision could not be read as an implied exception to the *Woolmington* principle.

Birch argues (see *The Hunting of the Snark*) that the reason the presumption of innocence principles were not given great prominence in *Hunt* was that *Hunt* was a decision about what constituted the actus reus of a particular offence of possession of a proscribed drug, rather than its mens rea. She contends that in a crime with a mental element offering a defence of 'lawful' excuse on the basis of the factors already mentioned in *Hunt,* the burden of proof is unlikely to shift. The typical s101 offence will, therefore, she says, be one which is not very serious, and lacking a mens rea requirement. If she is right, the element of defence should be independent of the definition of the offence and not too onerous for the defendant because it could easily be separated from the definition of the offence itself and the burden should not weigh too heavily on the defendant.

It is submitted that this kind of pettifogging approach lacks principle. If we are firm that, in our legal system, we have clear presumption of innocence, that must surface clearly in our law; we have a crystal clear – and famous – reaffirmation of that principle in *Woolmington*. What *Hunt* says, loud and clear, is that judges, on the basis of guidelines of statutory interpretation, can interpret a statute in a way that runs counter to that general (some would say foundational) principle of our legal system; they can find that in a criminal statute, in other words, when there are no clear words to that effect, a shift of this important and serious burden. Quite apart, too, from these considerations, there is the important interpretation principle that, for criminal statutes, ambiguities and unclarities *should be resolved in favour of the defendant.* I conclude, therefore, that *Hunt* was a retrograde decision when it allowed relatively flimsy reasons justifying the reversal of the burden of proof.

QUESTION FOUR

'To import the criminal standard of proof into a civil proceeding is to confuse the respective functions and needs of the criminal and civil processes.'
Discuss.

University of London LLB Examination
(for External Students) Evidence June 1990 Q3

Skeleton Solution

- General rule in criminal proceedings – exceptions.
- Express statutory exceptions – implied statutory exceptions.
- Civil proceedings – general rule in *Hornal* – exceptions – matrimonial cases and cases of extreme seriousness – *Halford* v *Brookes*.

Suggested Solution

In order to answer this question it is necessary to establish the distribution of the standard of proof in criminal proceedings. By this means it is possible to evaluate the extent to which the approach applied in such proceedings can be translated to civil proceedings.

The general rule in criminal proceedings is that the prosecution bears the legal burden in accordance with the *Woolmington* (1935) principle. The standard of proof on which the jury is directed is that the facts in issue must be proved beyond reasonable doubt (*Miller* v *Minister of Pensions* (1947)) or so that the jury are satisfied so that they are sure of the accused's guilt (*R* v *Summers* (1952)). To this general rule there are notable exceptions. The accused bears the legal burden in respect of the defence of insanity (*M'Naghten's Case* (1843)) and any statutory exception (*Woolmington*). This latter phrase incorporates both express statutory exceptions and where the exception is implied (*R* v *Hunt* (1987), confirming the assumption of what was said in *Woolmington*).

It is relatively easy to establish express statutory exceptions from the wording of the statute but implied exceptions can be more problematical and are governed by the criteria of *R* v *Edwards* (1975) and *R* v *Hunt*. They are where an offence is subject to exceptions, exemptions, provisos, excuses or qualification, which is the wording of s101 of the Magistrates' Court Act 1980 and declaratory of the common law (*R* v *Edwards*).

Where an exception to the *Woolmington* principle does apply, the standard of proof is the balance of probabilities (*R* v *Carr-Briant* (1943)). In other words, the jury is directed that the accused discharges the burden on him if they are satisfied that his version is more probable than not.

In translating this approach to the civil forum, the first and perhaps obvious point is that since very few civil actions are now tried with a jury, the form of the direction on the standard of proof could not appropriately be incorporated into the civil jurisdiction. In fact the tribunal in civil actions is usually the judge.

The next and more substantial point is whether there is any justification for importing a standard of proof beyond reasonable doubt as a general requirement for civil proceedings whilst at the same time leaving the current civil standard in place relative to the same matters which may be raised by one or other of the parties coinciding with the exceptions to the *Woolmington* principle which exist in civil cases.

It is submitted that to provide a standard of proof beyond reasonable doubt in civil proceedings would ignore the fact that in criminal proceedings the trial is for the liberty of the individual in which the State is a party, whereas in civil proceedings the trial is of 'equals' and the stakes do not amount to a threat to liberty of either party. The development of the criminal standard of proof very much reflects these features. Moreover, it would also conflict with existing authority, in particular with *Hornal* v *Neuberger Products* (1957), which establishes that the allegation of a crime in civil proceedings attracts the civil standard of proof. If the criminal standard were applied, application of a lower standard to coincide with the exceptions to *Woolmington* would have to be justified. Such justification is hard to see. Since a civil action is in a legal sense between equals for the settlement of a private dispute, it also follows that there can be no justification jurisprudentially for a lower standard of proof for insanity (if raised by the defendant) or for statutory exceptions on which the defendant seeks to rely. Yet a good deal of fuss was caused at the end of 1991 by a case decided by the High Court (QBD) – *Halford* v *Brookes & Another* (1991) – a civil action alleging battery was brought by the mother of a murder victim, against the alleged killers. The court decided that the criminal standard of proof should be adopted. Because of the serious nature of the allegations, the judge decided that the case should be conducted as if the defendants were being tried for murder in a criminal court. But the case causes problems – as a civil court it was allowed to draw adverse inferences when the defendant refused to testify, unlike in criminal cases. Also, hearsay evidence was allowed in under the Civil Evidence Act 1968 which would not have been at a criminal trial. Also, similar fact evidence would be more admissible. And, of course, there would be the usual problems of a trial within a trial when there is no jury. However, it is unlikely that this case would be followed in future for these very reasons.

There is, it is true, some other case law, particularly in the field presumptions and matrimonial proceedings, in which the criminal standard has been indicated. Examples are to be found in the old case of *Morris* v *Davies* (1837) (presumption of validity of marriage) and the relatively recent authorities such as *Preston-Jones* v *Preston-Jones* (1951) (proof of grounds for divorce). It is doubtful, however, how far these cases represent the present law, a view reinforced by the fact that that they have been largely overtaken by statutory intervention which has provided for a standard of proof on the balance of probabilities. To the extent that the degree of proof varies in civil proceedings, it is attributable to the fact that the courts require a greater weight of evidence before being satisfied on the balance of probabilities. In those cases in which the legal burden in civil cases is reversed, such as arises under s11 of the Civil Evidence Act 1968, the standard of proof is the usual civil standard and wholly consistent with the fact that civil proceedings are concerned with the settlement of disputes between private parties standing on equal terms in court.

Thus the only circumstances in which the proposition in the question would not be sound is, it is submitted, if the legal burden referred to in the question were the burden on an accused in cases where an exception to the *Woolmington* principle applies. That standard is a balance of probabilities – in other words, the present civil standard.

4 Competence and Compellability

4.1   Introduction

4.2   Key points

4.3   Analysis of questions

4.4   Questions

4.1 Introduction

Following the enactment of s80 Police and Criminal Evidence Act 1984 the competence and compellability of the spouse of an accused person has been simplified, and drastically changed. The compellability of the accused may well become an issue for the courts and Parliament if proposed changes to the right of silence become law.

4.2 Key points

a) *Distinguish competence and compellability*

   i)   Competence

      general rule is that all persons are competent as witnesses, ie they may give evidence. Exceptions to the general rule include children; persons of defective intellect; the accused as a prosecution witness.

   ii)   Compellability

      general rule is that all competent witnesses are compellable, ie they can be compelled (under threat of punishment for contempt of court as a last resort) to give evidence. This does not mean that the witness will always have to answer every question put to him (he may claim that his answer will tend to incriminate him, for example, or the matter may be the subject of legal professional privilege). Exceptions to the general rule of compellability are only two – the accused and his spouse.

b) *Children*

   The law used to be that a child's competence was tested by inquiring into his or her understanding of the oath. According to the result of that test, the child could give sworn or unsworn evidence in criminal proceedings, but could only give sworn evidence in civil proceedings. Now s52 of the Criminal Justice Act 1991 has changed this as far as criminal proceedings are concerned. Now all children's evidence in such proceedings is given unsworn, whether they understand the oath or not – s52(1) inserts this as s33A into the Criminal Justice Act 1988. A 'child' is defined for these purposes as someone under the age of 14: s33A(3). The question of competence is now governed by s33A(2A) which provides that 'a child's evidence shall (ie must) be received unless it appears to the court that the child is incapable of giving intelligible evidence'. For children over 14 the general rule is that the child is competent to give sworn evidence subject only to the inability to understand an oath because of unsoundness of mind.

As for civil proceedings, s96 of the Children Act 1989 (which came into force at the end of 1991) allows a child to give unsworn evidence in certain circumstances, for the first time.

Section 96 applies to any civil proceedings, and any child witness (which is defined in the Act as someone under the age of 18). If, in the opinion of the court, the child does not understand the nature of the oath, the child's evidence can be heard by the court if, in its opinion:

i)   he understands that it is his duty to speak the truth; and

ii)   he has sufficient understanding to justify his evidence being heard.

In civil cases there is no fixed age, obviously, at which a child becomes competent to give sworn evidence, though it has been suggested that this will normally be between the ages of eight and ten: *R* v *Hayes* (1977). It has also been stated that it would be most undesirable to call as a witness to give unsworn evidence in a criminal trial a child aged five: *R* v *Wallwork* (1958). This has clearly been overtaken by s33A(2A) with its mandatory form of wording.

c)   *Persons of defective intellect*

If a proposed witness appears to suffer from some impairment of intellect – which could be the result of mental illness or handicap, or drink or drugs, then his competence to give sworn evidence must be tested by the judge; if he does not understand the nature and solemnity of the oath, he is incompetent; if of defective intellect but nevertheless adjudged competent, the jury must decide how much weight, if any, to attach to the evidence of the witness. If the defect appears to be caused by drink or drugs there will be an adjournment before competence is tested.

d)   *The accused*

The accused is incompetent as a witness for the prosecution. A co-accused is similarly incompetent unless he has already been acquitted or convicted or unless he has otherwise ceased to be a co-accused, eg a successful application for separate trials has been made. Once the co-accused becomes competent for the prosecution he is also compellable.

Section 1 Criminal Evidence Act 1898 (as amended by the Police and Criminal Evidence Act 1984) states: 'Every person charged with an offence shall be a competent witness for the defence at every stage of the proceedings, whether the person is charged solely, or jointly with any other person. Provided as follows: (a) A person so charged shall not be called as a witness in pursuance of this Act except upon his own application ...' Therefore the accused may given evidence for the defence, but is not compellable either as a witness in his own defence or that of a co-accused.

e)   *Spouse of the accused*

Section 80 Police and Criminal Evidence Act 1984 has drastically changed the competence and compellability of the accused's spouse:

i)   spouse is always competent for the prosecution unless husband and wife are jointly charged with an offence, and is always competent for co-accused of other spouse;

ii)   spouse is compellable as witness for the prosecution or for co-accused of other spouse only if the offence charged involves assault on, or injury or threat of injury to the spouse of the accused or a person under 16, or if the offence charged is a sexual offence in respect of a person under 16;

iii) spouse is always competent to give evidence on behalf of the accused (even if both spouses jointly charged) and is always compellable *unless* both spouses are jointly charged;

iv) prosecution cannot comment on failure of spouse to testify, although there is no such prohibition upon the judge.

f) *Ex-spouses*

i) Civil cases

The effect of s1 Evidence Amendment Act 1853 and the Evidence Further Amendment Act 1869 is to make the spouse of a party in a civil trial competent and compellable. The 1853 Act has been construed strictly: *Shenton* v *Tyler* (1939), and therefore the decision in *Monroe* v *Twistleton* (1802) appears to remain binding, ie that an ex-spouse is incompetent to give evidence about events which occurred during the subsistence of the marriage.

ii) Criminal cases

Section 80(5) Police and Criminal Evidence Act 1984 states:

'In any proceedings a person who has been but is no longer married to the accused shall be competent and compellable to give evidence as if that person and the accused had never been married.'

The wording is unambiguous, and the effect is that an ex-spouse is competent and compellable whether for prosecution or defence, and whether or not the evidence relates to occurrences during the subsistence of the marriage: *R* v *Mathias* (1989). The case of *R* v *Cruttenden* [1991] 3 All ER 242 made it clear that the divorced spouse is competent and compellable in any proceedings which take place after s80(5) came into effect even if the events about which he or she was to give evidence occurred before it came into effect.

4.3 Analysis of questions

Competence and compellability of witnesses will very rarely constitute a self-contained question; it will often comprise a part of a problem question embracing other areas such as corroboration etc. Occasionally, since s80 Police and Criminal Evidence Act 1984 was enacted there have been essay questions especially on spouses' competence and compellability. Therefore the problem question which follows is NOT a typical degree or Bar Final question – but competence and compellability will appear again in later chapters as *part* of problem questions.

4.4 Questions

QUESTION ONE

Albert Jones was driving the family car with his wife Bertha in the front passenger seat and their 15-year-old son Charles and seven-year-old daughter Diane in the rear seats. The car was knocked off the road by an oncoming lorry which failed to stop. Charles was killed instantly, and Bertha and Albert both sustained cuts and bruises. Immediately before the incident Diane shrieked: 'Look out, Daddy!'; she was very shocked, but sustained no physical injury.

Albert has been charged with causing death by reckless driving. Bertha made a statement to the police to the effect that Albert was driving far too fast, could not negotiate a bend in the road and thus hit the lorry and was swept off the road; she now does not wish to testify for the prosecution. Diane made a statement: 'Daddy was on the proper side of the road – Mummy's side was near the fence – I shouted very hard when I saw a great big lorry slide across the road towards Daddy's car.'

Discuss the evidentiary problems.

Written by editor

Skeleton Solution

- Competence and compellability generally.
- Compellability of spouses – s80 Police and Criminal Evidence Act 1984 and its interpretation.
- Competence of children in criminal trials.

Suggested Solution

The prosecution will have to prove beyond reasonable doubt that:

- Albert was driving the car recklessly; and
- that reckless driving was a cause of the death of Charles; it is not necessary to prove that it was the only cause, so long as it was a cause of the death. (On causation in criminal cases, see textbooks on Criminal Law, and consider *R* v *Hennigan* (1971).)

Bertha, as the spouse of Albert, the accused, is now a competent witness for the prosecution (as she is not charged jointly with them – see Police and Criminal Evidence Act 1984 s80(1)(a)), but whether she is compellable depends on the interpretation of s80(3) Police and Criminal Evidence Act 1984.

Diane, aged seven, being a 'child' for the purposes of s33A of Criminal Justice Act 1988 (as amended by Criminal Justice Act 1991), will have her competence tested in accordance with s33A(2A). She can only give unsworn evidence, and there is therefore now no need to test her understanding of the oath. The case law before the 1991 Act suggested a child of the age of five should not be called to give evidence in a criminal case – *R* v *Wallwork* (1958), but above that age it was more likely that he or she would be called. However, the new test is, arguably, much less stringent and does not impose any particular burden of understanding concepts such as truth or lies.

If Diane gives evidence in Albert's defence her evidence does not need to be corroborated – s52(2) Criminal Justice Act 1991, and the judge is not required to warn the jury of the dangers of convicting without corroborative evidence, but the jury themselves may attach little or no weight to Diane's evidence, dependent on how she gives her evidence and withstands cross-examination by prosecuting counsel.

Section 80 Police and Criminal Evidence Act 1984 makes the spouse of an accused person a competent witness for the prosecution whatever the charge, unless the spouse is a co-accused. However, competence means that the spouse *may* give evidence if she wishes; Bertha can be compelled to give evidence against Albert only in the limited class of cases stipulated in s80(3), of which the relevant paragraph is s80(3)(a) which makes the spouse of the accused a compellable prosecution witness if:

'the offence charged involves an assault on, or injury or a threat of injury to, the wife or husband of the accused or a person who was at the material time under the age of 16.'

Section 80(3)(a) is not very clear, but in the situation in the question the offence charged involves injury to a person under 16, Charles, who was allegedly killed by Albert's reckless driving. If Charles had not died, but had suffered some non-fatal injury, the charge against Albert would have been reckless driving – therefore arguably it would not have been covered by s80(3)(a) as it would not have been in issue that Charles (and Bertha) had been injured, nor that Diane had feared immediate injury to herself. However, since Charles, under 16 years of age, has been fatally injured, and that injury must be part of the prosecution's case against Albert, then Bertha is a compellable witness for the prosecution against her spouse. Her attendance would probably be secured by a witness order or summons (Criminal Procedure (Attendance of Witnesses) Act 1965): if she does not attend when ordered or summoned to do so, a warrant may be issued for her arrest – *R* v *Bradford Justices, ex parte Wilkinson* (1990); if, having been sworn, she refused to testify, she would be in contempt of court. If she gave evidence, but contradicted her previous statement, and showed enmity to the prosecuting counsel, then with leave of the judge she could be treated as a hostile witness, and her examination by prosecuting counsel would resemble a cross-examination, with questions being put to her on her previous statement as to her husband's driving (see, for example, *R* v *Baldwin* (1986) and *R* v *Thompson* (1976)).

Albert cannot be compelled to testify in his own defence; if he does so testify then he can (and probably will) be subjected to rigorous cross-examination. If he elects not to testify, the matter is now governed by s35 Criminal Justice and Public Order Act 1994 which will allow for appropriate comments to be made upon his silence and for proper inferences to be drawn by the court in accordance with the guidelines suggested in *R* v *Cowan* (1995).

Given the unwillingness of Bertha to testify for the prosecution, her evidence if she is compelled is unlikely to carry much weight, therefore it could be that a plea by Albert's counsel of 'no case to answer' would be successful at the conclusion of the prosecution's case, ie the prosecution have not even discharged the evidential burden, therefore there is not even a *prima facie* case. If such a plea is unsuccessful, or is not made, then Albert would be well advised to testify in his own defence if the only other defence witness is a child of tender years who may be adjudged incompetent as a witness; and if allowed to testify, she is *not* an independent, disinterested witness. Bertha, once she has been called as a prosecution witness, is not permitted to give evidence for the defence (*R* v *Kelly* (1985)). Albert's counsel should also bear this in mind when deciding whether or not to call Albert (who must be called, if he is going to testify, before other defence witnesses).

QUESTION TWO

'When Parliament by the Act of 1898 effected a change in the general law and made the prisoner in every case a competent witness, it was in evident difficulty and it pursued the familiar English system of compromise.' (Viscount Sankey).

Discuss.

University of London LLB Examination
(for External Students) Law of Evidence June 1994 Q3

General Comment

This question permits wide discussion of the 1898 Act and its effects, especially with regard to the accused and evidence of his bad character. An understanding of the background to the Act is required, so as to put the quotation into context: the progression from the defendant being incompetent to the position today. Coupled with this, a critical assessment of the Act and its objectives is needed – does the defendant deserve protection and, if so, is it afforded by the Act?

Skeleton Solution

- The historical development of the competence of the accused.
- The 1898 Act.
- The balance/compromise of interests especially s1(f)(ii).
- Judicial discretion to disallow cross-examination.
- Discussion of the implications of this balance/compromise.

Suggested Solution

In criminal cases prior to the passing of the Criminal Evidence Act 1898, the accused was incompetent at common law. He was thus not permitted to give evidence in his own defence. This was because it was felt *first* that the defendant's personal interest in the outcome of the proceedings ought to preclude him from giving evidence and *second* that if competent, it was feared the defendant might be compelled to incriminate himself.

In the years leading up to the Criminal Evidence Act 1898 a number of statutes were passed, rendering the defendant competent in relation to certain offences. This piecemeal approach was clearly unsatisfactory; it was recognised that the defendant should be permitted to give sworn evidence in his own defence in *all* criminal cases. This was brought into effect by s1 of the Criminal Evidence Act 1898 (hereafter 'the Act').

The Act also changed the position relating to the competence of spouses. Spouses became competent (but not compellable) for the defence, subject to the consent of the defendant (s1(c)). Spouses remained incompetent for the prosecution (although various statutory exceptions were enacted). Since this part of the Act has now been repealed, and the spouse's competence and compellability is now governed by s80 of the Police and Criminal Evidence Act 1984, it is not proposed to deal with this area of the law in this suggested solution.

Returning to the defendant, s1 of the Act made defendants competent but not compellable in all criminal cases. However, it was recognised that whilst it was just for the defendant to be able to give evidence in his own defence, this also brought about serious potential risks – in particular the fear that he might be torn apart by cross-examination and be forced to incriminate himself. Cross-examination is 'a powerful weapon entrusted to counsel' (per Lord Sankey LC in *Machine and General Investment Co Ltd* v *Austin* (1935)).

The Act was with drafted with these issues in mind, attempting to strike a balance between these apparently conflicting considerations. How was this balance struck? The defendant was made competent but not compellable, hence he could give evidence in his own defence but only 'upon his own application' (s1(a)). If the defendant fails to give evidence, this may *not* be commented upon by the prosecution (s1(b)). *However*, the judge may comment on this (*R* v *Rhodes* (1899)), as may counsel for a co-accused (*R* v *Wickham* (1971)).

The Act places restrictions on cross-examination of the accused: s1(e) provides that the defendant may be asked any question notwithstanding that it would tend to criminate him *as to the offence charged* (but *not* as to any *other* offences).

As regards other offences (and the defendant's bad character in general) the Act places restrictions on cross-examination. The defendant may be cross-examined as to other offences for the purpose of proving *guilt*, if the evidence of the other offences is admissible under the similar fact evidence doctrine (s1(f)(i)).

The balance (or compromise) is apparent when one considers cross-examination with regard to offences which are *not* similar fact offences. The defendant is not fully protected, nor is he fully exposed to cross-examination.

Questions tending to show commission of, or convictions of, other offences (other than similar fact offences) or which show the defendant to be of bad character, are not permitted unless:

a) the defendant's good character is put in issue; or

b) imputations are cast on the prosecution or prosecution witnesses (s1(f)(ii)); or

c) the defendant gives evidence against a co-accused (s1(f)(iii)).

Hence, the defendant has the 'shield' of s1(f) unless one of the circumstances laid out in s1(f)(i), (ii) or (iii) arises, in which case the 'shield' is lost. Questions under s1(f)(ii) and (iii) go to credibility (although arguably questions under s1(f)(ii) indirectly go to guilt) (*Maxwell* v *DPP* (1935)). It should be added that the judge has a discretion to disallow such cross-examination by the prosecution (*R* v *Cook* (1959)), but this is purely a discretion, not a general rule to be relied upon by the defence (*Selvey* v *DPP* (1970)).

How successfully has this balance been struck? The compromise reached in s1(f)(ii) acts as a powerful disincentive to cross-examination of prosecution witnesses by defence counsel. If 'imputations' are cast, then the defendant loses his 'shield'. Whilst prima facie this may seem fair (ie that if a defendant seeks to sully the reputation of prosecution witnesses he should be equally open to such treatment) it is submitted that in reality this is rather unfair – prosecution witnesses are not on trial and are not at risk of conviction and penalty. The defendant is! Surely the defendant's interests are compromised as a result of this apparent balance. It may be said that this is redressed by the judge's discretion to disallow cross-examination but it is submitted that this cannot be used to justify the compromise. As explained above, the House of Lords has said that the judicial discretion is not an absolute rule (*Selvey* v *DPP*).

When one considers the Act in the light of these points it becomes apparent that a compromise has been reached; regrettably, this includes a compromise of the interests of the person most at risk – the defendant.

QUESTION THREE

Bill and Denis are charged with indecent assault on Freda, aged 17, and with raping Gertie, aged 15. Agnes, Bill's wife, made a statement to the police in which she stated that she had witnessed both incidents, but she is now unwilling to give evidence. Bill and Dennis assert that they have never touched the girls.

Consider whether Agnes is a competent, or compellable, witness for:

a) the prosecution;

b) Denis;

c) Bill.

Written by editor

Skeleton Solution

• Introduction; spouses as witnesses.

• Agnes – competent/compellable for:

a) prosecution;

b) Denis;

c) Bill.

• Brief discussion of problems raised by s80 Police and Criminal Evidence Act 1984.

Suggested Solution

The general rule at common law was that a spouse of an accused person was incompetent as a witness for the prosecution; by virtue of the Criminal Evidence Act 1898 the spouse was competent as a witness for the accused and competent, provided the accused consented, as a witness for a person charged jointly with the accused. The rationale of this general rule was that the law respected the sanctity of marriage and, recognising the unity of husband and wife, considered it undesirable (even abhorrent) that one spouse testify against the other, whether as a witness for the prosecution or as a witness for a person jointly charged with the other spouse as that evidence could be unfavourable to the other spouse's defence.

Even prior to the Police and Criminal Evidence Act 1984 there were numerous statutes which created exceptions to the general rule governing the spouse as a prosecution witness, but in 1979 the House of Lords held that, in all these exceptional situations, the spouse of the accused was competent as a witness for the prosecution, but *never* compellable (*Hoskyn* v *MPC* (1979)). Pre-1984, therefore, the law in this area was very complex; as a prosecution witness the spouse of the accused was generally incompetent, but was competent by virtue of numerous statutory exceptions; as a witness for the accused she was competent but not compellable; as a witness for a person charged jointly with the accused spouse the other spouse was competent with the consent of the accused spouse but not compellable. So, pre-1984 a spouse was either incompetent, competent with consent of the other, accused, spouse, exceptionally, competent – but *never* compellable as a witness.

Section 80 of the Police and Criminal Evidence Act 1984 swept aside these, presumably archaic, restrictions on competence, and, further made the spouse compellable in specified circumstances. The spouse is now competent in every situation, unless charged jointly with the other spouse, and is compellable as a prosecution witness if the offence is a sexual offence against a person under 16, or is an offence involving injury to that spouse or a person under 16.

Applying s80 to the given facts, Agnes is compellable as a prosecution witness to the rape of Gertie, as the offence with which Bill, her spouse, is charged is 'a sexual offence alleged to have been committed in respect of a person who was at the material time under 16' (s80(3)(a) and (b)). Whether she is compellable as a prosecution witness to the indecent assault on Freda depends on the age of Freda 'at the the material time', ie if, at the time of the alleged indecent assault Freda was under 16, then Agnes is a compellable prosecution witness; if Freda was 16, then Agnes is merely competent. Despite her reluctance, if Agnes is compellable then her attendance can be secured by a witness order or witness summons (Criminal Procedure (Attendance of Witnesses) Act 1965). If she still refuses to attend a warrant can be issued for her arrest – *R* v *Bradford Justices, ex parte Wilkinson* (1990) If, having attended, she refuses to testify, she may be punished for contempt of court; if she shows enmity towards the prosecutor in giving her evidence and contradicts her previous statement, then, with leave of the judge, she may be treated as a hostile witness – in which case her examination-in-chief will take the form of a cross-examination, and consequently her evidence will lack the cogency it might otherwise have had. The prosecutor, therefore, may be reluctant to call Agnes if she shows hostility and is adamant that she does not intend to testify against her husband. (Regarding the competence and compellability of Agnes, it is irrelevant that they were not married at the time of the alleged incidents giving rise to the charges – s80 is concerned with the marital status of the accused and the potential witness at the time of the trial. Conversely, if Agnes and Bill had divorced by the time of the trial, then Agnes will be competent and compellable as if she had never been Bill's wife (s80(5)).)

Agnes is now competent as a witness for Denis whether or not Bill consents to her giving evidence for his co-accused at their joint trial (s80(1)(b)). However, her compellability as a witness for Denis is subject to the same restrictions as outlined above regarding her compellability as a prosecution witness. Whether competent or compellable as a witness to testify for Denis, the competence or compellability of Agnes is not subject to the consent of Bill – since s80 became law the wishes of the accused spouse in this context are irrelevant.

Agnes is a compellable witness for Bill, despite her previous apparent willingness to give evidence against him (s80(2)). However, if Agnes is compelled to give prosecution evidence in respect of the rape charge (and, subject to Freda's age at the time of the incident, the indecent assault charge), then she is no longer available as a witness for the defence, whether for her spouse, Bill, or his co-accused, Denis (*R* v *Kelly* (1985)).

Several problems are caused by s80, not all of them by some ambiguities in its wording, and not all of them relevant to this problem. Those which are relevant are:

a) If a successful defence application is made for separate trials of Bill and Denis, then Agnes is compellable as a witness for the prosecution, or defence, at Denis's trial, and her marital status is irrelevant.

b) Whether or not Bill and Denis are jointly tried, if the counts of rape and indecent assault are severed, and therefore tried separately, then Agnes may be compellable as a prosecution witness at the trial for rape, but not at the trial for indecent assault, but at both trials she would be compellable as a witness for Bill, but not Denis.

c) If there are separate trials of Bill and Denis, or if they are tried jointly, and Agnes gives prosecution evidence under compulsion, she may have to be treated as a hostile witness, But if the compulsion is permissible only in respect of the alleged rape, not the indecent assault, it may be difficult to the point of impossibility to put her previous statement to her in her examination-in-chief without referring to both alleged incidents as they may be inextricably linked in her statement.

5 Corroboration

5.1 Introduction

5.2 Key points

5.3 Analysis of questions

5.4 Questions

5.1 Introduction

The requirement for evidence to be corroborated is exceptional in English law, and the exceptional circumstances where the court will concern itself with corroboration have been whittled away by s34 Criminal Justice Act 1988 and now, significantly, in s32 of the Criminal Justice and Public Order Act (CJPOA) 1994 which finally abolished the *mandatory* requirements for corroboration, as well as rendered more complex by decisions such as that in *R* v *Chance* (1988). In law degree and Bar Final examinations it is unusual to be faced with a question dealing solely with corroboration; as happens so often in Evidence papers questions about the area dealt with in this chapter will include a test of the students' knowledge of other, overlapping, areas such as burdens of proof, right of silence etc. Nevertheless, corroboration is an important issue in the law of evidence in criminal trials, although the effects of s32 CJPOA 1994 will be to reduce its importance considerably.

5.2 Key points

The following should be understood by the student who wishes to be conversant with corroboration:

a) *Definition of corroboration*

   The best definition is a combination of that given in *R* v *Baskerville* (1916) and *R* v *Scarrott* (1978), ie 'relevant, admissible and credible evidence, originating from a source independent of the witness requiring corroboration, and implicating the accused in a material particular.'

b) *Functions of judge and jury*

   It is the function of the judge to decide whether evidence (either in itself, or aggregated with other evidence) is capable of amounting to corroboration. If the judge decides this in the affirmative, he must then leave it to the jury to decide whether the evidence *is* corroborative. If the judge decides this in the negative, he must direct the jury to disregard that evidence because, for example, it is not credible, not independent etc.

c) *Corroboration a pre-requisite to conviction*

   Three statutes stipulate that an accused person cannot be convicted of the offences stipulated on the evidence of only one witness:

   i) The offence of driving a motor vehicle on a road at an excessive speed, contrary to the Road Traffic Regulations Act 1984. Section 89 provides that a driver cannot be convicted of exceeding the speed limit on the uncorroborated opinion evidence of one witness as to the speed of the vehicle. There are two caveats:

- the corroboration requirement arises only when the charge is exceeding the speed limit – so if the charge were driving at a speed or in a manner which was reckless, the corroboration requirement would not have to be met;

- corroboration is required of the *opinion* evidence of one witness, therefore if the evidence is of fact, eg a police officer's reading of a radar speed device, corroboration is *not* required.

ii) The Treason Act 1895 requires the evidence of two or more witnesses for a conviction of high treason.

iii) Section 13 Perjury Act 1911 provides that a person cannot be convicted of perjury on the uncorroborated testimony of only one witness as to the *falsity* of any statement made by the accused which is alleged to be false. Therefore, if the statement was believed to be false, but unbeknown to the maker happened to be true, then there is no corroboration requirement. Where corroboration as to the *falsity* is required, it does not matter if two witnesses give evidence as to the falsity of the defendant's statement, and each heard him admit its falsity together, on the same occasion: *R* v *Peach* [1990] 2 All ER 966.

The stipulation that an accused person could not be convicted of offences of procuration – for sexual intercourse or prostitution – of women contrary to the Sexual Offences Act 1956 has now been abrogated by s33(1) CJPOA 1994.

d) *Corroboration warning required as a matter of practice*

i) The evidence of children – always now to be given unsworn – does not require corroboration nor a corroboration warning – s52(2) of the Criminal Justice Act 1991 abolishing s38(1) of the Children and Young Persons Act 1933, and s34(1) Criminal Justice Act 1988. However, judges may continue as a matter of practice, rather than law, to give a corroboration warning.

ii) Accomplices testifying for the defence

An accomplice giving evidence in his own defence obviously has his own axe to grind, and will often give evidence which is unfavourable to his co-accused. Therefore, as a matter of practice, it is desirable that the jury be alerted to the dangers of convicting on that evidence if it is not corroborated. Every case must be treated according to its own particular circumstances, and the omission of a warning will not always lead to a conviction's being quashed on appeal: *R* v *Prater* [1960] 2 QB 464. Where there is no evidence pointing to the involvement of the witness in the crime of which the accused is charged, but nevertheless the witness may have some ulterior motive in testifying for the defence or for the prosecution, then the judge may direct the jury to treat that evidence with some scepticism, but a failure to do so will not necessarily result in the quashing of the conviction of the accused: *R* v *Beck* [1982] 1 WLR 461; *R* v *Lovell* [1990] Crim LR 111. The case of *R* v *Brown* (1991) The Times 13 December in the Court of Appeal, also makes it clear that even if the witness is not an accomplice, but his evidence might be suspect, the judge should not give a corroboration warning, but warn the jury of danger of relying on that evidence.

Similarly, where the spouse of an accomplice gives evidence which is supportive of the accomplice's evidence, the judge may give a warning to the jury to treat the spouse's testimony with caution: *R* v *Evans* [1965] 2 QB 295.

The requirement to give an accomplice corroboration warning as a matter of practice was abrogated by s32 CJPOA 1994 and the judicial discretion involved is now summarised in *R* v *Makanjuola* [1995] 3 All ER 730 CA.

Section 32 CJPOA 1994 also ended the requirement, as a matter of practice, to warn about the evidence of sexual offence victims.

e) *Identification of accused*

Evidence of identification does not need to be corroborated, and a warning against convicting on such uncorroborated evidence is not mandatory. However, because a witness identifying the accused can often be mistaken, albeit genuine, guidelines were laid down by the Court of Appeal (Criminal Division) in *R* v *Turnbull* [1977] QB 224, and any student of evidence should be conversant with the gist of what the court said, and of subsequent appellate decisions which qualify or amplify the *Turnbull* guidelines. Note further that identification from police photographs ought not to be put in evidence because it infringes similar fact rules: *R* v *Bleakley* [1993] Crim LR 203 and *R* v *Lamb* (1980) 71 Cr App R 198.

f) *Corroboration provided by the accused*

The accused may provide the necessary or desirable, corroboration of the evidence of prosecution witnesses:

i) If the accused tells a material lie (usually by making one statement, then retracting some, or all, of it and making another, contradictory, statement) then this *may* amount to corroborative evidence. Whether it will or not was exemplified in *R* v *Lucas* [1981] QB 720; briefly, to be corroborative the lie must be material, deliberate, and told because of fear of the truth because of a realisation of guilt. So, if the accused can give an explanation of his lies which is consistent with innocence, the lies will not amount to corroboration: *R* v *Dowley* [1983] Crim LR 168; *R* v *Ahmed* [1993] Crim LR 946.

Similarly, lies told by the accused when testifying in his own defence *may* corroborate other evidence, but do not necessarily, and the same criteria apply as those for lies told pre-court.

ii) The silence of the accused in court, ie the fact that he elects not to testify, can never amount to corroboration. But if the accused is accused of an offence by a person or equal terms with him, and he remains silent where it would be reasonable to expect some reply (such as a denial, an indignant retort etc), then his silence is capable of corroborating other evidence of prosecution witnesses: *R* v *Cramp* (1880) 14 Cox CC 390. Whether or not the defendant and his accuser are on equal terms is a question for the jury: *R* v *Horne* [1990] Crim LR 188.

Where the accuser is a person in authority, eg a police officer, then the silence of the accused, as the law stands at present, cannot be corroboration: *R* v *Whitehead* [1929] 1 KB 99.

iii) If the accused refuses, without any reasonable explanation, to provide samples or specimens when he is told the purpose for which they are required, then his refusal is capable of amounting to corroboration: *R* v *Smith (Robert William)* (1985) 81 Cr App R 286. This decision has been adopted in s62(10) Police and Criminal Evidence Act 1984, in respect of refusal by suspects to give intimate body samples, the phrase used being 'without good cause' rather than 'without reasonable explanation' as in *Smith*. (With regard to non-intimate samples, s65(3) of the 1984 Act provides for these to be taken without consent.)

5.3 Analysis of questions

Recent questions have tended to concentrate on evidence in sexual offence cases and evidence of identification. Corroboration in problem questions tends, still, to be combined with other evidential issues, but essay questions on the incidence and rationale of corroboration do also appear.

5.4 Questions

QUESTION ONE

'The purpose of corroboration is not to give validity or credence to evidence which is deficient or suspect or incredible but only to confirm and support that which as evidence is sufficient and satisfactory and credible ...' (Lord Morris).

Discuss.

University of London LLB Examination
(for External Students) Law of Evidence June 1994 Q4

General Comment

To attempt this question, a knowledge of the context of this quotation is vital since it is a dictum which has been *disapproved*! The quotation should be put in context and discussed with regard to the decision in *Wong Muk-Ping*. There is then ample room for discussion of the purpose of corroboration and the various scenarios in which questions of corroboration arise.

Skeleton Solution

- Put quotation in context: *DPP* v *Hester*.
- Discuss this dictum as considered in *Wong Muk-Ping*.
- Define corroboration and consider its need and purpose more fully with regard to types of case involving corroboration:
  - corroboration required as matter of law;
  - corroboration warning as matter of law;
  - corroboration warning as matter of practice;
  - identification cases.

Suggested Solution

This dictum is taken from the case of *DPP* v *Hester* (1973). Its clear implication is that the purpose of corroboration is to support evidence which is 'sufficient, satisfactory and credible' *in its own right* (ie when considered *without* any corroborative evidence). If evidence is not 'sufficient, satisfactory and credible' in its own right, then, Lord Morris suggests, it is not the purpose of corroboration to support it. (Dicta to similar effect can be found in other cases, eg per Watkins LJ in *R* v *Olaleye* (1986) and per Lord Hailsham LC in *DPP* v *Kilbourne* (1973).)

This proposition came before the Privy Council in the case of *Attorney-General of Hong Kong* v *Wong Muk-Ping* (1987), where it was submitted that where a judge gives a corroboration warning, the jury should be told to consider the credibility of the witness desiring corroboration (the 'suspect witness') in isolation from any other evidence. If they are satisfied as to the credibility of that witness, only then may they go on to consider any corroborative evidence, in order to decide whether or not to accept the evidence of the 'suspect witness'.

This submission was rejected. Lord Bridge said that it is precisely because the evidence of a suspect witness might be unreliable that the corroboration warning is given. Hence, the credibility of a suspect witness is not to be considered in isolation, but in the light of the corroborative evidence, which may assist in establishing its reliability. It should be added that in rare cases, if the suspect witness admits that his evidence-in-chief was false (and the prosecution depends upon it) *then* the judge should direct an acquittal: *Attorney-General of Hong Kong* v *Wong Muk-Ping*.

A more detailed examination of the purpose of corroboration can be undertaken by briefly considering first what corroboration entails, and second, when it arises in the law of evidence.

What is corroboration?

'It is a matter of common sense that the risk of conviction of the innocent is reduced if a conviction is based on the testimony of more than one acceptable witness:' per Lord Morris in *DPP* v *Hester*. Such additional evidence is termed 'corroboration'. However, there is *no* general requirement for corroboration in criminal law. A conviction, generally speaking, may properly and safely be founded on uncorroborated evidence. Therefore, generally, whilst corroboration may assist in proving a case, there is no general requirement for it to exist before a jury may convict.

There are, however, exceptions to this general rule. The reasons underlying these exceptions are simple:

a) the gravity of the allegation; and/or

b) the danger of acting on certain categories of evidence, if uncorroborated.

In order to amount to corroboration, evidence must meet certain requirements:

a) *It must be relevant* – this is true of all evidence!

b) *It must be admissible* – that is to say, not excluded by other rules of evidence; again this is true of all evidence.

c) *It must be credible.*

   The evidence providing corroboration must be credible. If a witness's testimony falls of its own inanition, the question of the witness being capable of giving corroboration does not arise: per Lord Hailsham in *DPP* v *Kilbourne*.

   It should be noted that this is a quite different scenario from the witness *desiring* corroboration (the 'suspect witness'), whose evidence does *not* fall of its own inanition but should be considered in the light of any corroborative evidence, as explained above in *Attorney-General of Hong Kong* v *Wong Muk-Ping*.

d) *It must be independent* – that is to say, extraneous to the witness who is to be corroborated: *R* v *Whitehead* (1929).

e) *It must implicate the accused in a material particular* – it must confirm both a material circumstance of the case *and* the identity of the defendant: *R* v *Baskerville* (1916).

When, and why, do questions of corroboration arise? These queries can be answered with reference to four types of case:

a) cases where corroboration *itself* is required as a matter of law;

b) cases where a corroboration warning must be given as a matter of law;

c) cases in which a corroboration warning is given as a matter of practice;

d) cases involving identification.

a) *Corroboration required as a matter of law*

Corroboration itself is *required* in very few scenarios. However, when required, if there is no evidence capable of amounting to corroboration, the judge will direct an acquittal.

Corroboration is required in the following cases:

i) Speeding – a conviction cannot be based on the opinion evidence of just one witness; corroboration is required (eg *another* witness's opinion evidence!): s89(2) Road Traffic Regulations Act 1984.

ii) Perjury – s13 Perjury Act 1911. The reason underlying this section is unclear, but may be a policy decision – it is felt that if prosecutions for perjury were too easy, witnesses might be discouraged from giving evidence (Criminal Law Revision Committee, 11th Report (Cmnd 4991, paras 178 and 180)).

iii) Treason – s1 Treason Act 1895. Technically, treason is punishable by the death penalty, hence corroboration (understandably) is required.

b) *Corroboration warning required as a matter of practice*

A warning used to be given because of the inherent unreliability of certain types of evidence. The warning was to the effect that it was dangerous to convict on the uncorroborated evidence of a witness, but if satisfied as to the truth of such evidence, the jury could nonetheless do so: *R* v *Freebody* (1935). It should be stressed that corroboration itself was *not* required – the requirement was that the warning be given.

The warning was given as a matter of law in only two types of case:

i) *Accomplices giving evidence for the prosecution* – the obvious danger was that the accomplice may minimise his own part, and maximise the rôles of others!

ii) *Sexual offences* – allegations are easy to make and difficult to refute. Dangers arise because allegations may be motivated by spite, shame, fantasy and so on (Criminal Law Revision Committee, 11th Report (Cmnd 4991, paras 178 and 180)).

Both of these requirements are now abrogated by s32 CJPOA 1996.

c) *Corroboration warning given as a matter of practice*

Two examples will suffice:

i) Accomplices giving evidence on their *own* behalf – a warning is desirable (but not required) because the witness may seek to minimise his own role, and increase the role of his co-defendants: *R* v *Cheema* (1993).

ii) Children – a warning is desirable because of the risks of childish imagination, suggestibility or poor memory: *R* v *Pryce* (1991).

d) *Identification cases*

Such cases carry with them the risk of mistaken identification. Whilst neither corroboration nor a corroboration warning is required, a warning is given to the effect that there is a 'special need for caution' in such cases, and telling the jury to look for 'supporting evidence' (which need *not* meet the strict requirements of corroboration), although the jury may convict in the absence of such supporting evidence. A detailed examination of this warning as laid down in *R* v *Turnbull* (1977) is beyond the ambit of this question.

In conclusion: the quotation discussed has a flawed foundation. The very purpose of corroboration is to enable the jury to consider the credibility of the 'suspect witness'. The categories of case in which a question of corroboration arises have been discussed, showing that in each category there is potentially unreliable evidence, hence the suspect witness's evidence should be considered in the light of any corroborative evidence so as to enable the jury to accept or reject it. The Privy Council's decision in *Attorney-General of Hong Kong* v *Wong Muk-Ping* thus firmly rejects Lord Morris' dictum from *DPP* v *Hester*.

QUESTION TWO

A is charged with indecently assaulting B, a six year old boy, and C, a ten year old girl. Both B and C are pupils at the same school. B's story is that A offered him a lift home in his car while B was walking to the bus stop just after school had finished and the assault took place in the car shortly before A dropped him off just round the corner from where B lived. D, B's mother, noticing a mark on B's leg that evening exclaims, 'Did someone do that to you?' and B describes what happened. He describes A as a short person with a beard, who wore sunglasses and 'had a funny smell'. C's story is that, the day after the assault on B, a man, wearing sunglasses and smelling of garlic, sat on the seat next to her at the bus stop while she was going home from school. He then put his hand on her thigh. She screamed and ran away. E, a passerby, can confirm that he heard C scream but that he only got a glimpse of a short man, who disappeared very quickly.

F, a policeman, sketches a picture in accordance with B's description and B subsequently picks out A in an identification parade. B is overwhelmed by the events of the trial and is unwilling to give evidence. C picks out A from five photographs shown to her from the police records. A claims an alibi for each charge.

Advise the prosecution on any evidential issues that might arise.

University of London LLB Examination
(for External Students) Evidence June 1992 Q6

General Comment

This is a very wide question covering many important evidential issues. You will not be expected to go into each evidential point in great detail; marks will be awarded for recognising the issues.

Skeleton Solution

• Children.

- Children's evidence.
- Competence and compellability.
- Corroboration.
- Warnings.
- Previous consistent statement.
- Complaints in cases of sexual nature.
- Identification evidence.
- Alibi.

Suggested Solution

The most important issue here is the competence of a child to give evidence. The general rule in criminal cases is that if a child is competent to give evidence for the prosecution, the child can be compelled to give evidence for the prosecution. B is overwhelmed by the events of a trial and is unwilling to give evidence. The prosecution will be able to compel B to give evidence.

It was established in the case of *R* v *Brasier* (1779) that the competence of a young child to give sworn evidence in criminal proceedings depends upon whether the child understands the nature of the oath but now the matter is determined by s33A(2A) CJA 1988 which requires that the child is capable of giving intelligible testimony. The question should be decided in open court but without the jury: *R* v *Hampshire* (1995). The evidence must be given unsworn: s33A(1).

The former requirements for obligatory corroboration warnings in respect of child witnesses and sexual complainants have now been removed by s32 CJPOA 1994.

The prosecution will wish to adduce evidence of B's complaint to his mother, D. It is well established that in sexual cases the fact that the victim made a voluntary complaint shortly after the alleged offence is admissible to show the victim's consistency. This rule applies even if the complainant is male: *R* v *Christie* (1914).

In the case of *R* v *Osborne* (1905), evidence of a complaint by a victim to his mother was admissible despite the fact that his mother's initial question elicited the complaint. The court held that a question such as 'what is the matter?' does not deprive the complaint of its voluntariness. The prosecution in this case may face difficulties in adducing the evidence of the complaint due to the fact that D's question went beyond the normal inquiry allowed; it could have prompted the complaint. Accordingly, the defence may wish to challenge the evidence in a voir dire.

If B does not give evidence then D will not be allowed to give evidence of the complaint as a witness can only give evidence of a previous complaint if the victim gives evidence: see *R* v *Wallwork* (1958).

E's evidence may be challenged by the defence on the ground that its prejudicial effect outweighs its probative value. In any event, if it is held to be admissible, the judge will give a warning to the jury about the dangers of convicting on identification evidence. The case of *R* v *Turnbull* (1977), set out the guidelines for identification evidence. The judge will give a warning as to the circumstances of the identification. For example, factors such as visibility, light, time of day, length or duration of identification will all be pointed out by the judge.

It is highly unlikely that the court will allow evidence as to the identification of A by C from the police photographs. The general rule is that where a witness identifies the accused from a photograph such an identification is admissible provided that the photograph does not come from the police files. The ratio behind this rule is that the prejudicial effect of such an identification outweighs its probative value (see generally: *R* v *Wainwright* (1925)).

The identification of A by B in the identification parade would be admissible provided that the identification parade was carried out in accordance with Code D of the Code of Conduct. Evidence of the identification of A can be given by B or by a police officer who witnessed the identification (see generally: *R* v *Beveridge* (1987)).

As to the alibi of A, the general position is that the defendant does not bear the evidential burden of proving his defence of alibi as the burden is on the prosecution to prove the defendant's presence at the scene of the crime. However, in the case of *R* v *Johnson* (1961) dicta can be found to the effect that the defendant does bear the evidential burden of proving his alibi. If the jury rejects the defendant's alibi the judge should tell them that the evidence that the defendant has lied about his location does not prove that the identifying witness was correct.

QUESTION THREE

N is charged with the rape of O, aged 16. O says that she was coming home from a disco late at night when N came up behind her and dragged her into some undergrowth where the rape took place, and that N then ran off. P, O's mother, says that when O came home she looked very dishevelled but said nothing until the next morning when, in reply to P's question 'Did something nasty happen last night?', O said 'I was raped'. Later that day, O said that it was someone who was tall, with fair hair and a purple jumper, who raped her. Q, a passer–by at the time of the alleged offence, can confirm that he heard a scream from O and that he got a brief glimpse of a tall person with fair hair who ran away. Two policemen go to N's place that night; when N opens the door, one of them says 'You raped O, didn't you?' N's response is to go bright red and slam the door in their faces. Later he denies to the police that he has ever met O. O picks N out at an identification parade, but in court, she cannot remember who it was that she selected. A policeman is able to give evidence both of O's selection of N at the parade, and of O's selection from police records of a photograph of N.

Advise the prosecution of any evidential issues that might arise.

University of London Examination
(for External Students) Law of Evidence June 1993 Q8

General Comment

This is a question on disparate items of admissibility; again, none of them is particularly difficult but it requires some skill to pick them all out. Basically they have to do with items arising during the course of evidence. This sort of question requires a good understanding of the rule against narrative and its exceptions and, particularly, its relation to the rule against hearsay. Remember that the rule against narrative is about witness *credibility*, whereas the rule against hearsay is about the *truth* of what is said. Credibility is supported by consistency and attacked by inconsistency and *truth does not come into it*. Many candidates come a cropper because they do not appreciate this distinction.

Divide this question up into a number of smaller questions; this makes so much more manageable. Note how, in all the problem questions answered, the answers *go straight into the question*; there is no beating around the bush in the form of 'I am asked to advise in the matter of ...' or a boring and silly repetition of the facts given!

It is not difficult. That does not mean that you should answer it in one page; rather, it gives you a chance to show the examiner what you know about the rationale for the rules (in particular, here, the operation and scope of the so–called 'rule against narrative.')

Skeleton Solution

- The rule against narrative.
- Sexual complaints (*Osborne)* and voluntariness.
- Question of corroboration.
- Silence in face of accusation (*Christie* and *Cramp*).
- Parties dealing on uneven terms.
- Identification evidence: 'fleeting glimpses' and *Turnbull* warning; breach of hearsay rule (*Osbourne and Virtue*) .
- Use of photograph from police records prejudicial.

Suggested Solution

O has made the serious accusation of rape against N and this amounts to a sexual complaint. Sexual complaints are admissible in evidence in the following way: they are to show that the testimony of the witness in court is consistent; the complainant gives evidence as to the rape in court and her evidence is bolstered by the fact that she complained a very short time after the alleged rape took place. It is not *corroborative* of that fact, since you cannot corroborate your own testimony, but it is thought to boost credibility (provided certain conditions are met) and, for that reason, sexual complaints are admitted as an exception to the rule against narrative. What is this rule? It prevents witnesses, in general, giving their own later testimony added strength: it prevents them from *manufacturing* their own evidence. Imagine the defendant who, having murdered his wife, races around saying 'It was an accident; it was an accident' (a fairly common occurrence, sad to relate). However many priests testify to this fact, it should not be seen to bolster his defence of accident in court!

But for sexual complaints to be admissible, two conditions, laid down in *Osborne* (1905), have to be met; the complaint must be as soon as is reasonably possible after the event and it must be voluntary, in the sense that it should not have been elicited by leading questions (it need not only go to consent, incidentally, and applies to sexual complaints other than rape). What is the position here? O doesn't complain immediately; however, this doesn't seem too important because she may have been so shaken that she needed to get rest immediately and whether this was so would depend upon what would be reasonable to expect in the circumstances, which would obviously involve reference to O's age. Is the complaint elicited by a leading question? It is not as if O's mother had just asked if anything was the matter; she asks 'Did something nasty happen last night?' and it could be argued that this is a leading question, negativing voluntariness, which suggests the answer 'yes'. But it is not a leading question so far as suggesting *rape*, or even a sexual offence of a lesser sort. In fact, given that O is dishevelled and P is O's mother, this would be a reasonable sort of question to put. It is fairly clear, therefore, that this sexual complaint would be admissible (not as truth of the facts contained within it) but to support the credibility of O's later testimony in court.

Another exception to the rule against narrative relates to identification evidence; the rationale is that identification being so fraught with inaccuracy, the closer the statement of identification to the time of the actual identification the better. Dock identifications are always frowned upon because of the obvious possibilities of mistake (an assumption that the police have got the right person; embarrassment on the part of the witness that he may have got it all wrong, etc) and so identification evidence in court (given by testimonial description as opposed to pointing to the dock) can be so bolstered. Clearly, O's statement about the assailant being tall, fair and with a purple jumper may be admitted to support her evidence and P will be able to go into the witness box to confirm what O said. Q's evidence is different though, because he only obtained a 'passing glimpse' of whoever might have been the assailant (he only hears a shout). This evidence is possibly admissible but, if so, the judge will have to give what is known as a *Turnbull* (1977) warning. This case actually gives the power to a judge to withdraw 'fleeting glimpse' type evidence from the jury where the evidence is largely or wholly of the circumstantial identificatory evidence sort. But there is other evidence (eg N's behaviour in the presence of the police) which might suggest otherwise; it would be sensible to consider the items of evidence separately before urging the judge to take this action, however.

A *Turnbull* warning requires the judge to warn the jury of the dangers of convicting a person on the basis wholly or largely of identification evidence alone; outside the fleeting glimpse type cases the jury *may* convict but only if the appropriate warning is given. The judge should point out such things as the circumstances obtaining at the time (light, distance, length of time of sighting), the state of mind of the witness (Was he familiar with the person identified? Did he have a special reason to notice?), the distinctiveness of the person's appearance (clothing, colour of skin, peculiar features) and so on. Note that it was held in *Chance* (1988) that where the identity of the alleged rapist is in issue, a *Turnbull* direction will suffice, and no separate corroboration warning as to the sexual nature of the offence is called for. The reason is that no question of the fantasising of the complainant arises. Why? Because the issue of the trial is the *identity* of the complainant, and not the question *whether in fact the complainant has been raped*. It would be different, of course, if the defence were that O had *consented*.

N's response to the policemen's accusation appears damning; but care is needed. In the first place, as has often been pointed out, going bright red, or remaining silent in the face of an accusation, is consistent with many things other than acknowledgement of guilt; one can question the relevance, therefore. On the other hand, the accusation is very direct and clear, specifying O and the circumstances, and an innocent person would, in the normal way, have responded by an angry denial (although sometimes denials, coupled with demeanour, can amount to admissions of guilt: see *Christie* (1914)). However, the real point here is that this evidence is not admissible; a person has a right to remain silent in the face of an accusation (in the sense that this silence will not be used as evidence against him) *where the parties are not dealing on even terms* (see *Parkes* (1976) and *Hall* (1971)). The police behaved disgracefully here; if they had grounds to suspect that he did this, they should have cautioned him immediately and arrested him; he could then not be questioned unless he was willing and had a solicitor present.

The policeman is allowed to give evidence of O's selection at the identity parade; this is in direct contravention of the hearsay rule because the policeman can only be giving evidence of a statement made by O ('This is the man') made out of court for the purpose of proving the truth of that statement; the policeman's statement cannot be bolstering the credibility of O's testimony in court *because O cannot give evidence on this point in court in order for it to be bolstered*. Nevertheless, despite *Myers* (1965), *Osbourne and Virtue* (1973) permits this position in the law. (A lazy counsel and a sleepy judge obviously were in that case – an astute counsel would have insisted that the policeman's hearsay evidence be excluded and would not have been dissuaded by the judge's remark – as occurred in *Osbourne and Virtue* – that 'it was not practical otherwise'.)

The policeman's evidence of a photograph from police records is not allowed as clearly prejudicial because it informs the jury that the defendant has had dealings with the police before: *Wainwright* (1875).

To conclude, there is little evidence here to maintain a conviction; basically is relies only on a sexual complaint and a 'fleeting glimpse'. If the judge, and he should be urged to do so by the defendant, withdraws the identification evidence of Q from the jury, we only have the sexual complaint and identification by O. The case by the prosecution therefore looks rather weak.

6 Hearsay – General Exclusion

6.1 Introduction

6.2 Key points

6.3 Analysis of questions

6.4 Questions

6.1 Introduction

Hearsay is one of the most important areas of the laws of evidence; the rule against hearsay is complex, but the rule and the many exceptions to it will always form the basis of at least one question (and frequently several) in any Evidence examination.

In this chapter the scope and application of the exclusionary rule against hearsay will be examined, together with the important common law rules which exceptionally allowed hearsay to be adduced.

In the next two chapters, admissibility by statute in civil and criminal cases respectively will be examined – only then will the full complexity of the hearsay rule emerge.

6.2 Key points

a) *Definition of hearsay*

Definitions of hearsay abound; to determine whether evidence is or is not hearsay (and therefore whether it is necessary to go any further and consider exceptions to the exclusionary rule) one should consider the purpose for which an out of court statement is tendered in evidence. If the statement is tendered as evidence of any fact (or opinion) expressed therein, then it is hearsay, ie if any out of court statement is tendered in order to invite the court to accept the truth of its content, that is hearsay. The statement may take various forms, ie it may be spoken, written, or in the form of a gesture:

i) Spoken, or oral hearsay

A good example of this is contained in the House of Lords decision in *R* v *Blastland* [1985] 2 All ER 1095, where their Lordships upheld the decision of the trial judge to exclude as inadmissible hearsay evidence of the content of a confession made by a person other than the accused. Blastland's counsel wanted this confession statement reported to the court as evidence of its truth, ie to further Blastland's defence. It was hearsay, and because it was not covered by any recognised exception to the hearsay rule, was therefore inadmissible.

Again, in *Sparks* v *R* [1964] AC 964, a white man was charged with indecent assault on a girl aged three. Sparks's counsel wanted to call as a defence witness the girl's mother to inform the court that shortly after the incident the girl had said that a coloured boy was the assailant. This evidence was being tendered to invite the court to believe the truth of the out of court statement by the girl (who did not give direct evidence herself), and was therefore hearsay, and, again, inadmissible because not covered by a recognised exception to the rule against hearsay.

ii) Written, or documentary hearsay

The same principles apply at common law as for spoken, or oral hearsay, so again the vital issue is the purpose for which the written, or printed etc, evidence is tendered.

iii) Gestures as hearsay

An affirmative nod or negative shake of the head may be hearsay just as the spoken or written affirmative or negative would be if tendered as an out of court 'statement'.

b) *The ambit of the hearsay rule*

If an out of court statement is tendered for a purpose *other* than to invite the court to accept the contents as true, then it is not hearsay. Therefore, if the fact rather than the content of the statement is what the person tendering it seeks to prove, it is not hearsay. For example, in *Ratten* v *R* [1972] AC 378 a telephone operator was permitted to give evidence that the wife of the accused had made an emergency telephone call in which she hysterically demanded the police a couple of minutes before she was fatally shot. The *fact* of the call contradicted Ratten's statement that his wife had made no telephone call; also the wife's hysteria tended to refute Ratten's defence that his gun went off as he was cleaning it and his wife was thus accidentally shot and died immediately. Therefore the evidence of the telephone operator was not hearsay. The case emphasises the point that the purpose for which the statement was tendered determines whether or not it is hearsay.

However, sometimes it is extremely difficult to know what that purpose is. In the case of *R* v *Kearley* [1991] Crim LR 282, there was the evidence of some police officers, who searched the defendant's house, that a number of people rang there to enquire about drugs. The court held the evidence to be admissible to prove that the defendant was the supplier of drugs. It was argued that the truth of the statements was irrelevant – what was important was the fact that the phone calls were made. However, it could be argued that the prosecution here was relying on the truth of the words said during those phone calls.

The case of *R* v *Harry* (1988) 86 Cr App R 105 concerned similar evidence which was held to be *inadmissible*, but the distinguishing point perhaps in this case was that the evidence was being used by one co-defendant against another. Both co-defendants were found at the same flat, but D1 wanted to use the words of the phone calls to show that it was D2 who was being asked for – hence D1 was certainly relying on the truth of the words, not just the fact that the phone calls were made.

c) *Implied assertions*

The hearsay rule applies undoubtedly to express assertions; there was some doubt as to whether implied assertions are covered by the hearsay rule. It would seem that most of the authorities (of which there is a paucity!) would support the view expressed by Lord Reid in *Myers* v *DPP* [1965] AC 1001 that implied assertions are admissible hearsay only if they come within a recognised exception to the hearsay rule. This seems to be the rationale upon which *R* v *Kearley* was decided and it should be assumed that the rule catches such matters.

d) *Statements on tapes, films, etc*

In *Taylor* v *Chief Constable of Cheshire* [1987] 1 All ER 225 a security camera in a shop made a video recording of Taylor stealing from the shop. Police officers watched the recording and identified Taylor; the recording was returned to the shopkeeper and was accidentally erased. The police officers were allowed to testify as to what they had seen on the video recording; it was *not* hearsay, in essence it was the same as if they had been in the shop and witnessed the incident, and then gave evidence as percipient witnesses. Similarly, a police officer may give evidence as to the reading on a radar speed meter, or the speedometer of his pursuing police vehicle, or a witness may state that an incident in issue occurred on a certain date because he looked at the newspaper he had bought or at his digital watch which displayed the date; throughout there is no element of hearsay in the evidence. In *R* v *Spiby* (1990) 91 Cr App R 186, the print-out from a machine used to monitor telephone call numbers and the length of the calls was not hearsay but real evidence because, like a speedometer, it is merely an instrument which can't contribute its own knowledge.

e)   *Admissibility of hearsay at common law*

When examining hearsay admissible at common law it must be borne in mind throughout that in many instances there has been statutory intervention. Some hearsay admissible at common law in both civil and criminal cases may now be admissible by statute in either civil cases, or alternatively in criminal cases.

i)   Informal admissions

A statement made by a party out of court, which is adverse to his interests in the case, is an informal admission and is admissible as evidence of the truth of its contents as an exception to the hearsay rule. In civil cases informal admissions are now governed by s7(1) Civil Evidence Act 1995 which supersedes the common law exception. In criminal cases informal admissions by the accused – confessions – are governed by s76 Police and Criminal Evidence Act 1984, with judicial discretion to exclude such admissible hearsay evidence being put on a statutory basis by s78 of the same Act.

ii)   Statements in public documents

Statements in most public documents are admissible at common law as evidence of the truth of their contents. The evidence was admissible as an exception to the hearsay rule because it was considered reliable and very often the official who compiled the document will have no recollection of the facts, or will have died or be unavailable, unfit etc. However, a lot of statutes now provide for the admissibility of particular classes of public documents, eg certified copies of birth certificates as evidence of a person's date of birth. In addition many statements in public documents may now be admissible in criminal cases by virtue of s24 Criminal Justice Act 1988 and in civil cases by virtue of s7(2) Civil Evidence Act 1995 which has the effect of preserving the common law on these matters.

iii)   Statements by persons since deceased

Statements by persons who have died by the time of the trial may be admissible at common law as evidence of the truth of their contents, the most common examples of which are:

• Declarations against interest

The rationale is the same as that for admissibility of informal admissions. The declaration must be against the pecuniary or proprietary interest of the declarant; a declaration against *penal* interest is not admissible under this head: *Sussex Peerage Case* (1844) 11 Cl & Fin 85.

- **Declarations in the course of duty**

  These are admissible in criminal proceedings – the declaration must have been made by a person acting under a duty to record some activity; the activity must have been undertaken and the declaration made sufficiently contemporaneously with the activity and with no motive to misrepresent the facts.

- **Dying declarations**

  These may be admissible at the trial for the murder or manslaughter of the declarant. The statement of the victim, oral or written, as to the cause of his injuries (usually who the assailant was) must have been made when he was under a settled, hopeless, expectation of death, and had he survived he would have been a competent witness. The rationale of this exception, that the knowledge of impending death will make the declaration as reliable as a statement given in evidence under oath, is questionable. That the judge must warn the jury to treat the declaration with some caution, and should point out that the declarant was not exposed to cross-examination is indicative of the modern approach, which accepts the admissibility but is more sceptical about the weight to be attached to such declarations.

iv) Res gestae statements

The main, and most important element of the res gestae concept is that of the admissibility of hearsay which consists of statements made with spontaneity and sufficiently contemporaneous to some relevant occurrence or some state of affairs. Though attempts are made by textbook authors to compartmentalise the different situations where *res gestae* statements are admissible, the categories adopted are merely sets of situations where the principle has been applied. In *Howe* v *Malkin* (1878) 40 LT 196 Grove J explained the rationale succinctly:

'Though you cannot give in evidence a declaration per se, yet when there is an act accompanied by a statement which is so mixed up with it as to become part of the *res gestae*, evidence of such a statement may be given.' To some extent 'so mixed up' begs the question, but the following main types of statement are those which examiners favour, with the most frequently recurring one first, for example:

- Spontaneous and contemporaneous statements

  At common law it was accepted that an occurrence could be explained by some spontaneous statement made in the heat of the moment by either a participant or a witness to the occurrence. The old cases, such as *R* v *Bedingfield* (1879) 14 Cox CC 341, evince the insistence of the common law on strict spontaneity and complete contemporaneity. The leading case is now *R* v *Andrews* [1987] AC 281 in which the House of Lords overruled *Bedingfield* as being far too strict and set out the modern criteria for admissibility:

  distortion or concoction must be safe to disregard;

  to ascertain that, it may be concluded that statements made because of involvement in, or the pressure of, the event will not be distorted or concocted, if they are made in conditions of *approximate* contemporaneity;

  to be sufficiently spontaneous for admissibility, the statement must have been so closely associated with the event which excited it that it can be safely inferred that the mind of the maker of the statement was still dominated by that event;

48

other factors which bear on the possibility of concoction or distortion must be considered by the judge, eg malice of the declarant, his sobriety at the time.

R v *Andrews* has relaxed the contemporaneity and spontaneity requirement, but they will still play a major role in assessing the reliability (and therefore admissibility) of such res gestae statements.

• Declarations as to physical or mental condition

Statements about the contemporaneous physical or mental condition of the speaker, including his emotions, are admissible under the *res gestae* doctrine with the necessary inference of spontaneity. Statements as to sensations, symptoms etc are capable of admissibility under this head, but *not* statements as to the reason for them (but they might be admissible under another exception to the hearsay rule, eg dying declarations).

• Statements of intention

A statement as to what the speaker intended to do is admissible as evidence of that intention on his part, but whether it is admissible as evidence of his carrying out that intention is uncertain. In *R* v *Wainwright* (1875) 13 Cox CC 171 a statement by a subsequent murder victim that she was going to visit the accused was inadmissible as evidence that she did so. *R* v *Buckley* (1873) 13 Cox CC 293 is in conflict, but the speaker was a police officer informing his superior officer of his intention to perform an act in the course of his duty, so the evidence of his intention may have been admitted as a declaration in the course of duty (supra).

• Statements explaining actions

The statement of the perpetrator of some act may sometimes be that of the best person to explain the proper significance of that act. Provided such a statement is made contemporaneously with the act, and by the actor as opposed to an observer, then it can be admitted as hearsay under the res gestae doctrine.

The case of *R* v *McCay* [1990] Crim LR 338 causes problems here. The Court of Appeal in this case held as admissible evidence given by a police officer as to the number chosen in an identification parade by the witness. The court appeared to use two possible grounds for the admissibility. First, that any identification carried out in accordance with Code D of Police and Criminal Evidence Act 1984 is admissible, whether hearsay or not. This can hardly be right. Secondly, it fell within an exception to the hearsay rule, res gestae. However, this goes against authorities which suggest that it does not, eg *Teper* v *R* [1952] AC 480.

6.3 Analysis of questions

Hearsay is a favourite topic of examiners, and in the case of the criminal rules excluding hearsay and the many exceptions to them it is quite common to find questions exclusively in that area. The following questions incorporate material referred to in previous chapters. In addition, you should pay particular attention to the extremely difficult area of implied hearsay as well as the distinction between hearsay evidence and non-hearsay circumstantial evidence as illustrated in *R* v *Lydon* [1987] Crim LR 407 CA.

6.4 Questions

QUESTION ONE

Albert is charged with the murder of Betty by stabbing. Discuss the admissibility of the following:

a) Charles, walking past Albert's house, heard a woman scream: 'Don't do it to me, Albert; put that knife down!' He knocked at the door as the screams continued, got no reply, so reported to the police.

b) When the police arrived at the house, Betty staggered down the path and collapsed. Shortly before her death in hospital she recovered consciousness and said: 'Albert's done for me, but I forgive him.'

c) Betty told her mother on the day of the stabbing that she intended to visit Albert.

d) When interviewed by the police, Albert stated that he was not at home on the day of the stabbing. Subsequently he retracted that statement, said he was at home but that after an argument with Betty he went out to the pub and when he returned the ambulance was departing, with the police following.

e) David, dying of cancer a month after the murder, confessed that he was the person who had stabbed Betty at Albert's house.

Written by editor

Skeleton Solution

- Examination of implied assertions and res gestae statements.
- Exceptions to hearsay rule – dying declarations and res gestae statements.
- Hearsay – statement of intention.
- Corroboration – lies told by the accused.
- Inadmissible hearsay and irrelevance.

Suggested Solution

If Charles is to relate to the court what he overheard at Albert's house, it must be relevant to the fact in issue at the trial – the murder of Betty – and must not infringe any exclusionary rule of evidence. The fact that he heard screams emanating from the house, and that they seemed to be those of a female, would be admissible if relevant, for example to prove that a female was present, and was in fear, or hysterical (*Ratten* v *R* (1972)). However, that may not be relevant if Albert is not denying the presence of a female, but rather is stating only that he was not present.

If Charles tenders in evidence the content of what was screamed, as opposed to the mere fact of the scream, then the utterance implies that Albert was holding a knife and was threatening or terrorising the female with it; it is an implied assertion that Albert was present, was wielding a knife, and was threatening a female in the house.

Therefore, Charles' evidence would be hearsay to the same extent as if the statement/utterance had been an express assertion of those facts, and thus would be inadmissible unless it came within a recognised exception to the hearsay rule (*Myers* v *DPP* (1965)). The only exception would seem to be that of res gestae statements; if the time of the stabbing is established, and the screamed statement was sufficiently contemporaneous, and the other criteria as to spontaneity, concoction and distortion, and any relevant factors which may be given to the court have been taken into account, then Charles may report to the court not only the fact of the utterance, but its content (*R* v *Andrews* (1987)); and, of course, the fact of the continued screaming as he knocked at the door.

Betty's statement to the police may be admissible as a dying declaration, provided she was in settled hopeless expectation of death and if alive would have been a competent witness (*R* v *Pike* (1829)). (It is assumed that she is neither a child of tender years nor a person of defective intellect who would have been adjudged incompetent.) If she is Albert's wife, then she would now be both competent and compellable (Police and Criminal Evidence Act 1984 s80).) If she lost consciousness almost immediately after the last thrust of the knife and remained unconscious until she made her statement, then it could be argued by the defence counsel that she had not had enough time to reflect on her situation and thus could not make a dying declaration (*R* v *Bedingfield* (1879) has not been overruled on that point, although the rest of its reasoning has been overruled by *R* v *Andrews* (above)). However, the content of her statement would seem to suggest that she is aware of her impending death and is resigned to it. If her statement is admitted as a dying declaration, the judge must warn the jury to treat its significance with caution, and must point out to them that Betty was not subjected to cross-examination on her declaration (*Nembhard* v *R* (1982); *Waugh* v *R* (1950)).

If Betty's statement is not admissible as a dying declaration, it may possibly be admissible as a res gestae statement dependent on the spontaneity, contemporaneity etc as stipulated in *R* v *Andrews*. If it does not meet the criteria for either a dying declaration or a res gestae statement, then it will be inadmissible hearsay.

Betty's statement to her mother is a statement of her intention. Her mother may relate this to the court as evidence of Betty's intention to visit Albert, but that is not as relevant as is whether or not she *did* visit him. As to the latter, it would seem that the mother's evidence would be excluded as inadmissible hearsay, as the weight of authority is against the admission of such hearsay to prove the intended act was performed (*R* v *Wainwright* (1875); *R* v *Thomson* (1912); cf *R* v *Buckley* (1873)). There is conflict in the cases, and it could therefore be argued that if the interval between Betty's statement to her mother and her being stabbed at Albert's house was short, then her mother should be allowed to report the statement to the court.

Albert's retraction of his first statement and contradiction of it in his second could amount to evidence capable of corroborating prosecution evidence against him. Although in this case there is no necessity for corroboration, or a corroboration warning, nevertheless Albert's lie could be supportive of prosecution evidence unless there is some explanation for it other than one consistent with his guilt (*R* v *Lucas* (1981)). The contradictory statements about a material issue, ie his presence at the scene and time of the crime, mean that if there is a case to answer then Albert will have to elect to testify and give an innocent explanation for his lying to the police.

If David is resigned to his death and has died by the time of the trial, his statement cannot amount to a dying declaration (he is not the homicide victim!). Again, if he survives, unless in the light of his statement a decision is taken to drop the charge against Albert and instead prosecute David, David's statement cannot be reported to the court at Albert's trial as it is not a confession statement of the accused, and is therefore inadmissible hearsay (*R* v *Blastland* (1985) and *R* v *McGillvray* (1993)). If he dies before Albert's trial, his statement is not admissible as a declaration against interest, as the declaration is not against David's proprietary or pecuniary interest, but rather against his penal interest, which does not bring it within that exception to the hearsay rule in English law (*Sussex Peerage Case* (1844)). In any event, as it is Albert, not David, who is charged with Betty's murder, an admission made by David, adverse to his interests, is not relevant to the guilt of Albert (*R* v *Blastland*).

QUESTION TWO

A is charged with the murder of B, his wife's lover, by stabbing him in the throat with a kitchen knife late one night. B was Australian. C, B's neighbour, states that on 1 June, he was awakened by a violent banging noise and, looking out of the window, he saw B stagger out of A's flat and on to the landing. B was distressed and pointed into the flat before collapsing. C rushed inside and, hearing a noise outside an open window, observed A scaling down a drainpipe. A's wife, D, was not present. D states that B had told her on 15 May that he 'intended to do something about A'. E, another neighbour, states that, on the afternoon of 1 June, he overheard an argument between A and another person who was male and spoke with an Australian accent, in which the Australian said 'Come on, sit down; we've got some talking to do'. Outside the flat, three days later, the police find a receipt for a taxi made out to B and signed by someone who is unidentifiable.

Discuss any evidential issues that may arise.

University of London Examination
(for External Students) Law of Evidence June 1993 Q5

General Comment

This question could be awarded very high marks if the candidate alone concentrated on the issue of relevance; look at all the false clues and slender inferences that are suggested by the wide variety of circumstantial evidence. If the candidate does not feel confident at answering the question in this unorthodox, but perfectly feasible way, the relevance of each piece of evidence should be pointed out at some stage. What, for example, is the point of the evidence of the taxi receipt? The main topic is, of course, hearsay evidence and this question really tests your ability to see hearsay when you see it; in other words, it is a *practical* question about the *definition* of the hearsay rule. A common sort of mistake is to skirt round this difficult question: don't. A further common problem is that candidates will often think that all the hearsay points can be answered by the Criminal Justice Act 1988; remember that only applies to *written* hearsay and has no application to oral hearsay.

The best way to do evidence problems is to work out the narrative order; use that to separate out the main question into a number of smaller ones. So we have C's testimony (one question); D's testimony; E's testimony; the police's testimony. Then start by, as suggested above, detailing the relevance of the pieces of evidence (noting relevance for whom - defendant or prosecution); then move to these four, relatively small questions. Simple, isn't it?

Skeleton Solution

• General relevance (evidence that B provoked or attacked A and thus A has defence of provocation and/or self-defence).

• C's testimony (evidence of opportunity for A and time and place of killing; is 'pointing' hearsay, if so, admissible hearsay?).

• D's testimony (evidence that B had motive to go round and provoke or attack; admissible hearsay by res gestae rule as to intention ripening into act?).

52

- E's testimony (is this evidence of B's motive? How otherwise is it relevant? Is the report of an *accent* hearsay?).
- Police evidence of receipt (relevance? hearsay? if so, is it admissible?).

Suggested Solution

The relevance of the various items of evidence points, albeit in a very circumstantial way, to A's being attacked or provoked by B, thus bringing about the killing of B by A. There is evidence as to the time of B's death at A's flat, from B's staggering out and pointing towards it; B has a reason for ridding himself of A, as A's wife's lover; A appears guilty since he runs away; the only other with a motive, A's wife D, is not present; there is evidence that about two weeks earlier, B had an intention to 'do something about A'; there is evidence that, earlier on the day of the killing A had been with a person with an Australian accent who said that they had a reason to talk, and it clearly can be accepted that B was Australian. Finally, there is evidence from the taxi receipt that B was in the vicinity sometime close to the killing.

If most or all of the evidence is admissible, it would certainly discharge the evidential burdens of raising the defences of provocation and/or self-defence; when admitted, it would probably be sufficient to raise a reasonable doubt as to A's guilt in a charge of murder. But some of the items of evidence need closer attention.

First, is evidence of an intention 'to do something about A' evidence of an intention to attack in some way? It is not entirely clear because the words alone are arguably consistent with an intention 'to ask A to leave his wife and face facts'. On the other hand, in the sort of context described here, these sorts of words are used to describe at the least an intention to *threaten*, which is relevant to defences helpful to A. Further, the words 'Come on, sit down, etc' are open to the same sort of argument, although it perhaps sits less well with the idea of threatening behaviour. Nevertheless, both statements, if admitted, tend to reinforce each other, especially in the context of the adulterous wrong B is perpetrating on A (although the full facts are not brought to light) and suggest that B has gone round in a less than fully reasonable mood.

Second, the receipt for the taxi does not help much. What does it tell us? That B was near A's flat at the time of the murder? But that is uncontroversial since, of course, his *dead body* was found there!

Having indicated problems relating to the ultimate relevance of the various items of evidence, it is now necessary to establish whether each piece of testimony will be admissible independently. C's evidence is straightforward testimonial evidence, albeit circumstantial (he doesn't *see* A kill B), of opportunity and time. He hears banging (consistent with a struggle); he sees B stagger and he sees A run off. The two points of importance are: (a), is B's pointing to A's flat, in a state of distress, evidence of A's having done something to him there? Pointing is language by gestures, and is therefore subject to the hearsay rule; that is right in principle (otherwise reports of what deaf and dumb people are saying using sign language would not be hearsay) and it is also clearly established in *Chandrasekara v R* (1937) where a woman could only point to her murderer because he had just cut her throat. But, (b), it will be admissible under the res gestae exception of the 'excited utterance'; in *Andrews* (1956) the House of Lords adverted to just this sort of situation when it overruled the ridiculous case of *Bedingfield* (1879). The fact that B, obviously in distress (he collapses shortly afterwards), is *outside* A's flat is quite irrelevant.

D's testimony is that B had said, just two weeks before, that he intended to do something about A; this is clearly hearsay since it is a report of an out-of-court statement put forward in order to prove its truth (as defined in *Subramaniam* (1956), as using Cross's famous definition, as echoed in s1 of the Civil Evidence Act 1968). However, it is admissible under a special category of the res gestae rule, as established in *Sugden* v *St Leonards* (1876) and *R* v *Buckley* (1873), as evidence that B had that intention (subject above to what precisely those words meant) *at that particular time* two weeks before. Of course, that a person has an intention at a particular time means that he probably has it two days later and, depending on the circumstances, even two weeks later. Further, since intentions are the sort of mental state which describe a decision taken about future *action*, this is arguably res gestae evidence that B did what he said he was going to do, as in *Buckley* (the case of *R* v *Wainwright* (1875) can be distinguished. There, the witness was a fairly young girl talking of her boyfriend, not a policeman talking of his policeman's duties; the differences are in the quality of determination of decision, not the general principle as laid down in the *St Leonards'* case).

E's evidence of overhearing a person talking with an Australian accent proves, if admissible, that there was an Australian with A, but nothing more, although the relevance is its strengthening of some contact between A and B on that day, although it doesn't particularly build on any other scenario which can be sketched from these facts. But it is admissible, if thought to be relevant, since the report is not of the truth of a statement (*what was said*) but of the way *of saying it* (see *Subramaniam*); in this sense, what was said is of no importance as long as it established that the person to whom A was speaking was Australian.

The receipt would be admissible in two ways; if it is only to be used as a piece of paper with B's name on it to prove that he was there about that time, then it is directly admissible, as original evidence, in the same way the airline ticket was in the controversial case of *Rice* (1963) (see Guest, *Law Quarterly Review* 1985). Alternatively, if it were necessary to rely on the truth of some implied statement (see *Teper* (1952)) made by an identified taxi driver, while an obscure idea (what, for goodness sake was the 'assertion' on the receipt that the taxi driver was making?) it would be hearsay, but, again with the caveat that the receipt is of any relevance to the case, admissible either under ss23 or 24 of the Criminal Justice Act 1988.

QUESTION THREE

'Considerable relaxation of the hearsay rule has been engineered by the courts, but the decisions constitute not so much a retreat from *Myers* as a partial abandonment of the hearsay/non-hearsay analysis of evidence.' (Ashworth and Pattenden).

Discuss.

University of London LLB Examination
(for External Students) Evidence June 1995 Q4

Skeleton Solution

Outline of what *Myers* says about the admission of hearsay.

Examples of analysis as real evidence.

Analysis as original evidence, not tendered to show truth of statements.

Discussion of wider view of res gestae.

Consideration of special view taken of certain ID evidence.

Suggested Solution

In *Myers* v *DPP* (1965), still a leading authority on hearsay at common law, the majority view was that there was no judicial discretion to admit even the most cogent hearsay evidence unless it fell within an established exception to the rule, and that any new extension must henceforth be a matter for Parliament. The courts have not, however, been inactive in this area since Myers, and this is particularly evident in the areas considered below.

a) *Analysis as real evidence*

There has been a huge increase in the amount of information produced mechanically or electronically, and much of this is tendered as a type of statement for the purpose of proving its truth so, conceptually, there are hearsay implications. In many cases the evidence given is that of someone who has observed the equipment and gives testimony of what he saw. In truth this is little more reliable than a person giving evidence of out-of-court statements, but the courts have consistently supported the view that if equipment has any sort of recording function then evidence of the record is real evidence not hearsay. This pre-dates *Myers* but has been much extended since that case. Examples include *The Statue of Liberty* (1968) (film record produced by radar), *R* v *Wood* (1982) (complicated computer results of spectrometer readings and calculations, far beyond a record, in stolen metal case), *Castle* v *Cross* (1984) (printout from intoximeter machine to show that no sample given), and *Taylor* v *Chief Constable of Cheshire* (1987) (evidence of police who watched video record, later erased, of offence). Although the question of computer printout admissibility is largely covered by statute, the willingness to make use of the inherent reliability of such equipment does seem to influence the courts away from hearsay considerations as can be seen from *R* v *Shepherd* (1993). The cases of *R* v *Rice* (1963) (pre-dating *Myers*) and *R* v *Lydon* (1987) show a willingness to sidestep hearsay problems by treating airline tickets and pieces of paper with writing pointing towards the persons accused as real evidence indicating circumstantial links. These cases illustrate the trend away from hearsay analysis, although many academics view this as a strained approach.

b) *Analysis as original evidence relevant to facts in issue, not tendered to show truth of statements*

In *Woodhouse* v *Hall* (1980) evidence of offers of sexual services, made to police officers by girls in a massage parlour, were held properly admitted, not to show the truth of what was said but to show that offers had been made. The limits of this approach are illustrated by *R* v *Harry* (1988), where evidence of phone calls to a house involving details of enquiries about drug sales were properly excluded on the question of whether a particular person was doing the dealing. The evidence would probably have been admissible on the question of whether the house was being used for dealing, had that been in issue. Similarly, in *Ratten* v *R* (1972), the Privy Council held that evidence of a telephone operator repeating a hysterical woman's plea to call the police was admissible to rebut a claim that no call had been made from the premises and that a fatal shooting about that time had been an accident. There was no need to examine the truth of any assertion contained in the statement.

c) *Analysis of the evidence as part of the res gestae where the maker is dead or unavailable*

The courts seem to have taken a wider view in recent time of the res gestae analysis of spontaneous statements made under the influence of startling or frightening events. *Ratten* v *R* is a good example of this and, provided that the mind of the speaker is dominated by the event, and there is no real possibility of fabrication or concoction, the statement is admissible despite its obvious hearsay nature. The matter has been considerably refined and analysed in *R* v *Nye & Loan* (1977), *R* v *Turnbull* (1984), and by the House of Lords in *R* v *Andrews* (1987). The courts seem to have abandoned the former view, from *R* v *Bedingfield* (1879), that statements were only admissible if they were proved to be part of the same 'transaction', a very demanding test. The test now is simply one of the dominating quality of the circumstance upon the consciousness of the speaker, so that a particularly horrific event may render a statement admissible despite a considerable time gap, as in *Andrews*.

d) *Indications of a special approach towards certain ID evidence*

The courts have used much ingenuity to sidestep hearsay problems where identification evidence is concerned. In *R* v *Osbourne*, *R* v *Virtue* (1973) evidence of two witnesses of their identification of the accused in a parade would have been completely useless without the additional evidence of a police officer as to the witnesses' actions in picking out the accused. This was clearly hearsay but no attempt was made to take the point. A similar situation occurred in *R* v *McCay* (1990), where the policeman's evidence was viewed as either an undefined exception to the rule or as original evidence. The cases of *R* v *Percy Smith* (1976) (sketch made by policeman to witnesses description), *R* v *Okorudu* (1982) (photograph of photofit), and *R* v *Cook* (1987) show that the view of the courts is that these matters and, presumably, any other means of creating an image from a witness perception, are sui generis and quite outside the hearsay rule.

It is suggested that all the above examples illustrate a determined effort by the courts to move away from an approach which relies upon a strict hearsay/non-hearsay analysis.

QUESTION FOUR

P, a police inspector, is investigating a theft and explosion at a factory. Knowing that O has a previous conviction for causing an explosion, P requests him one morning to come to the police station. P questions O for most of the next twelve hours without result. Eventually at about midnight, P says 'Look, I'm happy to go on all night. Why don't you do yourself a favour? Tell me who the other villains are and where the stuff is you nicked.' O, who is by now totally exhausted, says 'OK, you win, Q and I took the stuff. You'll find it in the old shed by the allotments. But I didn't want anything to do with the dynamite. Q threatened to kill me if I didn't help him.' P goes to the shed and finds the goods stolen from the factory, but, apart from O's statement, there is nothing to connect them with either O or Q. P then arrests Q, telling him that if he will produce any remaining dynamite he will not be charged with an explosives offence. Q hands over some sticks of dynamite, saying that it is all he has left.

O and Q are charged jointly with theft and causing an explosion. At the trial within a trial O admits that his statement to P was true.

Advise O and Q.

University of London LLB Examination
(for External Students) Evidence June 1990 Q8

Skeleton Solution

• Evidence of O – hearsay – exception needed – s76 Police and Criminal Evidence Act 1984.

• Oppression under s76 – definition – breach of Codes of Practice.

- Reliability under s76 – definition.
- Use of s78 instead.
- Advice to Q – hearsay – cross-examination of accused on his character – s76 Police and Criminal Evidence Act 1984.

Suggested Solution

Advice to O

The police do not have first hand knowledge and can give evidence only of what they were told by O. The evidence will therefore be hearsay and inadmissible unless an exception to the hearsay rule applies. O is not compelled to give evidence and is unlikely to oblige the prosecution by giving the evidence they wish in chief at trial.

The only relevant exception appears to be s76 of the Police and Criminal Evidence Act 1984. O should, however, contend the application of s76. This will then require the prosecution to prove beyond reasonable doubt (as required by s76) that the confession (defined in s82(1) as including any statement wholly or partly adverse to the accused) was not obtained by oppression or anything said or done by P (or anyone else) which in the circumstances existing at the time was likely to make any confession by him unreliable. Further, even if s76 is satisfied, O can contend that the judge should exclude the confession under s78 which enables evidence to be excluded if in all the circumstances, including the circumstances in which the evidence was obtained, it would be unfair to allow it in. Sections 76 and 78 are not mutually exclusive: *R* v *Mason* (1987). The basis of the submissions are suggested as follows:

Section 76. Oppression is partly defined in s76 as including torture, inhuman or degrading treatment. A working definition has been proffered in *R* v *Fulling* (1987) as exercise of authority in a burdensome, harsh or wrongful manner. Though O's treatment at the hands of P could hardly be regarded as torture, O can readily argue that P's conduct falls within the *Fulling* definition. O's questioning should have been punctuated by rest periods at about two-hourly intervals in accordance with the Code of Practice on questioning unless exceptional reasons applied; for example that people would be harmed or the outcome of the investigation prejudiced. Those grounds do not necessarily follow from the facts given. Moreover, it seems that questioning went on into the late evening, not finishing until midnight. Nor, it seems, was O cautioned, or even arrested, although it may be that up to that time P did not have the requisite grounds because he had got nowhere with O. Even if that were the case, the Code of Practice on questioning issued under the Police and Criminal Evidence Act would apply in the same way as it is applied to detained persons. Failure to comply with the Code is a matter to be taken into account by the court in deciding any question, including therefore the question of exclusion on the ground of oppression (s67(11)).

Not all breaches of the Code of Practice will render a confession inadmissible but where, as appears to be the case here, the breach is significant and substantial, O is entitled to submit exclusion with some force (*R* v *Keenan* (1990)). It certainly does not mean that the police must give up at the suspect's first denial, however: *R* v *Heaton* (1993).

In relation to oppression, it is unclear from the authorities whether there is a requirement that the action occasioning the oppression should be deliberate. Indications are that this is required (*R* v *Hughes* (1949) and *R* v *Fulling*) and therefore O's case for exclusion on this ground will be enhanced if the court takes the view that P deliberately flouted the rules.

There is no requirement to show that the confession was unreliable but causation must be established. O's utterance after a long detention is indicative of this, but in making the assessment O's ability to withstand harsh questioning will be considered (compare *R v Prager* (1972) decided under the common law) and O does apparently have a criminal background. He may therefore be more resistant than many, though other characteristics such as his age and health will also be relevant.

Additionally, and in the alternative, O can submit that the confession falls at the reliability hurdle. His contention would be that conditions of questioning made him 'say anything'. It must however be said that the terms in which O gave a confession and the fact that the goods were found where he had said rather point away from unreliability and towards the supposition that O simply decided to 'spill the beans'.

O can call upon s78 if he is unsuccessful under s76 (*Mason*). The courts have not taken the same restrictive attitude to the exclusion under s78 as they took for exclusion under the common law (see *R v Bailey and Smith* (1993)). The submission would be that putting aside whether the police conduct was technically oppressive or provoked unreliability, or issues such as causation, in all the circumstances, including the circumstances in which the evidence from O was obtained, that evidence should be excluded on grounds of fairness. All the breaches of the Code of Practice are significant and substantial (*R v Keenan*), which gives O a lever. Moreover, if O successfully submits that P acted in bad faith, it is likely that the evidence will be excluded (*R v Alladice* (1988) in which the Lord Chief Justice said that the courts will have little difficulty in excluding such evidence under this section). *Alladice* itself concerned access to legal advice, but indications are that the dictum is to be broadly construed.

Arguments about admissibility under ss76 and 78 will be taken on the voir dire. O will be free to give evidence without its being used against him at the main trial, save that if the confession is admitted, he may be cross-examined as to inconsistent statements made on the voir dire (*Wong Kam Ming v R* (1980)). It has been suggested that the position may be different with the subsequent enactment of s76, which makes confessions admissible, subject to the conditions of the section, in criminal proceedings quite generally. Whilst that may be the case in a technical legal sense, it is likely that the courts will exercise the s78 discretion to exclude so that the voir dire evidence is in general kept from the main trial in the same way as envisaged by *Wong Kam Ming*.

Advice to Q

If admitted, the confession by O to P in which Q is implicated will be no evidence against Q. It will be hearsay at common law: *R v Rudd* (1948). Nothing in s76 allows in such evidence because under that section the confession by an accused may be given in evidence against *him* as an exception to the hearsay rule.

If O goes into the witness box and then gives testimony along the lines of his confession, then that will be evidence against Q because no hearsay element is involved. If that happens, Q will be able to submit that O has given evidence against him because, manifestly, it will undermine Q's case. We are told that O has a previous conviction and if O gives evidence at trial, Q will be able, as an exception to the general embargo on the putting of evidence of bad character to an accused by the prosecution, to cross-examine him about it under s1(f)(iii) of the Criminal Evidence Act 1898 (*Murdoch v Taylor* (1965)). The leave of the judge for this cross-examination will not be needed and such evidence will go to O's credibility (*Murdoch v Taylor*).

It may also be possible for Q to cross-examine O about his confession even if that confession is ruled inadmissible in the main trial (*R v Rowson* (1985)). The basis of such cross-examination is the entitlement of a party to put to an opposing witness previous inconsistent statements, evidence of which goes to that witness's credibility. It follows that Q can only proceed to cross-examine O if O changes his story at the main trial. Whether Q would actually want to cross examine O rather depends on what O changed his story to. If at the main trial O did not refer to Q's complicity, then it would obviously not be in Q's interest for such cross-examination to be pursued.

Q's statement to P is against his interest and therefore a confession within the meaning of s76. P will accordingly be able to state what Q said unless the oppression or reliability hurdles are not satisfied, or there is exclusion of the evidence under s78. The criteria have been dealt with in the advice to O. The breach of the Code of Practice is the inducement by P that he will not be charged if he owns up. This breach Q can argue as significant and substantial.

The evidence of Q's handing over the dynamite is unlikely to be regarded as a confession, even though a confession is defined in s76 as any statement, whether in words or otherwise. To assume the hearsay rule applies to all conduct from which facts can be inferred would be to extend the scope of the rule unduly. The prosecution are likely to say that the acquisition of the dynamite by P is admissible whether or not Q's statement is excluded under s76, on the authority of s76(4) (facts discovered as a result of an inadmissible confession admissible). Q's best course then is to submit that the evidence of the handing over of the dynamite is confession-type material which should be excluded, citing *R* v *Barker* (1941) in support. This case has been criticised, and was decided under the common law, both features which the prosecution will doubtless point out. The defence can, however, refer to the fact that s76(4) merely puts the common law of *R* v *Warwickshall* (1783) on a statutory basis, and further submit that even if *Barker* is unsatisfactory, it points towards exclusion of the evidence as a matter of discretion under s78.

QUESTION FIVE

M is charged with the murder of N, the lover of M's wife O, by running him down in the street. M has stated to the police that N unexpectedly stepped off the pavement into the path of his car and that a collision was unavoidable. Four days before his death, N wrote in his diary that he was afraid because M had become enraged about the affair with O and that he intended to 'watch over his shoulder' from now on. On the day N died, P, a passer-by, heard an unidentified woman at the scene of the accident say, pointing to M, 'That man went straight for him; he gave him no chance.' O has stated that M told her later on the same day that N had been involved in an accident, adding that 'he got what he deserved'. M proposes not to testify himself at his trial but seeks to adduce psychiatric evidence that P is schizophrenic and that he, M, has a timid personality and is unlikely to behave aggressively.

Advise the prosecution on any evidential issues arising.

University of London LLB Examination
(for External Students) Evidence June 1991 Q7

General Comment

This question raises a number of issues relating to the application of the hearsay rule and its exceptions. Predominantly they concern res gestae. The admissibility of opinion evidence also features, and there is also a point on silence.

Skeleton Solution

- Admissibility of evidence as an exception to the hearsay rule under res gestae as a contemporaneous state of mind. Scope of the exception; possible use of the Criminal Justice Act 1988 s23. Res gestae exception to the hearsay rule exemplified by *Ratten* v *R* and *R* v *Andrews* – scope of the exception.

- Application of the hearsay rule to implied insertions; illustrative case law. Comparison of hearsay and original evidence and relevance of the latter to the facts in question. Evidential value of silence.

- Admissibility of expert opinion evidence in state of mind cases; exemplification by reference to *R* v *Chard* and subsequent cases, and *Lowery* v *R*.

Suggested Solution

The diary entry must first be proved as a document if it is to be produced. This can be achieved by the production of the original document and the calling of evidence identifying the handwriting of N. The original is available and so poses no difficulty. As long as the prosecution have a witness who knows N's handwriting (or there is material to compare and on which a handwriting expert can give evidence under the Criminal Procedure Act 1865 s8), the second requirement should present no difficulty either.

As to the uses to which the entry can be put, N's statement that he was afraid and intended to watch over his shoulder is receivable as evidence of that fact as an exception to the hearsay rule which would otherwise be infringed, since M is not giving evidence. The exception is that of res gestae – showing a contemporaneous mental state four days before the event. The jury is entitled to find that state of mind continued to the time of the event, its being circumstantial evidence of N's state of mind then. The res gestae exception does not however extend to the cause of the state of mind, even if it explains it. The evidence of the affair with O, and M's rage, will not be receivable under this head. The evidence is, however, relevant as it goes to motive. It is possible for the prosecution to argue that M's reaction is receivable under s23 Criminal Justice Act, being a first hand hearsay statement in a document, the writer, now dead, having personal knowledge of that reaction. Such reception is subject to a discretion to exclude in the interests of justice under s25 of the Criminal Justice Act 1988, though the fact that M might have to counter the allegation by giving evidence himself will not necessarily mean that the statement is excluded (*R* v *Cole* (1990)). The evidence as to the reason (the affair) would be receivable as original evidence explaining M's reactions.

P's testimony that a woman pointed and said M went straight for him is hearsay because P does not have personal knowledge of the facts stated, and the pointing is an implied assertion within the rule, *Chandrasekera* v *R* (1937). It will therefore be inadmissible unless an exception to the hearsay rule applies. The prosecution can argue that the res gestae exception is applicable. Statements made in circumstances of such spontaneity or involvement in the events concerned, that the possibility of concoction or distortion can be disregarded, are admissible (Lord Wilberforce in *Ratten* v *R* (1972)), an approach upheld by the House of Lords in *R* v *Andrews* (1987). In this case, the woman was at the scene of the crime, and on the assumption she was an eyewitness who made her statement at or shortly after the event, when it was still dominating her mind, the test appears satisfied. It is submitted that there are no 'special features' within *R* v *Andrews* having a bearing on admissibility, although the circumstances of the identification by P of M as the person pointed out by the woman will be relevant to the weight to be attached to the evidence by the jury and may be a case in which judge gives them a *Turnbull* (1977) type warning in respect of its potential weakness, inviting them to consider carefully the circumstances in which it was made. The defence could counter that this evidence amounts to a 'special feature' relative to the issue of error which goes to admissibility rather than weight, and may draw on support from certain passages in *Andrews* to support this claim.

The prosecution will not be able to use the evidence that the woman said N was given no chance. This is evidence of opinion and as such inadmissible because at common law witnesses must give evidence only of fact. There are some exceptions to this rule, most notably evidence given by experts, but none seems applicable here.

O's evidence

As evidence implicating N by both suggesting his presence at the scene of crime and that he may have been responsible for it, the prosecution's case is assisted. Taken as an implied assertion of those facts, it is likely that the defence will argue that it is hearsay (not being O's personal knowledge) and therefore inadmissible.

The prosecution can answer this in three alternative ways. First, they can contend that M's statement is an implied assertion outside the hearsay rule. Cases such as *Woodhouse* v *Hall* (1980), and more recently *R* v *Harry* (1988), can be taken as supporting the view that statements not intended to be assertive of the facts they are tendered to prove to fall outside the rule. But this is an uncertain area and the prospects for success on this line cannot be guaranteed.

The second available contention is that even if O's testimony is hearsay, it is nevertheless admissible because an exception to the rule applies by reason of s76 of the Police and Criminal Evidence Act 1984. Clearly, M's statement is against his interest and therefore a confession within the definition in s82 and, subject to s76(2), admissible under s76(1).

The grounds for exclusion under s76(2) (a confession obtained by oppression or in consequence of anything said or done which in the circumstances existing at the time was likely to render any confession unreliable) do not arise because M clearly made this statement voluntarily to O.

The third argument is that M's statement is produced to show M's knowledge rather than the truth of the facts stated, and as such is receivable as original evidence. On this basis, no hearsay problem arises. It is, however, doubtful whether the prosecution will succeed in this submission. In *R* v *Blastland* (1986) such an argument was rejected on the basis that the real purpose was to rely inferentially on the facts stated by the witness, and that the hearsay rule therefore applied.

Finally, the prosecution should bear in mind that O is M's wife. She is a competent witness for the prosecution under s80(1) of the Police and Criminal Evidence Act, but because M's offence does not fall within those described in s80(3), she is not compellable for the prosecution. If, therefore, O refuses to testify, the prosecution cannot oblige her to.

M's failure to testify cannot be used against him by the prosecution, and the judge's direction to the jury must not infer guilt from that failure: *R* v *Bathurst* (1968); *R* v *Sparrow* (1973). M is entitled to impugn the credibility of an opposing witness at common law, and this may be used as the reason for bringing medical evidence that the witness suffers from a condition which undermines his reliability: *Toohey* v *MPC* (1965).

The prosecution can however challenge M's right to bring psychiatric evidence about his own mental state. The cases are not easy to reconcile and there have been instances, notably *Lowery* v *R* (1974), where such evidence has been admitted. The balance of the authorities supported by *R* v *Chard* (1971), *R* v *Masih* (1986) and *R* v *Reynolds* (1989) leans heavily towards the view that to be admissible, the evidence must be tendered to establish mental illness, rather than a mere personality trait. The underlying principle being deployed is that expert opinion evidence is received on the basis that the matter is outside the experience of the average jury. The jury is able to assess the contentions about personality falling short of mental illness. The prosecution are therefore in a strong position to contend admissibility because the evidence adduced about M does not seek to establish mental illness or a condition which the jury could not establish for themselves.

7 Hearsay – Statutory Admissibility in Civil Cases

7.1   Introduction

7.2   Key points

7.3   Recent statute

7.4   Analysis of questions

7.5   Question

7.1 Introduction

The Civil Evidence Act 1995 (CEA 1995), which came into force on 31 January 1997, abolishes the rule against the admission of hearsay evidence in civil proceedings in England and Wales. In doing so, it gives effect to the recommendations of the Law Commission in its 1993 Report *The Hearsay Rule in Civil Proceedings* (Law Com no 216), and represents a fundamental shift of focus from admissibility to the more sensible question of reliability of evidence.

7.2 Key points

a) *Admissibility – s1 of the 1995 Act*

Section 1(1) CEA 1995 states that in civil proceedings evidence shall not be excluded on the ground that it is hearsay. Section 1(2)(b) defines hearsay as

'a statement made otherwise than by a person while giving oral evidence in the proceedings which is tendered as evidence of the matters stated'.

This is the standard definition used in most leading textbooks. However, the subsection continues and indicates that hearsay includes 'hearsay of whatever degree', and therefore the provisions of the Act apply whether the hearsay is first-hand (when A states what B said), second-hand (when A states what B said C had said) or multiple.

'Statement' means any representation of fact or opinion, however made: s13 CEA 1995. The Act only applies to civil proceedings which are defined as civil proceedings before any tribunal to which strict rules of evidence apply: s11 CEA 1995. Accordingly, it does not apply to the small claims court and industrial tribunals. Hearsay evidence which is admissible by virtue of other statutes is not affected by the Act.

b) *Safeguards*

The simple proposition in s1(1) CEA 1995 is subject to certain qualifications. There are two 'safeguards' built into the 1995 Act:

i)   notice provisions (to prevent a party exploiting any tactical advantage in resorting to hearsay rather than direct evidence);

ii)   weight of hearsay evidence (to ensure that the court takes account of how probative the hearsay evidence is).

Rules of court have been made under s3 providing that where a party to civil proceedings adduces hearsay evidence of a statement made by a person who they do not call as a witness any other party may, with the leave of the court, call that witness, not as their witness, but in order to cross-examine him on his statement as if it were evidence in chief. This is a further aspect of the first safeguard and is designed to stop a party taking tactical advantage of the use of hearsay evidence. It is also a recognition of the sad reality that in contested litigation parties and witnesses often have an interest in being untruthful or economical with the truth. The function of cross-examination is to expose untruths.

c) *Notice provisions*

  i) Generally

Section 2(1) CEA 1995 provides that a person wishing to adduce hearsay evidence shall

'... give to the other party or parties to the proceedings –

(a) such notice (if any) of that fact, and

(b) on request, such particulars of or relating to the evidence as is reasonable and practicable in the circumstances for the purpose of enabling him or them to deal with any matters arising from its being hearsay.'

Under s2(2) CEA 1995 rules of court have been made specifying classes of proceedings or types to which s2(1) does not apply and as to the manner in which the notice procedure is to be undertaken (see SIs 1996/3219 and 3218). The rules are simpler than those in force under the 1968 Act. The parties to dispense with the provision of notice by agreement between themselves: s2(3).

However, a breach of the s2(1) duty or the rules of court passed to enshrine that duty will not render the evidence inadmissible: s2(4) CEA 1995. Rather, it will be a consideration relevant to 1) the court's exercise of its powers with respect to the course of the proceedings (eg to the granting of adjournments) and to costs; and 2) the weight to be accorded to the evidence in question.

Under the 1968 Act, the judge had to exercise his discretion to decide whether to admit hearsay evidence if the notice provisions had not been complied with and if the other party objected to its admission. Under the 1995 Act, a judge has no discretion to exclude hearsay evidence for failure to comply with any designated notice provisions – the evidence is automatically admissible. It is likely, however, that judges will make use of their power in respect of costs and adjournments, eg by penalising a late application for admission of hearsay evidence with a costs order or equally will not require an adjournment/costs where ample notice is given. The most crucial point is that failure to give notice may be taken into account by the court as a matter adversely affecting the weight to be given to the evidence, ie the evidence may be rendered valueless, despite its admission: s2(4)(b).

d) *Weight of hearsay evidence*

Section 4 CEA 1995 states that the court shall 'have regard to any circumstances from which any inference can reasonably be drawn as to the reliability or otherwise of the evidence'. Section 4(2) specifies matters the court may take into account when weighing the evidence:

i)   whether it would have been reasonable and practical to have called the witness instead;

ii) how contemporaneous the statement was;

iii) whether it involves multiple hearsay;

iv) any possible motive of the maker of the statement;

v)   whether there has been any editing; and

vi) whether the evidence has been adduced as hearsay in order to prevent proper evaluation of its weight.

This second safeguard is designed to ensure that hearsay evidence is only given as much weight as its probative value deserves. The list in s4(2) is not an exhaustive checklist, but the listed matters are all fairly common sense considerations.

e) *Preservation of common law exceptions*

Section 9 CEA 1968 preserved a number of exceptions to the hearsay rule. For example, published works dealing with matters of a public nature (histories, maps, dictionaries etc) were admissible as evidence of facts of a public nature stated in them. Section 7 CEA 1995 provides that the common law rule effectively preserved by s9(1) and (2)(a) CEA 1968 – admissibility of admissions adverse to a party (eg after a road accident a driver gets out of his car and says: 'I'm sorry') – is superseded by CEA 1995. Such a hearsay statement of admission adverse to a party is now subject to the notice and weight provisions of the new Act. However, the common law exceptions concerning public records and documents etc are preserved by the effect of s7(2). The common law rules on reputation/character, including reputation or family tradition as to pedigree, marriage and other matters, are preserved by s7(3) CEA 1995.

f) *Proof of statements in documents and records*

i)   Section 8 CEA 1995 provides for a statement contained in a document admissible as evidence in civil proceedings to be capable of being proved by production of that document or by the production of a copy (or a copy of a copy) of it, authenticated in such way as the court might approve. This provision further confirms the death of the 'best evidence' rule.

ii) Section 9 provides that business records or records of a public authority, which are substantiated as such records by an officer of the business or authority to which the records belong, may be received in evidence without further proof. Accordingly, there is no need to call a witness formally to produce documents in these categories to the court, and a lot of time and expense will be saved. However, it is still open to a party receiving such a document to challenge its authenticity and to subpoena anyone the party considers relevant to answer questions about its contents. Hearsay implications based upon an absence of an entry in records are provable by an affidavit of an officer of the authority or business to which the record belongs.

iii) The Act recognises that while in general terms business records are likely to be a reliable class of evidence, there are bound to be exceptions. Section 9(5) provides a dispensing power: ... the court may direct that all or any of the ... provisions [ie of s9] do not apply in relation to a particular document or record or description of documents or records'.

g) *Computer records*

The absence of any provisions relating specifically to computer records is a noteworthy feature of the CEA 1995. The 1968 Act contained provisions to ensure that the computer was operating properly at all material times before records produced by it were adduced. The provisions were very complex (doubtless explained by the fact that computer technology was still in its infancy in 1968). Under the 1995 Act, it seems that computer records will be admissible if they constitute business records or records of a public authority, but of much wider importance, the definition of 'document' in s13 may be seen to extend to almost any type of computer-generated document.

h) *Miscellaneous matters*

Hearsay evidence cannot be given of a statement made by a person who at the time of that statement was not competent as a witness: s5(1) CEA 1995. The Act does not apply to proceedings begun before commencement.

7.3 Recent statute

Civil Evidence Act 1995

7.4 Analysis of questions

Admissibility under the 1968 (and 1972) Act has in the past been a favourite topic of examiners, usually in the form of multi-part questions which include other issues such as privilege, previous convictions etc, although the other issues constitute a minor part of the total question. The change in emphasis wrought by the Civil Evidence Act 1995, from admissibility to reliability of evidence, will certainly be reflected in examination questions.

7.5 Question

A is suing B Jewellers Ltd for the loss of two rubies from a ring which A handed in to them for restyling. B Jewellers Ltd are relying on an exemption clause contained in the contract exempting them from accidental loss. A possesses a written valuation of the ring from X Valuers Ltd, dated ten years earlier, in which it is stated that the ring is worth £10,000. Unfortunately, X Valuers Ltd since went into liquidation and the valuer cannot be traced. A has also obtained a photocopy of an internal memorandum at B Jewellers Ltd which implicates C, an employee, in the theft of precious stones from jewellery handed in by customers. This memorandum had been forwarded to the company's solicitors who have refused to release it. A has further obtained a copy of an entry in the books of D Pawnbrokers Ltd which shows that C had pledged two rubies as security for a loan. The entries show that the carat weight and the refractive index of the rubies as determined by the firm's computer tally with the weight and index of A's jewels.

Advise A on the admissibility of these items as evidence and the standard of proof applicable to the assertion that C stole the rubies.

University of London LLB Examination
(for External Students) Evidence June 1991 Q5

General Comment

The question requires a knowledge of the Civil Evidence Acts 1972 and 1995 and also opinion evidence, legal professional privilege and standard of proof. The points to be addressed are however fairly well compartmented and provide a framework for answering the question.

Skeleton Solution

- Status of opinion evidence – application of the Civil Evidence Act 1972 and the effect of Civil Evidence Act 1995.
- Notice procedure and establishment of expertise.
- Admissibility of evidence under s7 of the 1995 Act.
- Admissibility of business records under s9 of the 1995 Act.
- Legal professional privilege – lawyer/client/third party.
- Use of copies of privileged document – *Calcraft* v *Guest* and subsequent cases.
- Discretion to exclude evidence in civil trials.
- Admissibility of hearsay and non hearsay computer evidence, the principle in *Hornal* v *Neuberger Products*.

Suggested Solution

Issues bearing on the admissibility of the evidence are dealt with in the order in which they arise in the question.

The valuation

The fact that it is 10 years old goes to the weight to be attached to it, and not to its admissibility. It is however produced as evidence of the opinion stated on it. As it is not being given by the valuer in court, it is hearsay and the notice provisions of the Civil Evidence Act 1995 must therefore be satisfied. It must also be established to the court's satisfaction that the valuer could properly give evidence of opinion, that is, he is an expert. This is because of the effect of s3 CEA 1972 on the admissibility of expert opinion evidence. The mere fact that hearsay components will not prevent admissibility does not remove other obstacles to admisibility: s14(1) CEA 1995. Opinion evidence upon a matter requiring expertise would be generally inadmissible from a non-expert as an irrelevance. This is a matter for the judge but he may take the view that the corporate nature of the valuers was some indication of the expertise and decide to admit it, particularly if there were indications that X Valuers Ltd had been in business for a period of time. Even if admitted, it would be subject to the weighing factors in s4. There are procedural requirements here under O.38 r36 RSC for an application to the Court for directions concerning disclosure and, in the absence of agreement, the leave of the Court would be needed to admit expert evidence unless a directions application had been made. Order 38 r.41 would allow the Court to direct A as to which provisions of the Notice Rules should apply to the valuation.

The internal memorandum

The value of this to A is to establish B Jewellers' culpability through the employee. Its production will therefore be subject to the hearsay rule and its admissibility governed by the Civil Evidence Act (CEA) 1995.

Since the statement is self incriminatory, A falls within s7(1) which applies CEA 1995 to adverse informal admission. This means that the memorandum is admissible subject to the notice and weighing provisions.

It is possible however that A will face arguments that s7 is not applicable, because it is not self incriminating of B Jewellers, having been made (presumably) by an employee about another employee. This raises a difficult question on vicarious admissions. An answer cannot be given from the facts given, but if A is unsuccessful in contending admissibility under s7, an alternative approach is for him to use s9 of the 1995 Act.

Section 9 CEA 1995 allows for the admissibility of 'records' of a business or public authority. The requirement is that the document is 'shown' to be a record. This can be done by certification by the business, but presumably can be done by proof in the absence of a willing certifier. The intention of the Act seems to be to get away from the former rigid requirements in CEA 1968, but there could be some difficulties in showing this memorandum to be a record, although it might be put to the writer of the memorandum if that person were subpoenaed as a witness or called for cross-examination on the document under s3 CEA 1995. The memorandum will be generally admissible under s1 unless there is some separate, non-hearsay ground for exclusion. The fact that this is a photocopy of the memorandum is of no consequence as s8 allows for copies at any number of removes from the original, subject to the court's view on authentication: s8 CEA 1995.

The next problem which A will have to meet is that of legal professional privilege. On the basis that the internal memorandum can be taken as a communication of B Jewellers with their solicitors, the privilege will apply, since a legal relationship evidently existed between them and the purpose of sending the information was presumably relative to the securing of legal advice. On the other hand, it is possible for A to argue that the memorandum was a pre-existing document which has not become privileged simply because it was subsequently sent to the solicitors (*Ventouris* v *Mountain* (1991)). Further, A can contend that unless written by a very senior officer of the jewellers, it is a communication between lawyer, client and third party as to which privilege will only apply if the dominant purpose of the production of the memorandum was submission to lawyers in connection with actual or contemplated litigation; *Waugh* v *British Railways Board* (1980). If for whatever reason, legal professional privilege applies, A can nevertheless use the copy in his possession, under the principle in *Calcraft* v *Guest* (1898). He must establish authenticity if contended by B. B will also, however, be entitled to seek a pre-trial injunction: *Ashburton* v *Pape* (1913). But the injunctive relief can be resisted if A neither came by the copy by underhand means, nor received it as a result of an obvious mistake by B Jewellers or their advisers: *Goddard* v *Nationwide* (1986); *Guinness Peat* v *Fitzroy Robinson* (1987).

The admissibility of the copy entry in the books of D Pawnbrokers will not depend on the way A obtained it, even if that was improperly. The courts have no discretion to exclude evidence in civil trials on the basis of the way it was obtained: *Helliwell* v *Piggot-Sims* (1980). The entry is useful to A in showing disposal by an employee of rubies, and it is an implied assertion of that fact. Assuming, as is probable, that it is an implied assertion to which the hearsay rule applies, the same comments as made for the memorandum (above) apply here with respect to the status of the pawnbroker's book as a business record within s9.

It is not clear whether the entry as to carat weight and refractive index is produced directly, or copied from a computer printout. No hearsay point attaches to the fact that the calculations are not subject to oral evidence. They were prepared automatically as in *The Statue of Liberty* (1968). They are simply contained in a document. If the document can be shown to be part of the business records of the pawnbroker, there seems to be no confidentiality or privilege to be invoked here and, subject to the notice and weighing procedures, this evidence can be used.

68

The authenticity of the copy must also be established, this can be done in any way approved by the court: s8(1).

Finally, there is the question of the burden of proof. It now seems established that where a crime is alleged in civil proceedings, the standard of proof applicable is the civil standard of a balance of probabilities, that is, the allegation with regard to C is more probable than not: *Hornal* v *Neuberger Products* (1957). It has sometimes been suggested that there is a third or different standard applicable to serious allegations in civil trials (as here), but such suggestions are best treated on the basis that in deciding whether the scales have been tipped to satisfy the civil standard, the court has regard to the seriousness of the allegations.

8　Hearsay – Statutory Admissibility in Criminal Cases

8.1　Introduction

8.2　Key points

8.3　Analysis of questions

8.4　Questions

8.1 Introduction

The major statutory exceptions concern confessions (with quite recent legislation on which there has been a plethora of interpretative cases) and documentary hearsay, on which there has been very recent statutory activity. In criminal cases confessions constitute an important exception to the hearsay rule, and one which will remain topical for some years and always controversial.

8.2 Key points

Common law on admissibility of confessions was altered drastically by the Police and Criminal Evidence Act 1984.

a)　*Definition*

Section 82(1): '... "confession" includes any statement wholly or partly adverse to the person who made it, whether made to a person in authority or not and whether made in words or otherwise.'

Therefore a confession may be oral, written or by a gesture such as a nod of the head, and may be made to any person, not just a person in authority such as a police officer. Silence in the face of an accusation may amount, in some circumstances, to a confession.

b)　*Admissibility*

As a matter of law is governed by s76 (s77 in the case of mentally handicapped persons). If a confession is unfairly obtained yet nevertheless strictly admissible, there is a statutory discretion to exclude it given by s78, over and above the general exclusionary discretion preserved in all cases by s82(3).

Confessions are treated as inadmissible hearsay unless the prosecution proves (beyond reasonable doubt) that they were not obtained by oppression, or that they were not obtained in consequence of anything said or done which was likely to render them unreliable (s76(2)). If the defence raises the question of admissibility, that in itself is enough to put the prosecution to proof (ie the defence does not have to discharge an evidential burden). Without any representation being made by the defence the court may, of its own motion, put the prosecution to proof of reliability or absence of oppression (s76(3)). When the admissibility of a confession is challenged, by the defence or the court itself, then the issue will be decided on a voir dire – ie in the absence of the jury who, if the confession is ruled inadmissible, will hear nothing of it.

i) Oppression

Oppression is not defined fully in the 1984 Act. Section 76(8) gives a partial definition:

'includes torture, inhuman or degrading treatment, and the use or threat of violence ...'

In *R v Fulling* [1987] 2 All ER 65, oppression was an issue in respect of Miss Fulling's confession: in the Court of Appeal Lord Lane CJ preferred the OED definition of 'oppression' to the partial definition in s76(8) or to any common law definition; thus, oppression in this confession context is 'the exercise of authority or power in a burdensome, harsh or wrongful manner; unjust or cruel treatment of subjects, inferiors etc; the imposition of unreasonable or unjust burdens'. So, when conduct falls short of the extreme oppression in s76(8), it would appear that there must be deliberate misconduct by the police, and that there is some subjectivity in the test for oppression, ie the strengths and weaknesses of the suspect are relevant to the issue of whether the treatment was harsh, cruel or burdensome. The fact that a suspect finds detention in a police station oppressive, however, is not sufficient for any subsequent confession to be excluded on the grounds of 'oppression' under s76 – something (much) more than that is needed.

In the recent case of *R v Ismail* [1990] Crim LR 109, the Court of Appeal made it clear that breaches of the Police and Criminal Evidence Act 1984 and the Codes of Practice during one interview could not be cured by a later properly conducted interview, when the confession was made. To allow such evidence would be to condone the flouting of the statute and the Codes of Practice. However, in the case of *R v Barrett* (1991) 92 Cr App R 61, the court distinguished *Ismail* in similar circumstances saying that it depended on the individual concerned and Barrett had not been affected by the breaches the way Ismail had.

ii) Unreliability

Even the *likelihood* of unreliability in consequence of something said or done is enough for a confession to be inadmissible (s76(2)(b)). The laws of evidence are concerned with the reliability, but not the truth, of the confession – which seems to be a contradiction in terms, unless s76 is to be used to discipline the police or safeguard the rights of the suspect, irrespective of the guilt of the accused. However, in the case of *R v Tyrer* (1990) 90 Cr App R 446, the appellant claimed she was worried about her children and wanted to get home whilst being interviewed and that is why she confessed. She also claimed that the trial judge took into account evidence given against her which was not evidence given during the voir dire. The Court of Appeal ruled that although, strictly, s76(2)(b) does not allow the court to consider the truth of the confession, nevertheless, the issue of admissibility could not be tried in complete isolation from the background of the case, and so the confession was admitted. The cases are in conflict, presumably because of the ambivalence of the judiciary in the appellate courts, eg in *R v Alladice* [1988] NLJR 141, although the suspect was denied his right to a solicitor, his confession was allowed in evidence because by his own admission he knew his rights and understood the cautions administered to him, therefore his confession statement was reliable despite impropriety on the part of the police. In the latter case of *R v McGovern* (1991) 92 Cr App R 228, the appellant was wrongfully denied access to a solicitor, and the Court of Appeal held that it was right to exclude her confession even though she later admitted its truth. See also *R v Chung*

(1991) 92 Cr App R 314. In *R* v *Sat-Bhambra* [1988] Crim LR 453, the suspect was given a tranquilliser by the police doctor to steady his nerves, and therefore his subsequent confession was held unreliable despite the fact that there was no improper conduct by the police to induce the confession. In *R* v *Harvey* [1988] Crim LR 241, a confession was excluded as unreliable where there was no impropriety at all by the police, but the suspect, a psychopath with a low IQ, may have confessed in order to protect her lover; any unreliability was occasioned not by the words or conduct of the police but by the suspect's own mental condition. However, in the case of *R* v *Crampton* (1991) 92 Cr App R 369, the defendant was a heroin addict and was suffering from withdrawal symptoms when he was interviewed about the crime and confessed to it. The trial judge admitted the confession. On appeal, the Court of Appeal said the trial judge had been correct – because it was doubtful whether the mere holding of an interview when the appellant was withdrawing from the symptoms of heroin addiction was something 'done' within the meaning of s76(2)(b) of the Police and Criminal Evidence Act 1984. The court considered and agreed with the case of *Goldenberg* (1989) 88 Cr App R 285, where the defendant again was suffering from the withdrawal from drug addiction. The court there also held that this was not something 'done' within s76(2)(b) – ie the stimulus must be external to the suspect. It could therefore be argued that the decision in *Harvey* is correct because the stimulus did not come from the suspect but from a third party, ie the lover. But the case of *DPP* v *Blake* (1989) 89 Cr App R 179 makes it clear that the test in s76(2)(b) is objective in the sense that it is irrelevant that the police acted in perfect good faith. In *R* v *Fulling* (supra), however, there was impropriety on the part of the police but the suspect's confession was held *not* to be unreliable despite the emotional upheaval caused within her by the police statements – the conduct of the police was considered by the Court of Appeal to be merely 'unsporting'.

So inadmissibility on the grounds of potential unreliability (s76(2)(b)), or on the grounds of oppression falling short of s76(8) as provided for in s76(2)(a), as a matter of law is the subject of a mass of, often contradictory, case law. However, even though adjudged admissible a confession may nevertheless be excluded as a matter of discretion.

c) *Exclusionary discretion*

If a confession is ruled admissible under s76, above, it may nevertheless be excluded in the discretion of the judge if it appears that in all the circumstances its admission would have such an adverse effect on the fairness of the proceedings that the court ought not to admit it (s78(1)). The case of *R* v *Manji* [1990] Crim LR 512 stated that a voir dire should have been used by the trial court judge to decide if a caution had been given to the defendant, and so if he should use his s78 discretion to exclude the confession.

Where a suspect was wrongly denied access to legal advice, his confession, irrespective of its admissibility under the criteria in s76, was excluded under s78 on the grounds of unfairness: *R* v *Samuel* [1988] 2 All ER 135. Where lies were told to a suspect and to his solicitor in order to induce a confession, it was held that the confession, despite its reliability ought to be excluded under s78 because of the unfairness of the proceedings: *R* v *Mason* [1987] 3 All ER 481.

If the police are in breach of the Codes of Practice issued under s66 of the Act (these Codes replacing the old Judges' Rules), then that is a matter which must be taken into account by the court (s67(11)). Breaches of the Code on the Questioning of Suspects may be sufficiently serious to constitute oppression or render the consequent confession potentially unreliable, and therefore in either situation inadmissible under the provisions of s76. If breaches of the Code are not so serious, it is then a matter of judicial discretion, under s78, as to whether a consequent confession, albeit legally admissible, is excluded. The matter is substantially one for the judge to decide according to his discretion: *R* v *Bailey and Smith* [1993] Crim LR 681 and *R* v *Smurthwaite* [1994] Crim LR 53. So it is for the judge in any particular case to decide whether there is unfairness justifying his exercise of his discretion to exclude; only if he is obviously wrong will the Court of Appeal interfere.

At common law there was throughout the criminal laws of evidence a judicial discretion to exclude evidence where its prejudicial effect outweighed its probative value, ie an exclusionary discretion which would make for a fair trial. That general discretion has been preserved by s82(3) of the 1984 Act, but to what extent that exclusionary discretion and the s78 exclusionary discretion overlap has yet to be decided by the courts, ie given there is no unfairness justifying the exclusion of a confession (s78), is it conceivable that the confession could still be excluded under s82(3)?

d) *Facts discovered in consequence of confessions*

If a confession statement is allowed in evidence, then, as regards facts discovered in consequence there is no evidentiary problem. But where the confession statement is excluded, under (s76) then, unless the defence give evidence as to how the other facts were discovered, no reference can be made to the content, or the fact, of the inadmissible confession (s76(5) and (6)).

So, although the subsequently and consequentially discovered evidence can be adduced, it cannot be linked to the accused by any reference to the inadmissible confession. But, s76(5) and (6) prohibit reference to any confession excluded under s76 – therefore if a confession is excluded under s78 in the discretion of the judge, then presumably the common law still applies and it would be acceptable for the prosecution witness to say: 'In consequence of what the accused said, I discovered X at location Y ...'

e) *Silence as a confession*

When a person is accused of having committed a crime and remains silent, then in certain circumstances that silence is capable of amounting to corroboration of other evidence against him, as has been discussed above.

Similarly, silence in the face of an out of court accusation can amount in some circumstances to adoption of the accusation as a confession. If the accused and accuser are on even terms, and it would be reasonable to expect a response, eg an indignant retort, a refutation, then silence can be left to the jury as something from which they *may*, in that situation, infer that the accused adopted the content of the accusation as his confession, ie tacitly accepted what was said as true: *Parkes* v *R* [1976] 1 WLR 1251. But where the accuser is a person in authority such as a police officer, then the silence of the suspect – whether cautioned or not – cannot amount to acceptance of the truth of the accusation, ie by exercising in that situation his right to silence the suspect cannot be providing evidence of guilt: *Hall* v *R* [1971] 1 WLR 298. In one case it was stated that when a suspect is questioned by a police officer in the presence of his solicitor, then his silence can amount to evidence of guilt since the parties are on even terms: *R* v *Chandler* [1976] 1 WLR 585. However, the reasoning in that case has, rightly, been criticised.

f) *Editing confessions*

A confession may be only partly adverse to the person who made it (s82(1) Police and Criminal Evidence Act 1984) and therefore may contain exculpatory as well as incriminatory material; in that case the whole confession statement must be reported – but the jury informed of the lack of evidential value of the exculpatory (ie 'self-serving') material. But if the confession includes references to the accused's previous convictions, bad character or other prejudicial matters, then that material *must* be excised by editing of the statement. If such editing leaves an incoherent statement, then the judge may exclude the whole statement.

If a confession statement implicates a co-accused, then the jury must be instructed that the confession is *not* evidence against that co-accused (that part of it is inadmissible hearsay). Alternatively, the confession statement may be edited so that the co-accused is not identified: *R* v *Silcott* [1987] Crim LR 765; or in exceptional cases separate trials may be ordered to avoid serious prejudice to the co-accused: *R* v *Lake* (1977) 64 Cr App R 172.

g) *Documentary hearsay*

Several statutes make provision for the admissibility of documentary hearsay in criminal proceedings, the most important now being the Criminal Justice Act 1988. Sections 23–28 and Schedule 2 of the CJA 1988 replace the provisions in the Police and Criminal Evidence Act 1984 except those in s69 relating to documents produced by computers. The overall effect is to make documentary hearsay in criminal proceedings more widely admissible.

i) Trade, business etc documents

Section 24 CJA 1988 is similar to s4 Civil Evidence Act 1968 regarding the prerequisites for admissibility of documentary hearsay, but the conditions such as death, unavailability etc of the maker of the statement in the document do *not* apply unless the statement was prepared for the purpose of criminal proceedings or criminal investigations (s24(4)). In any event, s25 gives the criminal court a discretion to exclude such statements in the interests of justice, with mandatory considerations spelled out in s25(2). Where a statement seems to have been prepared for the purpose of criminal proceedings or investigations, then s26 stipulates that leave of the court is required before it can be adduced as hearsay evidence.

The case of *R* v *Cole* [1990] 2 All ER 108 explained the difference between ss25 and 26. Under s25 the court should admit the statement when the conditions laid down in ss23 and 24 are satisfied, unless it considers (looking at s25(2)) that it should be excluded. But under s26, the court should not allow the statement which satisfies the conditions in ss23 and 24 to be admitted, unless it concludes (looking at the wording of s26) that it should be admitted.

ii) Other documentary hearsay

Whereas s24, above, obviously covers second-hand hearsay in respect of trade or business documents (and liberalises s68 Police and Criminal Evidence Act 1984), s23 provides for the general admissibility in criminal proceedings of all first-hand hearsay in documentary form. The prerequisite for admissibility is that the maker of the statement is dead, unfit, unavailable etc (similar again to s4 Civil Evidence Act 1968), or that where the statement was made to a police officer the maker (in addition to the above disjunctive reasons), does not give evidence through fear or because he is kept out of the way (s23(3)), explained in *R* v *Acton Justices, ex parte McMullen* (1991) 92 Cr App R 98 as meaning a statement will be admissible in circumstances where someone was sought to place its maker in fear of attending court or has physically prevented him from doing so. Again, discretion to exclude (s25) and leave of the court to admit (s26) apply as in the case of s24 statements. Also, as in the case of s24 statements, Schedule 2, para 3 CJA 1988 makes provision for the weight, if any, to be attached to such hearsay statements, the court having regard to all the circumstances from which any inference can reasonably be drawn as to accuracy – similar again to the provisions in the 1968 Civil Evidence Act (s6).

iii) Depositions and witness statements

Several statutes provide for the general admissibility (subject to restrictions and usually subject to the overriding judicial discretion to exclude) of hearsay documents, for example:

- Section 102 MCA 1980 – written statements in committal proceedings.

- Section 9 CJA 1967 – written statements in criminal proceedings other than committals.

- Section 105 MCA 1980 – deposition of dangerously ill person, unavailable through illness or subsequent death to testify at trial.

- Sections 42 and 43 Children and Young Persons Act 1933, and s103 MCA 1980 – provision made for the admissibility of depositions of children or young persons as victims of certain crimes, and witness statements of children. These sections are no longer as important as they used to be. We now have s32 of the Criminal Justice Act 1988 which allows for children to give evidence via a live television link during the court proceedings. The conditions are that the crime is one of a particular group – ie assault, or cruelty to persons under the age of 16 (CYPA 1933); and indecency or sexual offences under the Sexual Offences Act 1956 – s32(1)(b) and s32(2) of Criminal Justice Act 1988. The trial must be a trial on indictment or an appeal to the Criminal Division of the Court of Appeal arising out of such proceedings. The section also applies to proceedings in Juvenile Courts ('Youth Courts' after the Criminal Justice Act 1991), and appeals to Crown Courts from there – s32(1A) of the 1988 Act, as inserted by the 1991 Act.

  The age of the child is also relevant. He or she must be under 14 if the charge is cruelty; or under 17 if a sexual offence – s55 Criminal Justice Act 1991.

  The Criminal Justice Act 1991 also extends the 1988 Act by allowing video recordings of children to be shown in court – s54 of the 1991 Act inserting s32A into the 1988 Act. It applies in the same circumstances as s32 does (above). The video recording must be of an interview between an adult and the child and must relate to any matter in issue in the proceedings. However, the child must still be called to be cross-examined in court.

8.3 Analysis of questions

Hearsay in criminal cases, and statutory exceptions to the hearsay rule, will always figure in LLB and Bar Final examinations in a variety of guises. Although sometimes questions will test knowledge of exceptions to the general, exclusionary, hearsay rule in both criminal and civil cases, it is quite common for there to be 'self-contained' criminal questions on hearsay, often concentrating on admissibility of confessions and quite commonly requiring also some knowledge of the rules relating to evidence of bad character (dealt with in Chapter 9).

8.4 Questions

QUESTION ONE

P is charged with a bank robbery of a bank in St. Austell at 3.00 pm. The day after the robbery, he was questioned by Inspector Q. P said that he had spent all the previous afternoon in Plymouth, fifty miles away, watching the football. Q then said, 'We have four witnesses who definitely identified you near the bank yesterday afternoon'. P replied, 'All right, maybe I was there, but I know nothing about the robbery'. In fact, only one witness, R, had identified P. After being shown a number of photographs by the police, R had pointed to the photograph of P and said 'That's probably him'. A few days later, R picked P out in an identification parade. At the trial, P claims that he was at the football match in Plymouth at 2.00 pm and left at 3.00 pm to attend the evening match in Manchester. He wishes to tender the stub of an airline boarding pass bearing his name, for a 3.30 pm flights from Plymouth to Manchester on the day the robbery occurred. He says that he only admitted his presence in St Austell because he has an obsessive fear of being kept in custody.

Discuss any evidential issues that arise.

University of London LLB Examination
(for External Students) Law of Evidence June 1994 Q8

General Comment

A question involving issues of identification, confessions and hearsay. Understandably, some students may be confused by the somewhat esoteric geographical references (St Austell is fairly close to Plymouth, but some distance from Manchester!) and this may create difficulties. Beyond this, a manageable question which merely requires organisation to bring all the relevant issues out.

Skeleton Solution

- P's admission – s82(1) Police and Criminal Evidence Act (PACE) 1984: confession – ss76, 78, 82(3).
- P's initial statement – previous inconsistent statement – s4 Criminal Procedure Act 1865.
- Identification – from police photos – *R* v *Turnbull*.
- The ticket – *R* v *Rice* – *but* effect of *R* v *Kearley*?

Suggested Solution

This question centres around the disputed identification of P as being involved in a robbery in St Austell. Following his arrest, P makes an admission, partly as a result of dubious police practices; he later recants this, and wishes to adduce a ticket a prove that he was elsewhere on the day in question.

i) *P's admission*

PACE 1984 s82(1) provides a wide definition of a confession, as being any statement adverse to the person who made it. P's admission 'maybe I was there' is within this definition and as such either the defence or the judge may require the prosecution to prove beyond reasonable doubt that the 'confession' was not obtained by oppression or in consequence of anything said or done which was likely to render the confession unreliable (PACE s76).

Oppression does not seem likely on the given facts, but it could be argued that the confession is unreliable because P says he only admitted his presence in St Austell because of his obsessive fear of being held in custody.

However, following *R* v *Goldenberg* (1989), this is unlikely to provide a ground of appeal since it is not external to the accused. The defence could still argue that the confession should be excluded under s78 (unfairness) or s82(3) (the common law), in the judge's discretion, and in this regard there exists a further ground, namely P is told that *four* witnesses definitely identified him, whereas in fact only one possibly identified him. This would appear to be unfair within the meaning of s78 and thus the defence could seek to convince the judge to exclude this confession in the exercise of his discretion (*R* v *Alladice* (1988)).

ii) *P's other statement*

P initially said he had spent the entire day in Plymouth. At trial, he claims to have flown to Manchester in the afternoon of that day. His original statement is inconsistent with the version he puts forward at trial. The original statement is not a confession, and therefore need *not* be tested under PACE s76. It may be put to P in cross-examination, and if he denies it, it may be proved, under s4 of the Criminal Procedure Act 1865.

The previous statement does not go to truth but merely goes to the credibility of P, and the judge should warn the jury of this (*R* v *Askew* (1981)).

iii) *Identification*

R identifies P initially from police photographs (and subsequently in an identification parade). It must be stressed that the fact that the initial identification was from police photographs must *not* be disclosed to the jury (*R* v *Wainwright* (1925)), the obvious risk being that the jury may take a bad view of the defendant if they know that he is already on police records.

Since the prosecution case rests on this identification, the *Turnbull* warning must be given to the jury (*R* v *Turnbull* (1977)). They should be told of the special need for caution in identification cases, and why there is this need. Their attention should be drawn to the circumstances of the identification (lighting, length of observation, distance etc), and they should be told to look for supporting evidence (which need *not* be corroboration in the strict sense). The judge should identify the evidence in the case which is capable of supporting the identification.

On the given facts, the only piece of evidence which is capable of supporting R's identification is P's alibi, *if the jury reject it.*

The judge must take care in directing the jury as to the use they may make of this. If the jury reject P's alibi, they must be told that this does *not* of itself mean that he was where the identifying witness (R) says he was. Defendants can raise false alibis for any number of reasons and the judge must tell the jury that it is only when they are satisfied that the sole reason is to deceive them, that the falsity of the alibi can support the identification.

Further, following *R* v *Goodway* (1993) it would seem that a *Lucas* direction (*R* v *Lucas* (1981)) should be given in these circumstances (ie, the lie, to support the identification, must be deliberate, relating to a material issue and motivated by a realisation of guilt and a fear of the truth).

Having said this, the judge must make it clear that, having considered the special need for caution, the jury can safely assess the evidence without any supporting evidence. If the quality of the identification is good, the judge may leave the issue to the jury; but if the quality of the identification is poor, then if there is no supporting evidence, the judge should withdraw the issue and direct an acquittal (*R* v *Flemming* (1987)).

iv) *The ticket*

P wishes to support his trial alibi by means of an airline ticket stub bearing his name and indicating that he flew to Manchester at 3.30 pm on the day in question.

This is clearly a piece of hearsay, especially in the light of *R* v *Kearley* (1992). It is an out-of-court statement from which it is possible to infer that P was on that flight. As hearsay it is submitted it should be inadmissible. Despite this logical reasoning, the present state of the law appears to make this evidence *admissible*. In *R* v *Rice* (1963), a case with a similar factual basis, it was held that a ticket would be admissible since it would seem logical that the person whose name appears on the ticket had actually used it.

Hence, it would seem that the ticket will be admissible in P's defence.

QUESTION TWO

Mike is charged with the murder of Andrew by running him over in his car. Andrew had been having an affair with Mike's wife, Barbie. Mike tells the police that Andrew stepped off the pavement in front of Mike's car and that 'hitting Andrew was unavoidable'. Two days before he died, Andrew wrote on his computer that he was afraid because Mike had discovered the affair Andrew was having with Barbie and that he 'would have to watch where he stepped' from now on. This message was recorded in a file. On the day Andrew died, Xenophanes, a passing preacher, heard an unidentified woman near the spot where the accident occurred say, pointing to Andrew's lifeless form, 'That man stood no chance; the driver meant to run him down.' Barbie has stated that Mike told her about six hours after Andrew died that Andrew had been involved in an accident, adding that 'Andrew deserved it'. Mike does not wish to give evidence at his trial but he does wish to call two social workers who will give evidence that Barbie is suffering from a mental disorder which causes anti-social behaviour and that he, Mike, has a timid personality and is unlikely to behave aggressively.

Advise the prosecution on any evidential issues arising.

University of London LLB Examination
(for External Students) Law of Evidence June 1995 Q7

General Comment

The question requires consideration of the hearsay rule and exceptions, particularly those relating to states of mind and res gestae, as well as the use of expert and non-expert opinion evidence

Skeleton Solution

Admission of evidence to show Andrew's state of mind, if relevant to the issues.

Admission of first-hand hearsay by s23 Criminal Justice Act 1988.

Res gestae exception for Xenophanes.

Barbie's evidence of Mike's call – hearsay implications.

Use of the social workers as expert witnesses.

Admissibility of good character.

Significance of Mike's refusal to testify.

Suggested Solution

Mike's defence is one of unavoidable accident, so the real issue in the case is that of intention. It could be highly relevant to this issue if there is some evidence that Andrew had some apprehension of the danger to himself. In *Subramaniam* v *Public Prosecutor* (1956) the Privy Council held that defence evidence of threats was wrongly excluded as the evidence concerned the state of mind of the defendant which was in issue, irrespective of the truth of the statements. Similarly, in *Ratten* v *R* (1972) a jury was correctly directed that a fearful state of mind could be inferred from a distressed woman's voice regardless of what she said or its truth. The significance here is that the apprehension is, in some way, connected to the affair and Andrew.

The message is on a computer file and can be retrieved, presumably by printout. This raises the question whether the 'computer' is a simple word processor or something more sophisticated. Section 23 Criminal Justice Act (CJA) 1988 certainly allows admissibility for first-hand documentary hearsay where the maker is dead as evidence of any fact to which the maker would have been allowed to testify, if alive. This is subject to s69 Police and Criminal Evidence Act (PACE) 1984 which covers computer records. Mike could certainly have testified as to his state of mind so there seems to be no problem here. If the instrument was a simple word processor it is probable that s69 would not need to be complied with, according to the Court of Appeal obiter in *R* v *Blackburn* (1992), because of the proliferation of such equipment.

Xenophanes heard an unidentified woman say that the driver meant to run Andrew down. Much depends here upon how long after the incident this woman spoke. If almost immediately afterwards, it might be admissible as a spontaneous declaration made under the impress of the event, even though she could not be identified according to dicta in *Teper* v *R* (1952). The longer the gap, the less chance of true spontaneity and the greater the chance for distortion or concoction as in *R* v *Gibson* (1887).

Barbie's statement that Mike told her about the accident six hours afterwards, and the additional 'he deserved it', can be treated in several different ways. It clearly is hearsay if repeated to show its truth. It might be used to show the state of the maker's mind or emotional condition, or to shed light on his intentions, previous or prospective, irrespective of the truth of what was said. In *R* v *Hagan* (1873) a person's out-of-court statement was admitted to show his dislike of his child, and *Re Fletcher* (1917) shows that there may be admissibility to show both past and future intention. The problem here is that the statement points more towards dislike than intention, but may evidence motive. The statement might be used to show Mike's awareness of the death at that time if it were in issue (*Thomas* v *Connell* (1828)). Barbie could give evidence that Mike actually spoke to her at that time without offending the hearsay rule.

Mike wishes not to give evidence but to use two social workers to give evidence of Barbie's mental disorder and his own personality. Any testimony of any witness can be challenged as to credibility on grounds of mental disorder affecting its reliability (*Toohey* v *MPC* (1965)). This needs to be done by an expert witness in the particular field because the matter is outside the experience of judge and jury. The social workers will not be able to shed light upon Barbie's mental condition as affecting her credibility, which is the issue. Anti-social behaviour may affect truthfulness, but on the authority of *R* v *Turner* (1975) the social workers will not be allowed to give expert evidence on her mental condition. Mike's behavioural characteristics are an issue here, and in *R* v *Bryant and Oxley* (1979) it was held that evidence of disposition or character which tended to show that the accused was not the type of person likely to commit the offence charged was admissible. This was confirmed in *R* v *Vye* (1993) and, in principle, evidence on this point by these witnesses seems admissible whether as expert or as non-expert witnesses to Mike's good character. If the latter, it will need to avoid evidence of specific acts to avoid falling foul of *R* v *Rowton* (1865), but it will be evidence going both to credit and to the main issues. It will need to relate to the period proximate to the running down (*R* v *Swendsen* (1702)). If Mike does not give evidence, his silence will allow prosecution comment and invite proper inferences to be drawn by the jury, as well as requiring the judge to direct as to the significance of the silence (s35 Criminal Justice and Public Order Act 1994 and *R* v *Martinez-Tobon* (1994)).

QUESTION THREE

Knowing of their previous convictions for dishonesty, Inspector H invites K and L to the police station to help with enquiries into a burglary. K demands a solicitor but is told that he will have to wait. K is then questioned for four hours without a break and, finally, K says 'I don't know why you bother; I'm used to this; what can you police do about it?' In reply, H says, 'If you tell us about it now we probably won't do much about it; we just want to clear the matter up'. As he does this, he loosens his tie and begins to roll up his sleeves. Thinking that H may be about to strike him, K blurts out 'OK I did it; the loot is at L's garage but L made me do it; he threatened me with a gun if I didn't go along with him'. K is then formally cautioned and charged with the burglary. The police then search L's place and discover the stolen property. Meanwhile, L, who was frightened to begin with, has become very agitated by having been left in a cell on his own for two hours. H begins questioning him by saying that the stolen goods had been found in L's garden shed. L then admits to the burglary.

Advise K and L.

University of London Examination
(for External Students) Law of Evidence June 1993 Q6

General Comment

Confessions questions are relatively straightforward, posing none of the conceptual difficulties of hearsay. Prepare these questions bearing in mind the chronological pattern of so many examination questions: the invitation to the police station, the refusal of a solicitor, the interrogation, the admission, the finding of the stolen property. Remember to have up your sleeve, a reasonable knowledge of the Codes of Practice, a prepared discussion of the meaning *and rationale* of 'oppression', of the differences between s76(2)(a) and (b) of the Police and Criminal Evidence Act 1984, and of the uses of discretion under ss78 and 82(3). You should also be well aware of how s76(4) and (5) work (and show how the law derived from *Warwickshall*).

Skeleton Solution

- H's invitation.
- Relationship between the 1995 Codes of Practice and the Police and Criminal Evidence Act 1984.
- K: refusal of solicitor; questioning without break oppression (*Fulling*) or s76(2)(b)?; inducement; perceived assault; confession with exculpatory part (*Sharp*).
- L: subjective oppression?

Suggested Solution

The police are always entitled to ask someone to come to the police station to 'help them with their enquiries'; it is only when they have grounds to suspect such a person of an offence that they should caution and arrest. It is clear that such grounds could not be those of K and L having previous convictions since the reasoning of the similar facts rules tells us that. Nevertheless, those people who are so assisting the police have, according to the Codes of Practice, the same 'absolute' rights as those who have been arrested (s58 says that a person arrested is entitled to a solicitor) and so there has been a breach of the Code when H refuses access to a solicitor (on the other hand, K should have left instead of putting up with 'You'll have to wait'; it is clear that those not taken into custody have a right to leave whenever they want).

The Codes are not law, however; this is discussed in ss66 and 67 of PACE. They are evidence that can be put into court and this means that breaches by the police are evidence from which the judge can conclude (in the voir dire) whether there has been 'oppression', or a cause of unreliability of any confession, or whether he should exercise his discretion to exclude evidence under ss78 and 82(3).

In addition to the refusal of access, what other breaches of the Code are there? Four hours' continuous interrogation breaches the requirement that those questioned be given short breaks every two hours; H's reply to K's rhetorical question about what the police can do, that the police won't 'probably' do much comes close to breaching the Code's requirement that police only say what they will do in response to a direct question and, in any case, appears to be a lie.

But these do not look like serious enough breaches to warrant 'oppression' (the advantage to which, to a defendant, is that, however reliable the induced confession is, it must be rejected). 'Oppression' refers to 'harsh, burdensome and wrongful behaviour' and even then, that is a common law, widened, interpretation of the words of s76(8) which refer to torture and criminal assaults. The facts are too ambiguous here to say whether H intended or was reckless as to assaulting K as in *R* v *Venna* (1976) (but recklessness cannot be ruled out; in which case there *would* be an assault and, therefore, oppression). One argument *could* be explored here. Although commentators like to say that, because of *Fulling* (1987), the definition of 'oppression' is objective, that is, independent of the subjective qualities of impressionability on a weak person, there is an argument that subjective qualities of the suspect can affect whether there is oppression whenever a policemen acts 'wrongfully' (the definition in *Fulling*) *by exploiting the suspect's weakness.* In other words, had H known that K was the sort of person who would weaken despite these relatively minor breaches of the Code, arguably the confession should be rejected however reliable it seemed.

However, there are easier ways to do it. This must be a situation where there is a reasonable doubt (because that is all that is necessary: s76(2)(b)) that K's confession has been rendered unreliable from things said and done. Section 76(2)(b) clearly covers the case where the suspect has weakened and, whether or not H committed an assault, it is relevant for this paragraph that K thought that H had assaulted him. Even if this argument is not accepted, K's confession has an exculpatory element which, if accepted by a jury, would provide him with the defence of duress (see *Hudson* (1971), for example). In fairness to the defendant and ignoring, so it seems, the hearsay rule (see *Myers* (1965), *Sharp* (1988)) permits the exculpatory part to go before the jury, although the Court of Appeal in that case made it clear that the jury should be warned that the exculpatory part of the judgment should be given less weight as it could be self-serving. Incidentally, there is *an* argument that there is no breach of the common law rules on hearsay; s82(1) defines a 'confession' as a statement which 'includes' an admission – 'partly adverse' – and this would allow K's whole statement, which includes the exculpatory part, because another part of that one statement is an admission.

What is the position with L? He hasn't asked for a solicitor; on the other hand, the police should have informed him of his right to have one, or a friend, present. L could have left; but it is not always easy at a police station to do this and he possibly has no idea of what rights he has. If he has become excessively agitated in the cell (although it is not such a long time) this could, in theory, have had the effect of rendering his confession unreliable; but what evidence is there otherwise that it is unreliable? The stolen goods were, after all, found at his place. On being confronted with them, he blurts out immediately his involvement in the offence. It is unlikely, therefore, that his confession will be rejected.

QUESTION FOUR

Sykes is charged with the murder of Nancy by stabbing. Oliver is prepared to testify that Nancy telephoned him and shouted: 'Come quickly, Sykes is threatening to kill me ...', the phone then going dead. Oliver raced to Nancy's house and found her lying in a pool of blood. She whispered: 'You're too late, he's done for me' and lapsed into unconsciousness. A doctor arrived, briefly examined Nancy, covered her with a blanket and accompanied her in an ambulance. The ambulance collided with a lorry and the totally charred bodies of the ambulance's occupants were recovered from the burnt out wreckage.

Oliver finds Sykes and tells him he will kill him unless he comes to the police station. Sykes is dragged to the station by Oliver; as Oliver lunges at him and punches him in the face Sykes shouts to the police officers who are present: 'Get him off me for God's sake! I killed her; the knife's down the drain outside her house.' A knife is found there, wiped clean of blood and prints.

Advise the prosecution on the evidentiary problems, given that Sykes refused to write out or sign any subsequent statement.

Written by editor

Skeleton Solution

- Res gestae statement; dying declaration – competence.
- Statement by conduct.
- Causation in murder; alternative verdicts.
- Confessions; reliability; oppression; admissibility – voir dire.
- Facts discovered in consequence of confessions.

Suggested Solution

Oliver may be allowed to report not only the fact but also the content of the phoned statement as a res gestae statement. If it was contemporaneous, approximately, with the stabbing and was sufficiently spontaneous to enable the court safely to ignore the possibility of concoction or distortion, and any other factors such as malice on Nancy's part are taken into account, then the judge can admit the content of the call as a res gestae statement (*R* v *Andrews* (1987)). Its admissibility is determined by the judge, who will advise the jury on factors affecting the weight they may attach to it.

The fact that Nancy was shouting or was hysterical can be stated by Oliver (*Ratten* v *R* (1972)) and is relevant to the spontaneity issue. As regards contemporaneity, this depends on how much time elapsed between the phone call and Oliver's reaching Nancy's side, since there will be no medical evidence available to pinpoint the time of the stabbing, nor very probably its severity. Given that the stabbing and the phone call were *approximately* contemporaneous, that is sufficient to satisfy the court as to that element of admissibility of the res gestae statement. Given also that Oliver found Nancy within a short time (say ten minutes) of the phone call, then her second statement could also be admissible. Such a lapse of time, coupled with questions to elicit the res gestae statement, has been accepted by the court (*R* v *Andrews*; *R* v *Turnbull* (1984)). The other major issue for the court is whether Nancy's second statement is mere narration or whether her mind is still dominated by the drama of the event – the prosecution must persuade the court of the latter for the statement to be admitted.

If the second statement is not admissible under the res gestae doctrine, it may be admissible as a dying declaration. Nancy's statement certainly implies that she entertains no hope of survival, but she must be in *settled* hopeless expectation of death (*R* v *Perry* (1909)) and therefore must have had sufficient time for reflection (*R* v *Bedingfield* (1879)). In addition, had she survived she must have been a competent witness (*R* v *Pike* (1829)); even if she is Sykes' wife she would nevertheless be competent (s80(1)(a) Police and Criminal Evidence Act 1984). Nancy's declaration does not in itself state expressly the cause of her injuries, but in conjunction with her earlier exclamation it is very relevant to their cause.

The prosecution will want Oliver to testify as to what he saw the doctor do, arguing that he would be giving evidence, as a percipient witness, of an act performed by the doctor. The defence contention would be that the doctor's covering Nancy is an implied assertion by him that Nancy is already dead, and that implied assertions, just like express assertions, constitute inadmissible hearsay unless they come within a recognised exception to the hearsay rule.

There is a paucity of authorities on implied assertions (see Lord Bridge in *R* v *Blastland* (1985) and *Cross on Evidence* (8th edition, 1995), but the reason for the law's suspicion of them is the danger of concoction by the observed doctor. There seems to be little doubt that the doctor would have no motive to fabricate evidence for the observers, therefore Oliver should be allowed to state what he perceived and the jury draw their own inferences. In the unlikely event that Oliver cannot give this evidence, there may be no acceptable evidence of causation and therefore Sykes could not be convicted of murder; he could nevertheless, if the prosecution can prove his specific intent to kill Nancy when he stabbed her, be found guilty of attempted murder as an alternative verdict (s6 Criminal Law Act 1967).

Sykes' confession is damning if it is admissible. However, it may well be excluded under s76 Police and Criminal Evidence Act 1984, given the likelihood of its unreliability in consequence of Oliver's conduct (s76(2)(b) Police and Criminal Evidence Act 1984). An alternative or additional reason for the confession's inadmissibility is oppression by Oliver, which would lead to exclusion of the confession (s76(2)(a) Police and Criminal Evidence Act 1984). Lord Lane CJ, giving the judgment of the Court of Appeal in *R* v *Fulling* (1987) defined 'oppression' in this context, and his definition implies that the conduct must be that of a person in authority such as a police officer. However, he was dealing with conduct falling short of violence or threats of violence, and a partial definition of violence in the Police and Criminal Evidence Act has not been affected. Section 76(8) states that 'oppression' includes torture, inhuman or degrading treatment, and the use or threat of violence', and there is no requirement that this sort of conduct must be that of a person in authority. So, unless the prosecution can prove beyond reasonable doubt that, despite Oliver's words and conduct the confession was not made in consequence of oppression and is not likely to be unreliable, the judge (on a voir dire) will rule Sykes' confession statement inadmissible, and the jury will therefore be unaware that it was made.

If the confession is excluded under s76, then no reference can be made to it by the prosecution in order to link Sykes to the knife found in the drain, ie a police officer will not be permitted to testify: 'In consequence of what the accused said I went to the drain outside the house of the deceased and found a knife ...' (s76(5) and (6) Police and Criminal Evidence Act 1984). Therefore, unless the knife is Sykes's or unless there is some other admissible evidence to link it to Sykes it is inadmissible real evidence because it has no apparent relevance; relevance cannot be given to it by any reference to the *fact* of, let alone the content of, a confession statement excluded under s76.

QUESTION FIVE

Able was taking his daughters, Baker aged 7 and Charlie aged 11, for a walk when a car horn sounded behind them. Able looked behind him and saw that a green Mercedes car had left the road and was approaching them at high speed across the wide grass verge. He pushed his daughters to one side and was run down by the car; although conscious he could not get to his feet. He saw the car stop, a man alight and chase Baker (Charlie had jumped behind a hedge); the man indecently assaulted Baker, got back in the car and drove off.

A police patrol car arrived at the scene, and both Baker and Able gave the registration number of the car as C454 VKV; Charles said the car was green. From this information Douglas was traced as the car owner, was interviewed by the police but refused to comment. He has been charged with indecent assault and reckless driving. Able, Baker and Charlie have made written statements, but Able is paralysed as a result of the incident and cannot attend court; Baker is still in shock and having to give evidence could damage her mental health.

Advise the prosecution.

Written by editor

Skeleton Solution

- Hearsay; exceptions to exclusionary rule.
- Applicability of statutory exceptions; action pre-trial.
- Corroboration; sexual offences; identification; children of tender years; competence of children.
- Silence of accused; evidential value.

Suggested Solution

If the police officer(s) in the patrol car are to repeat what A, B and C said to them, the only purpose is to invite the court to believe the truth of what is repeated, therefore that is hearsay and will be inadmissible unless it falls within a recognised exception to the hearsay rule (*Myers* v *DPP* (1965)). If A and B do not testify, then the same applies if a witness wishes to read their statements to the court. Therefore, unless there are common law or statutory provisions which permit this hearsay evidence in criminal proceedings it cannot be adduced.

If a doctor certifies that A is dangerously ill and is unlikely to recover, then a magistrate may take A's deposition out of court, and provided Douglas's lawyer was given notice of this and the opportunity to cross-examine A, then if A is, by the time of the trial, dead or so ill that it is unlikely that he will ever be able to travel to court or give evidence, his written statement can be read to the court (s105 Magistrates' Courts Act 1980 and s6 Criminal Law Amendment Act 1867 (an offence is indictable even though it may be tried summarily)). If any of these conditions do not obtain, eg A is not certified as dangerously ill, then his written statement may still be given in evidence if 'by reason of his bodily or mental condition' he is 'unfit to attend as a witness' (s23(1) and (2)(a) Criminal Justice Act 1988). If A's condition does not come within either of these categories, then his statement, as a 's9 statement' is unlikely to be admitted, since the defence must be served with a copy and will doubtless give written notice of objection (s9 Criminal Justice Act 1967).

In the case of B's statement, if a doctor certifies that her attendance in court would involve serious danger to her life or health (including mental health), then a magistrate may take her deposition out of court, since she is under 17 and indecent assault is an offence contrary to the Sexual Offences Act 1956 (s42 Children and Young Persons Act 1933). But Douglas's lawyer must be given notice of the taking of the deposition and the opportunity to cross-examine (s43 Children and Young Persons Act 1933). If there is no such 'serious danger' to her mental health, but rather in her shocked state she has an abject fear of a court appearance, then it is conceivable, subject to how s23 Criminal Justice Act 1988 is construed, her statement would still be admissible in evidence as would the deposition. Section 23(1)(ii) and (3)(b) provide for the admissibility of such written statements if 'the person who made it does not give oral evidence through fear ...' This was inserted in the 1988 Act to cater for witnesses to terrorist activities who might fear for their lives, but on a literal construction could cover our situation.

One drawback, if in the case of A's and/or B's statement resort has to be made to s23 CJA 1988, is that leave of the court is required before the statement can be admitted, and the court must have regard to all relevant circumstances, including in particular any risk of unfairness to the accused (s25 Criminal Justice Act 1933). Alternatively a video recording of an interview with Baker could be used, under s32A of the Criminal Justice Act 1988 (as inserted by the Criminal Justice Act 1991), which could be played back to the court to replace Baker's testimony. However, she would still need to appear in court for cross-examination. Alternatively, a live TV link could be used under s32 as she is under 14. However, there may be problems with the fact that only one of the offences Douglas is charged with (indecent assault) allows for s32 and s32A to come into play.

If A and B could not recollect the car number by the time they gave their written statements and therefore the number does not appear in those statements, then a police officer tendering in evidence their oral statements would be attempting to give hearsay evidence. If he wrote down the number at the time in his notebook, and A and B verified the entry as correct, then the officer could refresh his memory from the notebook and so could A and/or B if giving evidence (*Jones* v *Metcalfe* (1967); *R* v *McLean* (1968) and see *R* v *Eleftheriou* (1993)). If A and B do not give direct evidence, the officer could nevertheless, with leave of the court, give the particulars in his notebook as a 'statement in a document' under s24 CJA 1988 if A and B are unfit to attend or given the lapse of time cannot be expected to have any recollection of the number (s24(1) and (4)).

Charlie (C) may have relevant evidence to offer as to the identity of the assailant etc, and the fact that she is aged only 11 does not in itself necessitate corroboration or a corroboration warning (s34(2) CJA 1988). The former requirements for corroboration warnings with respect to child or sexual complainant witnesses have now gone and the matter of jury directions as to supporting evidence in both of these situations is very much a question of the judge's direction. If A saw not only the assailant but also the incident, there is more corroborative evidence. As regards the identity of the assailant, the evidence of one witness *may* be sufficient for the court to be satisfied, but supportive evidence (even though it does not amount to 'corroboration' as defined in evidence) is highly desirable where the accused was not previously known, sighting not very good etc – per the guidelines in *R* v *Turnbull* (1977). Even though A, B and C identify Douglas, the judge should still caution the jury, where the identification is disputed by the defence, on the general unreliability of visual identification evidence of this sort.

Douglas's refusal to comment when interviewed will amount to a Road Traffic offence if he refuses to state who was driving the car at the time, given that, presumably, he is the registered owner. But his silence when accused of committing the offences cannot amount to corroboration when his accuser is a police officer (*R* v *Whitehead* (1929); *R* v *Keeling* (1942)) nor can it in those circumstances amount to an adoption by him of the accusation as his confession, because he has a right to remain silent of which he should have been reminded (*Hall* v *R* (1971)). This must, however, be viewed in the light of *R* v *Chandler* (1976) on the point of accused and accuser speaking on 'even terms' and the very considerable statutory inroads made upon this so-called 'right to silence' by s34 CJPOA 1994.

9 Character Evidence

9.1 Introduction

9.2 Key points

9.3 Analysis of questions

9.4 Questions

9.1 Introduction

Character evidence, especially that of the accused and its admissibility in the course of the trial, is one of the most difficult areas of evidence, but one with which all students must be conversant as it will appear in almost every examination paper on Evidence. For example, there is often, in problem questions, a statement that a person has previous convictions; that should immediately alert the examinee to the fact that the bad character of that person (usually the accused) will require discussion. Any witness in criminal or civil proceedings is liable to be cross-examined as to character, including previous convictions, to destroy or damage his credibility as a witness; the one exception is the accused who elects to testify – that witness is given protection from such gratuitous cross-examination, except where he has discarded that protection or where evidence of his previous bad character has become relevant to his guilt on the charge he faces.

Although, therefore, evidence of the bad character of the accused is the major area of concern, something must be said, briefly, of character of parties in civil cases and of character of witnesses in civil and criminal cases.

9.2 Key points

a) *Parties to a civil action*

Dependent on what issues are raised in the pleadings in civil cases, the character of a party may be in issue – 'character' here referring to general reputation, disposition *and* particular conduct. A prime example is an action in defamation; if the defendant pleads justification of his assertion that the plaintiff is a rapist, then evidence of a rape conviction of the plaintiff can be adduced by the defendant; as regards damages in defamation the general reputation of the plaintiff is in issue, to assess the injury done to it.

Where evidence of disposition is admissible as character evidence to show that a party has a propensity to a particular kind of misconduct, because it is sufficiently relevant to the facts in issue, that evidence is known as 'similar fact evidence' and is dealt with in Chapter 10 (in both civil and criminal proceedings).

b) *Witnesses in civil and criminal proceedings*

All witnesses, whether or not parties, may be cross-examined as to credibility. The answers of the witnesses to such questions in cross-examination are almost invariably final, ie evidence cannot be adduced to contradict the answers, as the issue is a collateral one. However, one major exception is where the witness denies the commission by him of a criminal offence, in which event the appropriate conviction can be proved by the cross-examiner. For example, in the case of *R* v *Edwards* [1991] NLJ 91, the Court of Appeal held that police officers could be cross-examined about relevant criminal offences or disciplinary charges found proved against them, but could not be questioned about any previous misbehaviour not yet adjudicated upon.

c) *The accused*

   i) Good character

   As a general rule at common law the accused may adduce evidence of his good character despite the general prohibition on the prosecution's adducing evidence of his bad character – but evidence of bad character may be given to rebut the accused's evidence of his good character (see below).

   The evidential value of evidence of good character is unclear; in *R* v *Bryant* [1979] QB 108 it was held that such evidence goes not just to the credibility of the accused but also to his guilt or innocence. But in *R* v *Levy* [1987] Crim LR 48 it was held that where there are two co-accused, one of good character and one bad, the good character of one goes only to credibility not unlikelihood of offending – otherwise the bad character of the other would give rise to an inference that he was likely to have committed the offence, which would be unacceptable!

   The appropriate direction for situations where the defendant has given good character evidence is confirmed in *R* v *Wren* [1993] Crim LR 952 which confirmed the earlier case of *R* v *Vye* [1993] Crim LR 604. *R* v *Vye* is now seen to be the leading case and the guidelines given by the Court of Appeal show that a 'first limb' direction, ie that good character supports the credibility of the accused as witness should be given in every case where it is appropriate. A 'second limb' direction, ie that good character may shed light on the probability of guilt, should be given whether or not the accused testifies. This has clarified the law considerably. See also *R* v *Cain* [1994] 2 All ER 398 CA on the question of multiple defendants, some of good character, some of bad. See also *R* v *Aziz* [1995] 3 All ER 149 HL on the judicial discretions where character is mixed or questionable.

   ii) Bad character

   At common law, evidence of the bad character of the accused may be given by the prosecution if it is admissible similar fact evidence (see Chapter 10); it may also be given to rebut evidence given by the defence of the accused's good character. Such rebutting evidence will usually be as to the general bad reputation of the accused, but evidence of previous convictions has been admitted under the common law: *R* v *Redd* [1923] 1 KB 104; *R* v *Winfield* [1939] 4 All ER 164.

   Section 1 Criminal Evidence Act 1898 deals with cross-examination of the accused as to his bad character, and therefore *it applies only when the accused elects to testify for the defence*. Otherwise, the common law rules apply.

   The 1898 Act made the accused competent for the first time, and the legislators compromised between treating the accused exactly the same as any other witness and making him immune from cross-examination; the result was to give the accused protection (often called a shield) from cross-examination as to character, but protection which may be lost in circumstances set out in the provisos to s1(f) of the Act. The provisions in s1(e) and (f) should be known *verbatim* by every Evidence student who hopes to do justice to examination questions on character.

iii) Relationship between s1(e) and s1(f)

Section 1(e) permits cross-examination of the accused even though it tends to incriminate him as to the offence charged, and in that context allows 'any question'. Section 1(f) prohibits questions in cross-examination which tend to show that the accused has committed or been convicted of any other offence. There is thus apparent conflict between s1(e) and (f), because a question tending to show the accused has committed or been convicted of some other offence may well also tend to incriminate him as to the offence charged – such a question is apparently allowed by s1(e) but prohibited by s1(f). After several conflicting decisions, the House of Lords ruled (by a bare majority) in *Jones* v *DPP* [1962] AC 635 that s1(e) must be read subject to s1(f). The majority also ruled that 'show' in s1(f) means reveal or disclose to the jury for the first time, so if the jury is already aware of the bad character of the accused, the prohibition in s1(f) does not apply. The ruling in *Jones* v *DPP* was used by the Court of Appeal in *R* v *Anderson* [1988] 2 All ER 549, but the principles were not merely followed but extended, to the disadvantage of the accused who testifies: see discussion in [1988] Crim LR 298.

iv) Exceptions to the s1(f) prohibition

- Section 1(f)(i) allows cross-examination of the accused on similar fact evidence which is admissible as proof of his guilt. However, only where the similar fact evidence shows the commission or conviction of an offence (not other misconduct or previous charges which did not result in convictions) is cross-examination under s1(f)(i) allowed as to the bad character of the accused.

- Section 1(f)(ii) contains two exceptions (the two 'limbs'). The first is where the defence has attempted to establish the good character of the accused; the second where the defence involves imputations on the character of the prosecutor or prosecution witnesses.

Under the first limb, 'character' includes both general reputation *and* disposition: *R* v *Samuel* (1956) 40 Cr App R 8. Evidence of good character can go not merely to the credibility of the accused as a witness, but also to his innocence: *R* v *Bryant* supra. Yet the cross-examination under the first limb goes directly to credibility – any bearing on the guilt of the accused is the subject of controversy: *Maxwell* v *DPP* [1935] AC 309; cf *R* v *Samuel* supra. The better view would seem to be that the purpose of cross-examination is to discredit the accused as a witness, *not* to prove his guilt by disclosing prior convictions.

It is important that in this context the character of the accused is not divisible; if the accused puts any good aspect of his character forward then he may be cross-examined on his character, not just the aspect on which he relies: *R* v *Winfield* [1939] 4 All ER 164; *Stirland* v *DPP* [1944] AC 315.

Under the second limb of s1(f)(ii), the accused may be liable to cross-examination as to his bad character if imputations have been cast on the character of the prosecutor or prosecution witnesses or the deceased victim (this last having been added by s31 of the Criminal Justice and Public Order Act 1994, which inserts at the end of s1(f)(ii) the words 'the deceased victim of the alleged crime'). For the 'shield' to be lost under this limb, there must be something more than an emphatic denial of guilt – but it can be difficult to draw the line between a robust denial and an imputation on the character of a witness: compare, and reconcile *R* v *Nelson* (1978) 68 Cr App R 12 and *R* v *Tanner* (1977) 66 Cr App R 66. The second limb can be brought into play by implied, as well as express, imputations on the character of prosecution witnesses. (NB: it must be an imputation cast on the character of someone called as a witness for the prosecution; if the accused attacks the character of a person not called as a witness, the shield is not lost under the second limb: *R* v *Lee* [1976] 1 WLR 71.)

Even if casting imputations is necessary as a part of the defence case, nevertheless the shield is dropped: *Selvey* v *DPP* [1970] AC 304; *R* v *Bishop* [1975] QB 274. See also the case of *R* v *Lasseur* [1991] Crim LR 53 – the defendant suggested to an accomplice that he was only giving evidence against him so as to get a more lenient sentence. The Court of Appeal held that the shield had been dropped.

One very important point, made in *R* v *Turner* [1944] KB 463, and approved in *Selvey* v *DPP*, supra, is that where consent is in issue in a rape trial the accused can allege consent by the complainant (and even gross indecency on her part) without losing his shield, the reasoning being that a defence of consent is merely a denial that an element of the offence has been proved and thus is not an imputation. Evidence of the sexual activity of the complainant with the accused, and (with leave of the judge) with other males, again goes to the issue of consent and therefore will not result in s1(f)(ii) being activated (somewhat incongruously perhaps!)

• Under s1(f)(iii) an accused is liable to cross-examination as to bad character by a person charged in the same proceedings when he gives evidence against that person. It is not necessary that he attacks the person's character, only that he gives evidence that supports the prosecution's case against him.

In *Murdoch* v *Taylor* [1965] AC 574, the House of Lords stated that the determinant is whether, objectively, the evidence undermines the other's defence or strengthens the case against him – regardless of whether this was intended. A denial of involvement by one accused, or evidence from him which appears to be in conflict with evidence given by the other, may, dependent on the particular facts, amount to evidence under s1(f)(iii): *R* v *Varley* (1982) 75 Cr App R 242.

Under s1(f)(iii) the co-accused can cross-examine the accused who loses his shield as of right, ie leave of the judge is not required and the judge cannot restrict the scope of the cross-examination, the effect of which is to attack credibility, not to go to the issue of guilt.

v) Judicial discretion in cross-examination

The discretion of the judge to refuse the prosecution leave to cross-examine the accused as to his character was given the ultimate seal of approval in *Selvey* v *DPP* supra.

The judge must ensure a fair trial, and even where bad character of the accused goes to credibility rather than guilt, it would prejudice a fair trial if, for example, the accused had a bad record with many previous convictions, or one conviction for a very grave crime and the instant charge was relatively minor and/or the imputation on the prosecution witness was relatively slight. Alternatively, there may be a number of charges against the accused and an attack was made on the character of a prosecution witness to one charge only. Again, the greater the similarity of the previous convictions to the instant charge the greater the prejudice to the accused if they are all revealed. Finally, an allegation that a prosecution witness was mistaken may, objectively, amount to a necessary imputation of fabrication of evidence. Guidelines for the exercise of judicial discretion were laid down in *R* v *Britzmann & Hall* (1983) 76 Cr App R 134, and a detailed summary of the current law is given in the judgment of Neill LJ in the Court of Appeal in *R* v *Owen* (1986) 83 Cr App R 100. An important guideline case in this area is *R* v *McLeod* [1994] 3 All ER 254 CA concerning judicial control and discretion in situations where the earlier offences are similar in type or detail to the offence charged.

9.3 Analysis of questions

The typical question on this topic is a problem question raising a number of the issues of detail under common law, and especially under the 1898 Act. Detailed knowledge of s1(f)(i) is rarely tested – this tends to appear in self-contained questions on similar fact evidence. Again, it is rare for problem questions to include character in civil cases. Occasionally essay questions are set on the subject of character, but these again tend to concentrate on criminal proceedings and particularly on permissible cross-examination of the accused under s1 of the 1898 Act. What is virtually certain is that evidence of character will appear in any examination paper; not so certain is that it will always be a question dealing *solely* with character.

9.4 Questions

QUESTION ONE

H is charged with raping J. The prosecution allege that H met J through an introduction agency, took her to a disco and then raped her afterwards at her flat. K, J's flatmate, testifies that she came home later that night and found J weeping. When asked whether 'something had been done to her', J said that H had raped her. There is medical evidence that J had bruises to her face and upper thigh area. Inspector L says that he interviewed H's friend, M, who told L that H had told M at the disco that he was planning to have sex with J that night 'whether she wanted it or not'. M can no longer be found but Inspector L says that he has a record of the interview. The defence wishes to establish that J consented to sex with H. Defence counsel wishes to cross-examine J to the effect that she has met a number of men through this particular dating agency and has invariably agreed to have sex with them. H has decided not to testify.

Discuss any evidential issues arising.

University of London LLB Examination
(for External Students) Law of Evidence June 1994 Q6

General Comment

This question brings together several areas of the law of evidence, and requires the student to have a sound knowledge of a number of topics. Beware of assuming that every question involving a sexual complaint only requires a discussion of corroboration. Time should be spent, initially, in sorting out the issues – once these have been isolated, this question is in fact fairly easy to tackle.

Skeleton Solution

• Isolate issues:

  – confessions/hearsay;

  – character (complainant and defendant).

• Previous consistent statement: admissibility; goes to consistency *and* to negative consent.

• Confession/hearsay:

  – H's out-of-court statement to M;

  – definition of confession: s82(1) PACE;

  – s76 PACE;

  – ss78 or 82 discretion.

• Character:

  – of complainant: s2 Sexual Offences (Amendment) Act 1976;

  – of defendant: s1(f) Criminal Evidence Act 1898; and common law.

Suggested Solution

The evidential issues arising in this question fall broadly into three categories:

a) supporting evidence/corroboration;

b) hearsay/confessions;

c) character (of defendant and complainant).

These will each be dealt with in turn.

a) *Supporting evidence/corroboration*

Considering the facts in this case, is there any evidence capable of amounting to corroboration or supporting evidence equivalent to the earlier requirement for 'corroboration' properly so called? We will look in turn at:

i)   J's distress;

ii) J's complaint to K;

iii) J's injuries;

iv) evidence of H's statement to M.

i)   *J's distress*

This is unlikely to meet the requirement of independence. It could all be part of an act staged by J, and cannot be said to be within the special circumstances in *R* v *Redpath* (1962). (See *R* v *Whitehead* (1929) on independence.)

ii) *J's complaint to K*

As above, this is not capable of amounting to corroboration since it too lacks the quality of independence: *R* v *Whitehead*. However, the evidence of this complaint may be admissible for two other purposes:

• Consistency – evidence of this complaint may be admissible, not as evidence of the facts complained of, but to show that J has maintained the same story throughout: *R* v *Osborne* (1905).

Note: it will be *crucial* that J gives evidence if this statement is to be admissible. Without J's evidence there is nothing for the evidence of her complaint to be 'consistent' with: *R* v *Wallwork* (1958).

- To negative consent – evidence of the complaint made shortly after the alleged incident is clearly inconsistent with consensual intercourse, hence evidence of this complaint is admissible to negative consent: *R* v *Lillyman* (1896).

To be admissible this complaint must meet the requirement of *voluntariness*. The fact that it was made in response to a question ('whether something had been done to her') will not affect the voluntariness of the complaint so long as the question merely anticipates a complaint which the complainant was about to make: Ridley J in *R* v *Osborne*.

iii) *J's injuries*

The evidence of injuries is certainly independent but on its own it will not implicate the accused: *James* v *R* (1970). But, in this case, intercourse is admitted. The issue is that of *consent*. As such, the injuries are capable of corroborating J's version of non-consensual intercourse: *R* v *Ensor* (1989).

iv) *H's statement to M*

As an 'admission', this evidence is capable of amounting to corroboration. Problems do arise with regard to this statement, due to the fact that it is an admission, and that M cannot be found. This will now be dealt with.

b)   *Confession/hearsay*

H's statement to M is made out of court. If it is sought to adduce this statement for the purposes of proving its *truth*, it will be caught by the rule against hearsay. This statement is clearly adverse to H, and as such falls within the definition of a 'confession': s82(1) Police and Criminal Evidence Act (PACE) 1984. A 'confession' can be made to any person, not just a person in authority: *Deokinanan* v *R* (1969).

Hence, for this statement to be admissible (as an exception to the rule against hearsay), it must comply with s76 PACE. The prosecution must prove beyond reasonable doubt that the confession was *not* obtained by oppression, or in consequence of anything said or done which was likely in the circumstances existing at the time to render the confession unreliable.

If the prosecution fail to prove that this confession was *not* obtained in such a way then the confession *will* be inadmissible: s76(2) PACE.

If, however, the prosecution *do* manage to prove this, the defence may still seek to convince the judge to exercise his discretion under s78(1) PACE (fairness of proceedings) or s82(3) (the common law, eg that the confession is more prejudicial than probative: *R* v *Sang* (1980).

The issue as to the admissibility of this confession will be decided on the voir dire (ie in the absence of the jury).

It is submitted that the best defence argument regarding this confession is that it is more prejudicial than probative – H made this adverse statement before the alleged incident – it cannot be said that he actually carried out this stated intention.

c) *Character*

The defence wish to cross-examine J on her sexual experience with men other than the defendant. There is no restriction on cross-examination concerning sex with the defendant since this would clearly go to the issue of consent: *R* v *Riley* (1887).

The position is different, however, with regard to the complainant's sexual experience with persons other than the defendant. Under s2 of the Sexual Offences (Amendment) Act 1976, no evidence may be called, and no question asked in cross-examination by or on behalf of the defendant, relating to the complainant's sexual experience with *other* persons except with leave of the judge. Leave will only be granted if the judge is satisfied that it would be *unfair* to the accused to disallow such evidence or cross-examination.

The purpose of the calling of such evidence should *not* simply be to blacken the complainant's character: *R* v *Lawrence* (1977). The test is: would it lead the jury to take a different view of her evidence?: May J in *R* v *Lawrence*. The evidence can go to *both* credibility of the complainant, *and* to an issue at trial (eg consent): *R* v *Viola* (1982). Note, though, that the *Lawrence* text is not appropriate to a defence based on reasonable belief in consent: *R* v *Barton* (1986).

Finally, the conduct of this defence is likely to involve an attack on J's character. Does this have any implications for H? Were he to decide to give evidence, he would lose his shield under s1(f) of the Criminal Evidence Act (CEA) 1898 since he would be 'casting imputations' within s1(f)(ii). However, s1 CEA 1898 only applies to a defendant who gives evidence. H has decided *not* to give evidence, hence this statute does not apply.

Under the common law, H will not lose his shield since he is not putting his good character into issue: *R* v *Butterwasser* (1948).

QUESTION TWO

Beater and Thwack, two school teachers, are jointly charged with severely beating a little girl Pettle, a six year old, who is at their school. Consider the following questions:

a) What issues arise in the law of evidence if Pettle is to be called as a witness for the Crown?

b) If Pettle gives evidence in the case, what use could be made of a statement made by Pettle to her mother the day after the alleged beating that Pettle did not 'ever want to be in Mr Beater's or Mr Thwack's classes'?

Would it make a difference if Pettle had told her mother the day after the alleged assault that Beater and Thwack had assaulted her?

Would either of the above statements be admissible if Pettle does not give evidence?

c) If Beater and Thwack give evidence on their own behalf, what use could be made of Beater's previous convictions for assault and causing grievous bodily harm if he denies in evidence that he made a confession to the Police (which was permitted in evidence after a voire dire) which was allegedly made during the course of a one hour interrogation. He also says that Thwack and he had admonished Pettle for being naughty but that he had left the room leaving Thwack with Pettle; Thwack says he had never spoken to the child.

University of London LLB Examination
(for External Students) Evidence June 1989 Q4

General Comment

With the enactment of the Criminal Justice Act 1988, it must have been expected that the question of evidence of children would appear. Other than in the context of an essay question on corroboration, competence etc, it was obvious that it would be one of several issues in a 'problem' question. The question raises quite a few issues, and the trap for the unwary candidate is to assume that the assault is a sexual assault – often the sort of offence specified when covering these issues – and thus to deal with some irrelevant material; a good example of the necessity to read questions with the utmost care.

Skeleton Solution

- Competence of children of tender years; corroboration of evidence of children; special provision for their giving evidence.
- Circumstantial evidence; self-serving statements; recent complaints, inadmissible hearsay.
- Casting imputations on prosecution witnesses – s1(f)(ii) Criminal Evidence Act 1898.
- Giving evidence against co-accused – s1(f)(iii) Criminal Evidence Act 1898.

Suggested Solution

At the outset it must be stressed that the specific charge which Beater and Thwack face is not stated – the question states 'severely beating'. If the dominant purpose of the beating were sexual gratification rather than (immoderate) chastisement, then the charges could include one of indecent assault, otherwise the charges would be of assaults contrary to the Offences Against the Person Act 1861, ss47, 20 and/or 18. Whether a sexual or non-sexual offence is charged is very relevant when dealing with part ii) in particular.

a) Pettle will be treated as a competent witness provided that the judge is satisfied that the test in s33A(2A) CJA 1988 is met. Pettle would then have to give evidence unsworn by the action of s33A(1).

At common law the sworn evidence of a child of tender years required the judge to give a corroboration warning to the jury, ie there could be a conviction on that evidence alone provided the jury had been alerted to the dangers. In the case of unsworn evidence there could be no conviction unless the evidence was corroborated. These common law rules have been abrogated by s34 Criminal Justice Act 1988, so there is now no requirement for a warning nor for corroborative evidence merely because the witness is a child or because she is a complainant of a sexual offence: s32(1) CJPOA 1994. Section 34 refers only to trials on indictment, and in addition it merely states that a corroboration warning is no longer obligatory. As Pettle is only six, the judge *may* consider it advisable to direct the jury to treat her evidence with some circumspection and in the absence of corroboration to convict only if sure of her credibility. See *R* v *Pryce* (1991) on the judicial discretions here.

As Pettle is a witness to an assault charge, whether or not a sexual assault case, s32 Criminal Justice Act 1988 provides that, as she is under 14 (or under 17 if a sexual case), she may be allowed to give her evidence through a live television link if Beater and Thwack are tried on indictment. She may be able to give a video recording of an interview to replace her testimony at court (s32A Criminal Justice Act 1988, as inserted by the Criminal Justice Act 1991). However, she will still have to turn up to court to be cross-examined.

b) Pettle's mother's statement regarding Pettle's never wanting to be in Mr Beater's or Mr

Thwack's classes could be excluded in that such testimony being given by the mother is hearsay and does not fall into any recognised category of exceptions to the general rule excluding hearsay in criminal trials. Arguably the statement by Pettle is not legally relevant in any case, so whether or not it is hearsay might not have to be decided (*Agassiz* v *London Tramway Co* (1872)). However, there is authority to support the proposition that a statement about the speaker's emotional state is admissible, when reported by another, if it is relevant to an issue before the court – its relevance is restricted to the emotional state of the speaker. Under this authority, Pettle's mother would be permitted to give evidence of the content of Pettle's first statement as circumstantial evidence (*R* v *Hagan* (1873); *R* v *Vincent* (1840); *Subramaniam* v *Public Prosecutor* (1956)).

Pettle's assertion to her mother that Beater and Thwack had assaulted her is a self-serving statement and therefore usually it would be inadmissible hearsay if the mother tried to relate it to the court (*R* v *Roberts* (1942)). If the defence alleged that Pettle's story was recently fabricated, then her assertion to her mother could be admitted to show consistency and thus tend to refute the allegation of fabrication, but in the absence of such a specific allegation the mother's evidence would not be admitted, and in any event it could never corroborate Pettle's evidence (*R* v *Baskerville* (1916); *R* v *Whitehead* (1929); *R* v *Oyesiku* (1971)). If the assault charged was a sexual assault, then the mother could report Pettle's statement, albeit not to corroborate Pettle's evidence but merely as evidence of a 'recent complaint' to show consistency (*R* v *Osborne* (1905)). There is some authority that such evidence of recent complaint is admissible in all cases involving violence whether of a sexual nature or not (*R* v *Wink* (1834)); however, the latest authority was in 1918 (*Jones* v *South Eastern Railway* (1918)), and the authorities seem to be strongly against admissibility of recent complaints except in criminal trials of sexual offences (*R* v *Whitehead*).

If Pettle does not give evidence in any form, then her assertion that Beater and Thwack had assaulted her could not be reported by her mother, as it would be a classic example of inadmissible hearsay (*R* v *Wallwork*). With regard to her other statement to the effect that she did not want to be in the teachers' classes, this circumstantial evidence would have little relevance (and little, if any, weight) if Pettle did not give evidence, and therefore would be ruled inadmissible, or if held to be technically admissible would be excluded by the judge in his discretion, as being more prejudicial than probative.

c) A denial by Beater that he made a confession is more than a mere denial of guilt, and in these circumstances goes beyond an assertion that the police officer(s) were genuinely mistaken – it amounts to an imputation on the character of prosecution witness(es), thus causing Beater's 'shield' to be dropped. Therefore, under the provision in s1(f)(ii) Criminal Evidence Act 1898, the prosecutor may, with leave of the judge, cross-examine Beater on his previous convictions (*R* v *Britzman & Hall* (1983)).

There has been some recent dispute over whether the judge should permit the prosecutor to cross-examine about offences similar to that of which the accused stands charged, as the purpose of revealing such bad character is not to prove guilt on the instant charge, but to indicate to the jury the credibility of the person casting the imputations on the character of prosecution witnesses (*R* v *Watts* (1983); *R* v *Bishop* (1975); *R* v *Burke* (1985); *R* v *Powell* (1985)). See now, the guidelines in *R* v *McLeod* (1994).

The revealing of similar offences having been committed by the accused can be gravely prejudicial to the defence case, but this is a matter for the judge to take into consideration when exercising his discretion to allow unlimited, limited, or no cross-examination. The very close resemblance of the other offences (eg Beater's previous convictions for assault and gbh) to the offence charged does *not oblige* the judge to refuse the requested cross-examination (this is the view of Lord Lane, giving the judgment in *R* v *Powell* (above)). Only if the judge manifestly errs will the Court of Appeal interfere with his exercise of his discretion (per Ackner LJ in *R* v *Burke*).

Beater's evidence about he and Thwack admonishing and his leaving Thwack with Pettle, given that Thwack denies speaking to Pettle, is evidence given against Thwack, his co-accused. On the assumption that Thwack had already testified, or the defence Thwack was running was obvious, then Beater's evidence undermines Thwack's defence, therefore Beater loses his shield, and Thwack's counsel may cross-examine Beater as to his previous convictions as of right (s1(f)(iii) CEA 1898 and *R* v *Varley* (1982)). Leave of the judge is unnecessary, and therefore the considerations discussed above when dealing with the casting of imputations on the character of prosecution witnesses are irrelevant (*R* v *Burke*). Only if the prosecution seeks leave to cross-examine under s1(f)(iii) does the judge need to avert his mind to the relevant considerations before exercising his discretion (*Murdoch* v *Taylor* (1965)).

QUESTION THREE

X and Y have been charged with shoplifting at Harridges, as a result of being apprehended by Z, one of the security staff. X was apprehended in the street 100 yards from the store and Y was apprehended inside the store. At their trial, where X decides not to testify himself, he calls a priest who attests to his belief in the Christian nature of X's character. The priest adds that, although X has been in trouble with the police before, in connection with a case of assault, X has never been involved in 'anything to do with dishonesty'. The judge then allows X to be cross-examined on his previous conviction for assault, in particular on the fact that the assault had occurred in Harridges and had been in response to an accusation by Z that X had been shoplifting. Y testifies that he was with X inside Harridges but was not involved in any shoplifting. He adds 'Besides, Z was gunning for X, after that last time'. The judge then allows X's counsel to cross-examine Y on four previous charges of indecent assaults against children. X and Y are convicted of theft.

Advise X and Y on the possible grounds for appeal.

University of London Examination
(for External Students) Law of Evidence June 1993 Q7

General Comment

You must be careful on these questions since there are pitfalls arising from the most unsatisfactory area of the law of evidence, namely, the cross-examination of the accused. It should be clear that this is a question on the Criminal Evidence Act 1898. The best way to prepare is to have a checklist: the reason behind the act, the tension between (e) and (f), f(ii) first and second limbs, and f(iii); the major cases for answering problems with (bearing in mind the sort of question that is commonly set) are: *Jones, Selvey, Britzman, Varley, Rowton, Winfield*. There are other cases, as you know, but these are the important ones for finding your way through the maze.

Actually, these questions are not as difficult as many candidates suppose; they don't require so much a detailed knowledge of case law (like hearsay) but instead need your intelligence, during the examination, to separate the issues. For example, this question has an unpleasant little trap in it: note that X has decided not to give testimony, yet the prosecution is given leave to cross-examine him and the prosecution, in fact, does so. You shouldn't be bothered about this sort of thing. You know that it is X's right not to be cross-examined; he could have refused to answer and the answers that X gives, which are damaging to him, are wrongfully admitted and would be the subject of a successful appeal. On the other hand, it is always possible (the facts aren't clear) that X had changed his mind by this stage, so it is necessary to see what the effect of his giving evidence would be. In a question like this, it is fatal to ignore this sort of point; if you skirted over it, an examiner would think that you lacked flexibility (after all, a barrister would have to be alive to this sort of thing).

This is not such difficult question from the point of view of law; it largely depends on native intelligence and 'getting straight into it'.

Skeleton Solution

- X: right not to give evidence; meaning of 'good character'.
- *Rowton*, *Maxwell* and *Winfield*; effect of priest's phrase 'X has been in trouble with the police before'.
- *Jones*; effect of cross-examination; Y: attack on co-defendant undermining his defence.
- *Varley*; attack on prosecution witness.
- *Selvey*; effect of cross-examination.

Suggested Solution

X elects not to give evidence as a defendant is not a compellable witness; but his witness is able to give character evidence on his behalf. This evidence may be both to disposition as well as reputation, since the largely ignored common law rule in *Rowton* (1865) (which assumes evidence of disposition to come under the rule against the reception of evidence of opinion) does not apply to the Criminal Evidence Act 1898 which governs the cross-examination of the accused: *Maxwell* (1935). The priest is clearly giving evidence of disposition. Unfortunately, the priest adds that X has been in trouble with the police before, which means that, because the jury now know that X has, because of the effect of *Jones* (1962), where the same situation occurred, the prosecution may question X on his character. Why? The shield of s1(f) only applies, according to that case, where character questions are put to elicit facts that have not yet been revealed to the jury. While there are unsatisfactory aspects to *Jones* (for example, the meaning of 'indirect question' – virtually meaningless, including to the minority judges), since the point of the shield is to *shield*, this aspect seems satisfactory. There is no point in bolting the door when the horse has fled!

But the judge was wrong to compel X to give testimony; it is clear from s1(a) of the Act that X need only give evidence 'on his own application'. It is conceivably possible that X had decided to give evidence; he may have thought (we don't know if he is represented) that he would be able to clear up the bad impression that the priest inadvertently gave. X has thrown away his shield under the first limb of s1(f)(ii) and so the prosecution (subject to the leave of the court) may question him on character; this line of questioning is particularly damaging because it refers to a similar incident in which X was involved. Should the prosecution have been permitted to ask these questions as they related to this incident?

In the first place, the charge is one of theft, not assault and it might appear that the line of questioning is irrelevant. But this argument does not work: it is clear from *Winfield* (1939) that the character of a man is to be judged 'whole': you cannot split up the 'dishonesty' bits from the 'assault' bits, as it were. That seems reasonable. True, there are sexual perverts who are utterly honest and vice versa; but they all have something in common, which is that they have committed offences! But, for another reason, the line of questioning is very prejudicial; it is in fact the sort of line of evidence prohibited by the similar facts rules because it will tend to suggest to the jury that, because this has been done before by X, he did it again on the particular occasion for which he is currently being prosecuted.

The answer to this question relies upon the rationale for allowing the prosecution, under s1(f)(ii), first limb, to question about character; it is that the defendant has raised the issue of character and, therefore the prosecution have a right to attack it, in the interests of a balanced and fair trial. That seems reasonable enough; the defendant didn't have to raise the question; he shouldn't be able to get away with saying he is of good character (which has a bearing on whether his plea of not guilty is *truthful*). So the prosecution should be able to attack his character. The rationale does not extend as far as raising questions about *issue*, however. Some cases, *Richardson and Longman* (1969), for example, have hinted that this is a possibility, but the argument cannot stand up. Why? The whole point of the Criminal Evidence Act is that it is to shield the defendant (now given the right to give evidence on his own behalf) against *prejudicial* character evidence of the *similar* fact type sort. It would be ridiculous if, by merely giving evidence of his good character, the defendant was not protected from the similar fact rules (and, in any case, one would wonder what the point was of s1(f)(i), which expressly allows questions admissible in their own right under the *Boardman* (1975) and *Makin* (1894) principles. The obvious conclusion is that these questions were wrongly put and that there are good grounds for appeal.

Y's testimony undermines X's plea of not guilty because it involves the allegation that X was in Harridges at the time, corroboration of the evidence that X had been involved in the previous incident, although, it should be noted, it also includes the suggestion that X has been framed. On the other hand, the test in *Murdoch* v *Taylor* (1965) and *Varley* (1982) is *what the effect on the whole is to the jury*. Therefore, X would be entitled (*Varley*), independently of the leave of the court, to question Y on Y's character, because Y has begun to act, vis-à-vis X, as a witness for the prosecution.

Y also casts a serious imputation (more than a mere rejection, perhaps couched in layman's language, as in *Rouse* (1904) and *Rappolt* (1911)) that Z was involved in a malicious prosecution. It is easily within *Britzman* (1983) and *Selvey* (1970) and this means that, under the second limb of s1(f)(ii) the prosecution are entitled to question X on his character. The rationale for this questioning is the 'tit for tat' principle, which arises out of the need to maintain balance and fairness in the trial. After all, it would be unfair if the defence could make all sorts of unsubstantiated attacks on the prosecution when the prosecution has clear evidence of the bad character of the person making these accusations. The judge is right, therefore, to allow the questioning and, because of *Winfield*, it does not matter that these questions are about the offences which seem entirely unrelated to the subject-matter of the prosecution.

To conclude: X has clear grounds of appeal but Y does not.

QUESTION FOUR

'When Parliament by the Act of 1898 effected a change in the general law and made the prisoner in every case a competent witness, it was in an evident difficulty, and it pursued the familiar English system of compromise.' (The House of Lords in *Maxwell* v *DPP*).

Evidence

Discuss in relation to s1(f) of the Criminal Evidence Act 1898.

What changes, in your view, would be desirable?

University of London LLB Examination
(for External Students) Evidence June 1991 Q2

General Comment

A question requiring critical discussion of the interpretation of s1(f) of the Criminal Evidence Act 1898, coupled with an appreciation of the circumstances in which character evidence may be given at common law. A knowledge of the law before 1898, other than the surviving principles, is not required.

Skeleton Solution

- The common law governing the adduction of character evidence against the accused – the *R v Rowton* principle; *R v Redd*; the 'similar fact' rules.

- Requirements and interpretation of s1(f)(i) – comparison with common law (*Jones v DPP* and *R v Anderson*); s1(f)(ii) first and second limbs; comparison with common law noting in particular the extension offered by the second limb; efficacy of the case law; the role of discretion. Section 1(f)(iii) – comparison of requirement with common law on cross examination of opponents and witnesses: *R v Murdoch & Taylor*; the potential unfairness of *R v Varley*.

- Desirable changes – the interpretation of 'tending to show'; achieving consistency in evidential effect and reversal of *R v Powell*; reforming of the rule in *R v Varley*; clarification of use by prosecution of s1(f)(iii) and by co-accused of s1(f)(ii).

Suggested Solution

In making the accused competent to testify, Parliament had to address the extent to which an accused exercising the new right should be protected from hostile cross-examination designed to show him to be a dog with a bad name.

The practice of juries in inferring guilt from bad character was then, as now, a well recognised problem, and even before the 1898 Act, there were restrictions on the circumstances in which the prosecution could adduce such evidence. These remain today. Accordingly, only where the defence first gives evidence of the accused's good character can the prosecution retaliate with evidence of adverse general reputation or prior convictions: *R v Rowton* (1865); *R v Redd* (1923). The prosecution is also allowed to adduce evidence of the accused's misconduct on other occasions where that conduct is specially relevant to the issues in the case under the 'similar fact' principle laid down in *Makin v Attorney-General of New South Wales* (1894) and subsequent cases. Evidence under both heads go to the accused's guilt as well as his credibility.

The 1898 Act recognises the existing common law allowances for bringing evidence of the accused's past misdeeds, but provides a self-contained code within which cross-examination of the accused on character may take place.

Section 1(f) provides that no question in cross examination shall be asked tending to show the accused has committed, been convicted of or charged with any offence, other than one subject of the proceedings, or is of bad character unless (1(f)(i)) the prosecution would be allowed to give evidence in chief; (1(f)(ii)) the accused (or his witnesses) have given evidence of good

100

character, or imputations have been cast on the prosecutor or prosecution witnesses; or (1(f)(iii)) the accused has given evidence against a co-accused in the same proceedings.

Section 1(f)(i) is wholly consistent with the similar fact principles at common law. Where the prosecution is allowed to adduce character evidence in chief, it is only reasonable that the accused should be amenable to cross examination. The jury has already properly heard the evidence and the protection which 1(f) is intended to afford does not arise for consideration. In fact, as a result of the decision in *Jones* v *DPP* (1962) and more recently, in *R* v *Anderson* (1988), where character evidence is properly made known to the jury before cross-examination occurs, there is no need to rely on s1(f)(i) because 'tending to show' in s1(f) has the meaning 'made known to the jury for the first time'. It is clear from the terms of s1(f)(i) and the common law rules that when evidence is adduced under 1(f)(i) it goes to guilt as well as to credit of the accused as a witness.

The subsection is, therefore, a recognition of the common law and does not seek to extend it. It is a sensible compromise between allowing cross examination and protecting the accused's legitimate interests.

The first limb of s1(f)(ii) is relatively straightforward and reflects the common law *Rowton* rule. An accused who gives evidence of his own good character can be cross-examined by the prosecution. If the prosecution can lead evidence, the matter is before the jury, and no purpose is served by disallowing cross-examination. But there are some differences in approach, although it is far from clear that they were intended by Parliament. Good character is not confined to evidence of general reputation as at common law, but extends to evidence of particular acts: *R* v *Dunkley* (1927). In this sense, the ability to cross examine has been liberalised. Second, what may amount to good character under s1(f)(ii) is generously interpreted in the prosecution's favour as argument in *R* v *Coulman* (1927) (in which the accused's statement that he was a family man and had employment was regarded by the court as an allegation of good character) demonstrates.

The second limb of s1(f)(ii) provides recognition of the fact that an accused who questions the integrity of prosecution witnesses should not, as the common law supposed (*R* v *Butterwasser* (1948)) leave the prosecution powerless to retaliate. The requirement of the casting of imputations was the chosen mechanism to effect the compromise between the common law and this recognition. The provision has received considerable judicial attention. The interpretation of 'tending to show' in the case of Jones and more recently Anderson demonstrate that the protection does not apply where an aspect of the accused's bad character has been indicated to the jury before the cross examination occurs. In the early cases, there was a certain degree of reluctance to find that an imputation had been made. For example, in *R* v *Rouse* (1904) an accusation that a witness was a liar was held not to be imputation. But more recently, with the formal recognition in *Selvey* v *DPP* (1970) of a discretion to disallow cross-examination, this reluctance has tended to evaporate so that in *R* v *Lasseur* (1991) such a contention was held as capable of being an imputation as a matter of law. In addition to establishing the judicial discretion in s1(f)(ii), Selvey laid down other principles which are helpful in deciding the question of what amounts to an imputation. These are however, rules of case law. There is nothing to indicate that Parliament had such results in mind. Likewise, with the role of discretion in disallowing cross-examination, the guidance to be derived from *R* v *Britzman and Hall* (1983) for police interviews can hardly be distilled from the wording of 1(f)(ii). The compromise here is perhaps that Parliament decided to set out a new rule as a framework provision, thus leaving the common law to develop in a way best suited to the general objectives the section is intended to meet. It must, however, be questionable how far such an expectation has been fulfilled through the case law.

Nothing is said in the section about the evidential effect of either part of s1(f)(ii). If that was intended as a compromise with the common law by allowing the latter to take its course, it is doubtful whether the results are satisfactory. Predictably, both parts of s1(f)(ii) have been treated as going to credit rather than guilt of the accused (*Maxwell* v *DPP* (1935); *R* v *Vickers* (1972)). But according to *R* v *Powell* (1986) (not following the earlier case of *R* v *Watts* (1983)) the danger that a jury may be inclined to treat a conviction as going to guilt because they are similar in nature is no reason to disallow the cross examination in the exercise of judicial discretion. The danger is to be dealt with by directions from the judge. It must be doubtful how effective such directions are in practice. The matter has now been clarified to some extent by the Court of Appeal in *R* v *McLeod* (1994).

Section 1(f)(iii) allows cross examination where an accused has given evidence against a co-accused. This provision was evidently designed as a compromise between the common law which would allow the testifying co-accused to be treated in the same way as any other opposing witness, allowing the cross examining co-accused to ask character questions and about prior convictions, and prove them on denial, and the undue prejudice which might be caused to accuseds if such cross examination were allowed unfettered. 'Evidence against' is normally interpreted in accordance with authorities of *R* v *Murdoch and Taylor* (1965) and *R* v *Varley* (1982). The co-accused is at risk of cross examination if his evidence advances the prosecution's case or damages his co-accused's or if his defence necessarily means that if he did not do it, then his co-accused did. But the problem of such an approach is that co-accuseds with a criminal past may in effect be hamstrung. It is common for one co-accused to blame the other (a 'cut-throat defence'). This will, according to *Varley*, put him on risk of cross examination and the exposing of his past to the jury. That is likely to put a co-accused without a criminal past, whose colleague with a criminal past seeks to shift the blame, in a strong position to secure an acquittal.

The following changes are desirable. The meaning of the phrase 'tending to show' should be redefined so that revealing to the jury for the first time merely by indicating some unrelated aspect of prior misbehaviour before the cross-examination does not make an accused susceptible to cross-examination on prior convictions. In other words, this is to reverse the trend apparent in *Anderson*. The evidential effect of good character and retaliation evidence of bad character should be rationalised so that there is consistency between evidence adduced under the *R* v *Rowton* principle at common law, and under the first limb of s1(f)(ii). Under the second limb of s1(f)(ii), it would be very desirable to enable the judge to exclude cross examination where the jury are likely to infer guilt on account of the similarity of the prior misconduct; in other words, to restore the law as decided under Watts; and if greater reliance is to be placed on the role of discretion by interpreting what amounts to an imputation more restrictively, then further ground rules on the way it is to be exercised are desirable.

With s1(f)(iii) perhaps the major point is the potential harshness of the rule in *Varley* for an accused with a criminal past who is running a cut-throat defence, especially since cross-examination under 1(f)(iii) is of right and not subject to exclusionary judicial discretion.

A final point which has not hitherto surfaced much in the case law but which would benefit from clarification is the extent to which a co-accused can utilise cross-examination under 1(f)(ii) or the prosecution cross-examination under 1(f)(iii). The rules as they have developed assume cross-examination by the prosecution under 1(f)(ii) and a co-accused under 1(f)(iii). There is a case for making this a formal requirement if only to ensure a greater certainty in the ground rules for the future, because it is desirable that an accused's legal advisers should be as clear as possible as to what the circumstances in which he will be susceptible to cross-examination are.

QUESTION FIVE

Ludwig and Bertrand are charged with maliciously wounding Freddy. Thomas is charged with assisting Ludwig and Bertrand by doing an act with intent to impede their apprehension.

Freddy testifies that he was attacked by Ludwig and Bertrand at a public lavatory one night and that one or other stabbed him. Inspector Bentham testifies that when he visited Thomas to enquire of Ludwig and Bertrand's whereabouts Thomas informed him, falsely, that they had gone to Italy. Ludwig, who is conducting his own defence, testifies that Freddy struck the first blow and claims that he hit back in self-defence. He says that he has no idea how Freddy sustained a stab wound. He adds that Freddy has a disposition towards violence. Bertrand testifies in his defence that he and Ludwig had made up their minds to assault Freddy, but says that Freddy's injury must have occurred when he slipped and fell coming towards them. When asked by counsel for the Crown whether he had a knife with him that night Bertrand refuses to answer. Thomas claims that during a short conversation with Inspector Bentham he said that he had no idea of Ludwig and Bertrand's whereabouts.

Ludwig has previous convictions for assault and theft. Bertrand has a previous conviction for perjury. The prosecution can prove that the perjury consisted of giving false testimony providing an alibi for friends charged with offences, and furthermore that Thomas was acquitted of perjury on another occasion in respect of a similar allegation.

Advise Ludwig, Bertrand and Thomas.

University of London LLB Examination
(for External Students) Evidence June 1995 Q8

General Comment

This question concerns the circumstances in which a defendant's shield against reference to his previous convictions and character may be lost by the working of the Criminal Evidence Act 1898, and the extent to which judicial discretion operates on this point.

Skeleton Solution

Criminal Evidence Act 1898 – Ludwig's potential imputations on Freddy.

Bertrand's evidence against Ludwig and judicial discretion in this situation.

Bertrand's silence about the knife.

Thomas's and Inspector Bentham's evidence – s1(f)(ii).

Examination on acqittals.

Significance of lies – *R* v *Lucas*.

Suggested Solution

Ludwig testifies that he merely defended himself against Freddy's attack and has no idea about the injury, but states that Freddy has a violent disposition. Ludwig's convictions, if

103

brought out, may damage his case. The matter is governed by s1 Criminal Evidence Act (CEA) 1898 and he does have a shield againt such evidence, but it may be lost in the three ways provided by the section. Here, s1(f)(iii) is in issue, that is that the nature of his defence involves imputations on the character of the prosecutor or prosecution witnesses. If there was an unavoidable implication that Freddy was lying, this would cause the shield to be lost, but it is possible in these circumstances that Ludwig is only giving his view of a confused situation, perhaps in a badly lit fracas. *R* v *Britzman*, *R* v *Hall* (1982) indicates that the judge should exercise his discretion in favour of the accused in these circumstances. Ludwig goes further, though, in dealing with Freddy's violent disposition. The fact that this is a necessary part of his defence will not prevent loss of the shield (*Selvey* v *DPP* (1970)), but it does look more like a vigorous denial of the offence so as not to lose the shield, as in *R* v *Rouse* (1904).

If the shield is lost, any cross examination can only be as to credibility (*Maxwell* v *DPP* (1935) and *R* v *Watts* (1983)). The trial judge is, in any case, more likely to exercise his discretion in favour of an unrepresented defendant and he should warn of the danger in appropriate circumstances (*Selvey* v *DPP*).

Bertrand has a previous conviction for perjury and will not want this to come out. He makes no imputation about Freddy, but he does give evidence against Ludwig when speaking about the plan to assault Freddy. Any evidence which supports the prosecution case in a material respect, or which undermines the defence of the co-accused, will activate s1(f)(iii) (*R* v *Varley* (1982)), whether in cross examination or in chief. There is a direct conflict between the two and once it is decided that evidence has been given against Ludwig by Bertrand the judge will have no discretion to prevent Ludwig examining him (*Murdoch* v *Taylor* (1965)), although he will have discretion as regards examination by the Crown (*R* v *Seigley* (1911)).

Bertrand's refusal to answer about the knife may now be the subject of comment by the prosecution, and the judge may invite the jury to draw proper inferences (s35 Criminal Justice and Public Order Act 1994). This will be of great significance if Bertrand loses his shield. Although the evidence of the conviction should only go to credibility, there is a danger here of the judge failing to direct the jury that Bertrand's silence may have other explanations than that he must have had a knife. There is a possibility of a misdirection here.

Thomas's evidence is completely at odds with the Inspector's and creates a clear implication that the Inspector is fabricating his version (unless there was some problem such as excessive noise or a hearing defect) so Thomas is likely to lose his shield under s1(f)(ii). *R* v *Tanner* (1977) shows that this will be so no matter how the point is worded. Thomas's previous trial finished in acquittal. The subsection is worded with respect to offences 'committed', 'convicted' and 'charged' but it seems unlikely that it is permissible to examine as to acquittals (*Maxwell* v *DPP*), although there may be a possibility that the circumstances of such an acquittal might be looked at if there is a possibility of bringing the matter within s1(e) in respect of similar fact evidence. Such a situation was seen *R* v *Ollis* (1900) and *R* v *Shellaker* (1914). If Thomas does not give evidence, his bad character will not be admissible as he would not be 'called as a witness' (*R* v *Butterwasser* (1948)).

The judge will be obliged to give a *R* v *Lucas* (1981) warning as to the significance of Thomas's lies. The Court of Appeal in *R* v *Goodway* (1993) made it clear that in all cases where the accused's lies may be relied upon to support the prosecution evidence, such a warning is mandatory.

10 Similar Fact Evidence

10.1   Introduction
10.2   Key points
10.3   Analysis of questions
10.4   Questions

10.1 Introduction

When evidence of the misconduct of the accused is admitted in the form of previous convictions, its relevance is generally to the credibility of the accused as a witness. This admissibility of convictions etc as evidence of bad character at common law and under the Criminal Evidence Act 1898 was dealt with in Chapter 9, where it was stated that evidence of bad character could sometimes be admitted as similar fact evidence – ie to prove the guilt of the accused on the instant charge. Usually it is not permissible for the prosecution to lead evidence of the propensity of the accused towards misconduct (whether or not criminal), or of specific misconduct by him, since this would be prejudicial and thus prevent a fair trial.

However, exceptionally, evidence of misconduct, for example the details of how the accused misbehaved, not purely the fact of conviction (there may not have been one) may be admissible as 'similar fact evidence', ie to tend to show that the accused, given the similar fact evidence, committed the crime with which he is charged. In the main the topic centres on this issue, but similar fact evidence is sometimes admissible in civil cases, and is occasionally admissible in criminal cases by statute when certain crimes are charged.

10.2 Key points

In *Makin* v *Attorney-General for New South Wales* [1894] AC 57, Lord Herschell LC made a pronouncement on similar fact evidence which has been referred to on innumerable occasions. In effect, he stated that, if evidence of other misconduct of the accused did no more than show a general disposition to commit crime or a particular crime, then such evidence is inadmissible; but if the evidence goes further than that, and is 'relevant to an issue before the jury', then it may be admissible. This relevance to an issue before the jury led to attempts being made to categorise circumstances where the evidence was admissible, eg to rebut a defence; to show design; to prove a system; to prove 'guilty relations'; as identification of the accused. This elaborate and complex systemisation did not help to clarify the law on similar fact evidence, and is to some extent responsible for the confusion which still prevails, despite the attempt by the House of Lords to move away from categories of relevance to degrees of relevance in *DPP* v *Boardman* [1975] AC 421. In other words, their lordships concentrated on the striking similarity between the conduct of the accused alleged in the instant case and that of which the prosecution seek to adduce similar fact evidence.

However, in the cases since *Boardman* there is evidence of some disquiet with the application of the test of 'striking similarity' to the exclusion of all other tests for admissibility; in *Boardman* itself it is considered that the standard of striking similarity was set somewhat low. Two Court of Appeal decisions soon after *Boardman* evinced the difficulties which the striking similarity test was to cause; on almost identical facts the court admitted evidence of similar facts to prove guilt in one case and rejected it in the other: *R* v *Johannsen* (1977) 65 Cr App R 101; *R* v *Novac* (1976) 65 Cr App R 107.

Recent, post-*Boardman*, cases have also confirmed that similar fact evidence is admissible not only if strikingly similar to the fact of the offence with which the accused is charged but also if strikingly similar to the circumstances in which the offence was committed, eg *R* v *Scarrott* [1978] QB 1016. Further, it has been held that such evidence of circumstances does not need to show the actual commission of the evidence, providing it goes beyond merely proving a propensity to commit that type of crime, or crime generally: *R* v *Barrington* [1981] 1 WLR 419; *R* v *Butler* (1987) 84 Cr App R 12; *R* v *Tricoglus* (1976) 65 Cr App R 16. But the problem still remains of the difficulty, to the point of impossibility, in formulating a test of striking similarity, and evidence has been admitted by apparently applying a standard lower than that in *Boardman* itself – see eg *R* v *Seaman* (1978) 67 Cr App R 234.

In the recent case of *R* v *Brookes* (1991) 92 Cr App R 36, the defendant was charged with sexual offences against three of his daughters. The Court of Appeal held that it was not enough for the facts to be similar, they must tell the court something useful. The court must enquire into what the evidence was being used to prove, and whether that evidence was then probative of that fact. In this case, the similarity alleged was the common coin of evidence in the case of father-daughter incest, and there was a real risk that the daughters had colluded. Therefore, separate trials were ordered.

Where, as in *Boardman*, the similar fact evidence consists of testimony by another witness or witnesses as to conduct of the accused on other occasions similar to that alleged by a prosecution witness or witnesses on the occasion giving rise to the charge, then the court must satisfy itself that there has been no collusion between the witnesses and therefore no question of concoction: *R* v *Barrington*, supra.

Similar fact evidence continues to be admitted post-*Boardman* to rebut a defence raised or which is reasonably open to the accused (this pre-emptive adducing of the evidence by the prosecution being permitted to avoid a successful defence submission of 'no case to answer'). In *R* v *Lunt* (1987) 85 Cr App R 241 evidence of other misconduct by the accused was admissible to rebut a defence of innocent association; in *R* v *Anderson* [1988] 2 All ER 549 evidence was admitted to prove how implausible was the defence which the accused raised. 'Striking similarity' was not the test applied, but rather the positive probative value of the evidence.

See now also the case of *R* v *Carrington* [1990] Crim LR 330, where the function of the similar fact evidence was to show the defendant's intent in relation to the charge of threatening to kill the victim, the similar fact evidence being a threat made in a similar (but not strikingly similar) way to the victim a few months before.

Consider also the important recent House of Lords' decision in *R* v *P* (1991) 93 Cr App R 267. Here the House of Lords held that it had been correct to admit evidence that the defendant (a father) had similarly abused children of the family other than the complainant, in the absence of collusion, despite the absence of 'striking similarities'. The essential feature, the House of Lords said, of the evidence which was to be admitted was that its probative force in support of the allegation that the defendant committed a crime was sufficiently great to make it correct to admit the evidence, notwithstanding that it was prejudicial to the defendant. Probative force can be achieved by striking similarity, but there are other means. Here, the evidence of the girls described a prolonged course of conduct by the accused, including threats, use of force, and payment for abortions. This, the court felt, gave strong probative force to the evidence of each of the girls. The important question here was not who had committed these crimes, but had they been committed at all. 'Striking similarity' is more concerned with identifying the assailant when the fact that the crime has taken place is not in issue.

A particularly important decision followed in *R* v *Hepburn* (also reported as *R* v *H*) [1995] 2 All ER 865 HL, where their Lordships decided, on a majority decision, that the possibility of collusive witnesses was not, as formerly, a question of admissibility for the judge. By contrast, it was to be a question of weight for the jury. It is submitted that the combined effect of *R* v *P* and *R* v *H* in cases where identification is not in issue but the possibility of collusion exists, may well produce surprising results. This matter may, perhaps, be back with their Lordships in the not-too-distant future.

Where a defendant is charged with two or more offences and similar fact evidence is adduced to support his identification in relation to the later offence, the jury should be directed to consider first whether they were sure the accused had committed the first offence (see *R* v *Gurney* [1994] Crim LR 116). However, the jury should be told to consider the defendant's guilt as regards the first offence in isolation – ie without consideration of the other offences before his guilt as regards the first offence can be used as similar fact evidence with the other offences. Common sense? But what about the coincidence theory? – ie if the accused is said to have committed several different but similar offences by several independent witnesses, he must have committed the offences otherwise those witnesses would not have all told the same story against him.

It seems, therefore, that generally the prosecution may adduce similar fact evidence in chief if it shows some unique linking characteristic or is of sufficiently striking similarity to be positively probative of guilt. But, similar fact evidence would appear to be admissible despite lacking that degree of striking similarity, dependent on the particular facts in issue, for example to rebut a defence raised, to prove opportunity, identity etc where any of these is in issue, or where the probative force outweighs the prejudicial value.

Arguably, in the general run of cases, the judge has a discretion to exclude similar fact evidence if its prejudicial effect will outweigh its probative value; given these two factors should be weighed by the judge in deciding admissibility, it seems that there is no scope for discretionary exclusion – but the courts continue to recognise its existence. In *R* v *Butler*, supra, it was stated that where the similar fact evidence constitutes the commission by the accused of other offences there is greater prejudicial effect, which is relevant to the exercise of the judge's discretion.

Two important statutory provisions in criminal cases are:

a)   s27(3) Theft Act 1968: allows the prosecution to prove mens rea on the part of the handler of stolen goods by evidence which shows a general propensity to dishonesty; judicial discretion to exclude this evidence in the interests of a fair trial of the accused is recognised without argument: *R* v *Perry* [1984] Crim LR 680

b)   s1(2) Official Secrets Act 1911: allows evidence of disposition of the accused to prove that his purpose was prejudicial to the safety or interests of the State.

In civil proceedings, similar fact evidence is admitted more easily than in criminal proceedings, because the civil courts are not concerned with the fair trial of an accused and therefore prejudicial effect and probative value do not have to be weighed.

In *Mood Music Publishing Co Ltd* v *De Wolfe Publishing Ltd* [1976] 1 Ch 119, similar fact evidence was admitted even though some of it had been obtained by the plaintiff's setting a trap for the defendant; that was not considered oppressive or unfair to the defendant, who had had notice of the plaintiff's intention to adduce the evidence during the course of the pre-trial procedure.

10.3 Analysis of questions

Similar fact evidence in criminal proceedings is a favourite with examiners, either as a 'self-contained' essay question or as a problem question where it will almost invariably be accompanied by issues such as evidence of character under the Criminal Evidence Act 1898. The incidence of problems approximate that of essays, so it is advisable to be conversant with similar fact and character evidence.

10.4 Questions

QUESTION ONE

What is the rationale for the similar fact rules? What, in your view, are the tests that should be applied in determining whether the relevance of the similar fact evidence overrides prejudicial effect?

University of London Examination
(for External Students) Law of Evidence June 1993 Q1(a)

General Comment

This sort of question comes up year after year and there is no excuse for being unprepared for it. The important thing to remember about 'rationale' type questions is that you should have some views in advance; do you think there is something important or wrong or silly about the rules? If so, your examiner will be impressed if you give reasons in an ordered and knowledgeable fashion. Don't go straight to *Boardman* or *R* v *P* just because they are the latest or most important recent cases. The question requires a discussion of *Makin* and *Boardman*: those two cases set the scene. You must contrast the so-called 'ticket of admission' approach with the 'probative force outweighs prejudicial force' approach and then *try to make some sense of them!*

Skeleton Solution

- General discretion of judge.
- Law before *Boardman* v *DPP*.
- Categories or cases under similar fact evidence rule.
- *Boardman*.
- Moving away from categories.
- Striking similarity and probative force.
- Chain of forbidden reasoning.
- Prejudice of certain types of previous convictions.
- Law since *Boardman*.

Suggested Solution

The similar facts rules in general permit a trial judge the discretion to exclude evidence the prejudicial effect of which outweighs its probative force. It is not fully accurate to say that the judge has a discretion since once he has decided that the probative force of the evidence does not outweigh prejudicial effect then he has a duty to exclude it in order to ensure a fair trial (see, for example, *R* v *List* (1965)). However, he must use his judgment when considering whether he can reduce possible prejudice by a careful direction to the jury. To this extent the decision he makes is a matter for him and not for an appellate court, and so could be said to be a discretion.

Before *Boardman* v *DPP* (1975) the courts classified situations in which the prosecution might wish to use similar fact evidence, and laid down rules allowing it where a particular defence was put forward, or the offence charged was of a particular type. In *R* v *Sims* (1946), for example, the Court of Appeal held that whenever offences involving homosexual acts are alleged against an accused who is himself homosexual, then the jury may be told of his homosexuality. In *R* v *Bond* (1906) it was held that a defence of accident could be rebutted by evidence of the accused's propensity to commit acts of the type alleged. Accident soon became a special category of defence such that whenever the defence was 'Yes, I did it, but it was an accident,' so the prosecution could adduce evidence of disposition. Similarly, the defence of ignorance became a category, so that in *Blake* v *Albion Life Assurance Society* (1878) a principal's plea that he was ignorant of his agent's fraudulent conduct was rebutted by evidence that on previous occasions the agent had acted fraudulently to the benefit of the principal.

A third category was innocent association, which is a defence that, although the opportunity existed for the act alleged to have been done by the accused, that opportunity was not taken. In *R* v *King* (1967), for example, a man was charged with having committed various indecent acts with boys who were staying at his house. In his defence he admitted that the boys were there but said that nothing indecent took place. The Court of Appeal held that evidence of the accused's homosexuality was admissible to rebut this defence.

A fourth category was cases where the accused alleged that the wrong man had been arrested. For example, in *Thompson* v *R* (1918) the accused was identified by boys as the man who had previously made indecent advances to them; his defence that they had picked out the wrong man was rebutted by evidence of his homosexual propensity. The final category was a case where the prosecution wished to show various acts committed by the accused in order to show that he was engaged in systematic behaviour of the type alleged. In *R* v *Ollis* (1900) the accused faced several charges relating to the use of fraudulent cheques. Evidence was held to be admissible that on previous occasions he had acted fraudulently by use of false cheques.

These categories developed because of the large number of cases of their type which come before the courts each year. If all cases were essentially the same, then it would, indeed, make sense to have such categories so that at trial the allegation or the defence merely had to slot into the appropriate category in order for the judge to know whether similar fact evidence should be admitted. But cases are not all the same and each revolves around its own facts; the use of strict categories may, therefore, operate unfairly to the accused.

The House of Lords, in *Boardman* v *DPP*, held that the old categories should be discarded and each case looked at individually. In that case the House considered whether similar fact evidence was any different from other types of evidence, and made clear that in essence all evidence is the same – it is all adduced in order to assist the jury to reach its verdict. When evidence of the disposition of the accused towards a particular type of conduct is adduced there is always the risk that the jury will jump to the conclusion that because the accused is inclined to commit the type of conduct alleged, so he must have done so at the time alleged. Lord Hailsham referred to this as the 'forbidden chain of reasoning'. Whether evidence is admissible depends simply upon whether it is relevant, in other words whether it assists the jury to reach a verdict. The fact that the accused is inclined to commit offences like the one charged will only be relevant where that disposition can be properly treated by the jury as evidence of guilt.

For example, if the accused is charged with speeding, it does not really help the court one way or the other to show that he has been convicted of speeding on previous occasions; evidence of that disposition is almost wholly irrelevant. On the other hand, if the accused is charged with murder, the fact that he has murdered on previous occasions may be probative so far as it shows that he is one of the relatively few people who could commit the offence alleged. Furthermore, if the accused is charged with having committed certain homosexual acts whilst wearing the headdress of a Red Indian chief (see the example given by Lord Hailsham in *Boardman*'s case), evidence that he had done this on previous occasions is highly probative because it narrows down the group of suspects considerably. It can be seen from these three examples that evidence of the accused's disposition to commit the type of crime alleged may be probative or not depending on the nature of the allegation made.

Inevitably there is always only a certain number of people who could have committed the offence charged and anything which narrows down the group of suspects such that at the end of the trial the jury can say that the group has been reduced to one, the accused, will be of some assistance. It cannot be said that in the very wide categories which are mentioned above, the evidence of disposition will always assist the jury in its deliberations, any more than it would in other cases falling outside these categories, and this was expressly recognised in *Boardman* v *DPP* by the abolition of the categories.

The fact that evidence of disposition may lead the jury to jump to the conclusion that the accused committed the offence is no objection to the admission of that evidence if, in fact, the jury is right to jump to such a conclusion.

But there is the difficulty, which Lord Hailsham recognised, of the jury jumping to a false conclusion. For example, if the accused is charged with indecent assaults on children, the fact of his previous conviction for a similar offence may lead the jury to conclude that he must have done it this time, simply because of the feelings of horror and outrage which such offences excite. The jury may not be capable of bearing in mind the chance that the wrong man is in the dock and may give such weight to the previous conviction that other evidence in the accused's favour is not considered or is not properly weighed. To attempt to ensure that the jury does not give undue weight to such evidence, the trial judge must examine whether it really is as probative as the jury may think it is. If there is clear evidence that the accused has undergone treatment so that he no longer has the urge to commit such offences, then the trial judge may decide that justice is best done by omitting reference to the previous conviction.

But it is submitted that the House of Lords' decision in *R* v *P* (1991) is superior in that the court moves away from 'striking similarity' as these cases are not about who committed the crimes but whether the crimes were committed at all. In other words, each case must be looked at individually, and what the evidence is to be used for is very important.

The balancing act between the probative force of the evidence and its prejudicial effect was said to be at the heart of the similar fact rules in *Boardman* so that the admissibility of similar fact evidence is simply a matter of relevance. In many cases the judge will be able to reduce the prejudicial effect of the evidence of disposition and will allow it to go to the jury with an appropriate warning. It is not necessary for the probative value of the evidence greatly to outweigh its prejudicial effect, provided that it outweighs it sufficiently to lead to a fair trial. Indeed, where the evidence of previous misconduct is so probative that it proves that the accused must have committed the offence, then prejudicial effect is wholly irrelevant.

In *R* v *Straffen* (1952), for example, the evidence of the previous strikingly similar murders was such overwhelming proof of guilt that it would have done no harm for the jury to ignore all other evidence and convict solely on the basis of the accused's virtually unique disposition. Since *Boardman* the Court of Appeal and House of Lords have both dealt with similar fact cases on several occasions and, generally, have applied the balancing test between probative value and prejudicial effect. The only exception to this seems to be *R* v *Lewis* (1982) in which the old categories of admissibility re-appeared (but it is only a brief report). Nevertheless, that case has been the subject of so much criticism that it is unlikely to have any long term effect on the way in which similar fact cases are dealt with.

QUESTION TWO

'Where the identity of the perpetrator is in issue, and evidence of this kind is important in that connection, obviously something in the nature of what has been called in the course of the argument a signature or other special feature will be necessary. To transpose this requirement to other situations where the question is whether a crime has been committed, rather than who did commit it, is to impose an unnecessary and improper restriction upon the application of the principle.' (Lord Mackay in *R* v *P*).

Discuss.

University of London Examination
(for External Students) Law of Evidence June 1993 Q1(b)

General Comment

The same sorts of comments could be made about this question which is very much the same as the first (and therefore should cover much the same ground); the difference is that you are invited to get into the question of the categories of admission approach, especially in relation to the question of identity. *Thompson* is a very good case in point here and there are a number of ways that it could be explained, justified and criticised. The answer given below is actually one of quite a number that would suffice as an answer.

Skeleton Solution

- *Makin* versus *Boardman*.
- The general issue of identity and its particular application to 'stock-in-trade' in *Straffen*.
- The 'rationale' approach and the rapid dissatisfaction by judges (see *Lewis*).
- The 'ticket of admission' approach in general.
- The homosexual cases.
- The reasoning in *R* v *P*.
- Conclusion that Lord McKay's remarks do not apply across the board.

Suggested Solution

There are two major sources for discerning a rationale for the similar fact rules, namely, *Makin* v *AG for New South Wales* (1894) and the more recent case of *DPP* v *Boardman* (1975). It is the tension between these two cases which provides some help. Historically, the view has always been taken by the courts that character evidence was always of suspect relevance and this makes some good sense; if a person has been convicted before, or is a well-known liar, it does not follow that, on the particular occasion which is before the court, that he has committed the offence, or failed to tell the truth.

Boardman had the great advantage that it brought to the fore the real reason for occasional exceptions to the similar facts rule: that there could be circumstances where the degree of relevance was so high that it could outweigh any prejudicial effect. What does this mean? The cases illustrate it well; take *Makin* itself. There was evidence that the Makins had lived in houses in the recent past where dead babies had been found buried in the garden; there was evidence, too, that they had taken babies in for adoption for money at times when they had lived in these houses. They were charged with having committed murder by claiming to adopt a child, receiving money for it, and then murdering it and burying it in the garden. You have to be quite straightforward about his sort of case; the Makins said that it was just bad luck on their part that babies had unfortunately been buried in previous houses in which they had lived. This must be nonsense; the relevance of these previous occurrences just overwhelmed any possible prejudicial effect caused by the jury learning of the Makins' past history.

Another case is that of *Straffen* (1952). Here Straffen was charged with the murder of a young girl in unusual circumstances, was admittedly at large from Broadmoor in the area, and had been placed in Broadmoor for having committed two other such murders. Again, the relevance of his particular 'stock-in-trade' was overwhelming: it *could only have been Straffen.*

But the rationale espoused in *Boardman* is not all that useful as a test in practical courtroom circumstances, for all it does is to say that when the probative effect of particular evidence outweighs the prejudicial effect the evidence is admissible, otherwise it is excluded under the general rule. It is for this reason that judges in later cases than *Boardman* have been keen to stress, as in *R* v *Rance and Herron* (1975), that something more was required to establish the requisite degree of relevance. In that case the judges said that it had to have 'positive probative force', for example. Indeed, in later years, in *R* v *Lewis* (1982), the attitude of the judges appeared to be that a return to the principles in *Makin* would be in order.

What were these principles? One was that if offences involving homosexual acts are alleged against an accused who is himself homosexual, then the jury may be told of his homosexuality. For example, in *R* v *Bond* (1906) it was held that a defence of accident could be rebutted by evidence of the accused's propensity to commit acts of the type alleged. Accident also became a special category of defence such that whenever the defence was 'Yes, I did it, but it was an accident,' then the prosecution could adduce evidence of disposition. Innocent association was another, being a defence that, although the opportunity existed for the act alleged to have been done by the accused, that opportunity was not taken. An example is *R* v *King* (1967) where a man was charged with having committed various indecent acts with boys who were staying at his house. In his defence he admitted that the boys were there but said that nothing indecent took place. The Court of Appeal held that evidence of the accused's homosexuality was admissible to rebut this defence. Yet another category was where the accused alleged that the wrong man had been arrested. The accused in *Thompson* v *R* (1918), for example, was identified by boys as the man who had previously made indecent advances to them; his defence that they had picked out the wrong man was rebutted by evidence of his homosexual propensity. And another well-known category of case was that where the prosecution wished to show various acts committed by the accused in order to show that he was engaged in systematic behaviour of the type alleged: *Makin* is the classic case.

It was the relatively large number of cases of their type which came before the courts that gave rise to the development of these categories. If it were so that all cases were essentially

112

the same, then it would, indeed, make sense to have such categories so that at trial the allegation or the defence merely had to slot into the appropriate category in order for the judge to know whether similar fact evidence should be admitted. You can see the good practical sense of this approach, what Hoffman called the 'ticket of admission approach.' But the House of Lords, in *Boardman* v *DPP*, held that the old categories should be discarded and each case looked at individually; it is for this reason that the rationale of the rules became so clear but also the reason why, in cases such as *Lewis,* there was the hint of a revival of the old 'ticket of admission' approach.

The reasoning in *R* v *P* (1991) shows a curious mixture of both the *Boardman* and *Makin* approaches. Lord McKay obviously wanted to get away from fixed formulae, such as bedevilled the field of similar fact in the past. The phrase 'strikingly similar', for example, was thought to be not the end-all of the test of relevance, echoing the remarks made as early as six months after the decision of *Boardman*, in *R* v *Rance and Herron*. In *R* v *P* there had been a series of similar assaults by a father on his two daughters but there was not anything in particular that was 'strikingly' similar, although evidence of previous actions towards the daughter were similar enough, and over a sufficiently long period, in the House of Lords' opinion, to justify its reception into court. In this way, Lord McKay was supporting the line of approach in *Boardman*. Don't be hampered by the technicalities of either the 'ticket' approach, or colourful phrases like 'strikingly similar'; for this reason, Lord McKay's views are to be supported.

On the other hand, in the quotation of the question, Lord McKay asserted that there would be special circumstances for the introduction of that sort of case where there was some kind of 'hallmark', namely, cases where there is an issue of identification. Here we hark back to the *Makin* type approach by having establishing a category. In cases of mistaken identity, if there is some kind of 'strikingly similar' hallmark (eg the disposition of the defendant in *Straffen*), there is a presumption in favour of admission.

The test is whether Lord McKay's suggestion can stand up to closer analysis. It is submitted that he does not establish as strong a principle as might first appear. Admittedly, it will work for many cases (and we could bear in mind here, Lord Hailsham's famous example of the crime committed by a defendant wearing a Red Indian ceremonial headdress) but not for others. Take, for example, the famous 'hallmark' case of *Thompson*. Some boys gave evidence that they had been indecently assaulted by a person who had arranged to meet them at a particular lavatory and at a particular time, three days later. At the precise time and place, Thompson appeared. It was held that, because he bore the 'peculiar hallmark' of homosexuality (he admitted it; and so it is unclear what the relevance was of his carrying a powder puff and of his having indecent photographs at his flat was), this fact of his disposition was admissible at his trial under the similar fact rules.

But *Thompson* cannot now be thought of as a 'hallmark' type case, given *Boardman*, and should not have been thought of as one at the time. After all 'being a homosexual' is nowhere near the category into which we would place Straffen ('a person who has the disposition to murder young girls in a unique way'). But it *is* an identity case, in which the evidence of Thompson's disposition is relevant in another way: not to establish that Thompson, by his homosexuality has the disposition to commit the crime, but to strengthen the prosecution's case by eliminating the possibility of coincidence. It would have been too greatly against the odds if *another* homosexual had turned up at that precise time and place.

To conclude, while Lord McKay's statement makes a deal of sense in the *Straffen* type case, one has to be careful not too return to much to the rigidities of the old *Makin* 'ticket of admission approach'. But, because of the case of *Thompson*, the statement has to be watered down to the extent that some cases of identity cannot be decided in the way that Lord McKay suggests.

QUESTION THREE

L is charged with the murder of her elderly aunt, M. M was found dead at her home having died of asphyxia from a plastic bag which had been placed over her head. L, who visited M regularly, says that M had been ill and depressed for a long time and had expressed suicidal thoughts. She says that it is very likely that M had committed suicide. L's elderly father, N, whom L had been looking after for some time before, had died a year ago in similar circumstances. Further, L subscribes to an organisation, known at the 'The Dying Light', whose members advocate the legalisation of euthanasia, and L is found to have in her possession a book published by 'The Dying Light' in which various methods of carrying out euthanasia are described, including causing death by placing plastic bags over peoples' heads. In this book, passages relating to this method of killing are underlined in red ink. Further, O, who works in the same office as L, says that when O's mother had been suffering from a terminal illness three years ago, L had urged her to 'give her an overdose and end her suffering'.

Advise L.

University of London LLB Examination
(for External Students) Law of Evidence June 1994 Q7

General Comment

This is a question in which the issues are fairly easy to isolate.

A brief explanation of the basis of admissibility of similar fact evidence is useful, but since this is a problem question, such discussion should be kept fairly short. Each item of evidence can be subjected to the same basic test of 'probative value' but a sound knowledge of the relevant case law is required to fully explain the side issues which arise – without this, any answer to this question would be rather too short!

Skeleton Solution

• Isolate issues:
  – evidence of father's death;
  – book;
  – O's evidence.
• Brief explanation of basis of similar fact evidence admissibility:
  – probative value (*R* v *P*);
  – applicable in any case (no 'categories of relevance').
• Father's death:
  – probative value/striking similarity;
  – nature of defence raised;
  – does the absence of charge/conviction re father's death lead to bar to admissibility of similar fact evidence?
  – *Noor Mohamed* v *R*.

- Book:
  - probative value;
  - 'incriminating article': *Thompson.*
- O's evidence:
  - Hearsay or original evidence;
  - probative value;
  - circumstances surrounding offence as opposed to actual commission of the offence.

Suggested Solution

The issues raised in this question involve the topic of similar fact evidence, that is to say, evidence of other 'similar' acts, admissible to prove the guilt of the defendant.

There are three items of evidence which should be discussed:

a) evidence of the death of N (L's father) in 'similar' circumstances, whilst in L's care;

b) evidence of L's membership of 'The Dying Light', a pro-euthanasia organisation, and in particular the book found in her possession, with underlined passages;

c) O's evidence of the advice given to her by L (suggesting the 'mercy killing' of O's mother).

Before considering each of these issues, it is useful to consider the basis for the admissibility of similar fact evidence. In exceptional circumstances, the defendant's guilt may be proved by adducing evidence of disposition. Such evidence is termed 'similar fact evidence'.

It must be stressed that such evidence is only admissible in exceptional circumstances. The reason for this severely restricted admissibility is that whilst evidence of disposition is clearly relevant, juries may often attach greater weight to similar fact evidence than it perhaps deserves. Hence, more often than not, probative value is exceeded by prejudicial effect.

However, when evidence is 'so very relevant that to exclude it would be an affront to common sense', then it *may* be admitted: per Lord Cross in *DPP* v *Boardman* (1975). This does make it clear that in order for similar fact evidence to be admissible it must be highly relevant – would it be an affront to common sense to exclude it?

The test of admissibility can therefore be defined simply – it is a test of probative value: *R* v *P* (1991). This 'probative value' can be supplied in many ways – it *was* thought that striking similarity was required but *R* v *P* has confirmed that this requirement is only necessary in cases involving identity, where evidence is given by another victim of the alleged offender. Nor is the principle of similar fact evidence only applicable in certain types of case. It is potentially admissible in any type of case, categories of relevance having been rejected: *Harris* v *DPP* (1952).

It is now necessary to consider each of the items of evidence arising in this case, to determine whether any of them may be admissible as similar fact evidence.

a) *Evidence of the death of L's father (N) in similar circumstances whilst in L's care.*

   As stated above, 'categories of relevance' have been abandoned, hence there is no limit to the type of case in which similar fact evidence may be admissible. That having been said, the nature of the defence raised (one of these so called 'categories of relevance') can nevertheless be of importance.

As explained above, the test for the admissibility of similar fact evidence is probative value: *R* v *P*. This may, but need not, be provided by striking similarity. Striking similarity requires some 'unusual feature' – perhaps, for example, a Red Indian headdress worn during the commission of the offence: *DPP* v *Boardman*.

Can it be said that there is such striking similarity between M and N's death? It is certainly arguable, but plastic bags on heads are not quite in the 'Red Indian headdress' league of similarity!

In assessing the relevance (and hence the probative value) of an item of similar fact evidence, the defence raised becomes an important factor. In deciding whether evidence of other conduct is sufficiently relevant to an issue in the case it is necessary to take account of the defence, otherwise the issue may not be clear enough (Criminal Law Revision Committee 11th report (Cmnd 4991) para 81). Hence, similar fact evidence may be admissible to show the implausibility of a defence: *R* v *Anderson* (1988). The fact that L has sought to explain M's death as suicide is thus of great importance in deciding the probative value of the similar fact evidence.

It will be observed that L has not been charged or convicted of any offence relating to N's death. This, however, is no bar to the admissibility of the similar fact evidence The evidence will be admissible even if the jury might not accept that the event ever occurred, so long as they *might* conclude as a possibility,that it occurred: *Harris* v *DPP*.

To conclude, in advising L with regard to the admissibility of this evidence the case of *Noor Mohamed* v *R* (1949) is instructive. Factually, it is similar to L's case (evidence of a previous killing which could have been (but was not proved to be) caused by the defendant), this evidence was held to be inadmissible. In that case, Lord du Parcq said that evidence which is impressive merely because it shows a person to be more likely (from his character) to have committed the offence, *being otherwise of no real substance*, is inadmissible.

On this basis, it is submitted that evidence of N's death is likely to be insufficiently relevant, and hence more prejudicial than probative – the jury would almost certainly attach too great a weight to this evidence.

b) *The incriminating book found in L's possession (and L's membership of 'The Dying Light')*

Again, one must assess the probative value of this evidence.

As stated in *R* v *P*, striking similarity is not the only means of providing probative value. Here, there is evidence of L's possession of an incriminating article. Obviously there is no 'striking similarity' between possession of a book and the commission of the alleged murder, but the book may still be admissible under the similar fact doctrine. Articles which could have been used in the commission of the offence (but which are not proved to be) can still identify the accused as the offender: *Thompson* v *R* (1918).

Again, the defence raised will be of importance in assessing the relevance (probative value) of the articles: *R* v *Reading* (1966).

Clearly, if the evidence merely shows L's disposition (ie that she favours euthanasia) it will not be enough, but if it goes beyond this it may suffice: *R* v *Taylor* (1923).

Here, the underlining of certain passages relating to a particular style of killing may take this evidence beyond merely showing disposition and hence, it is submitted, the book itself may be admissible. Mere evidence of her membership of the organisation is unlikely to go beyond simple disposition, and hence is less likely to be admissible.

c)   *O's evidence*

First, this is clearly an out-of-court statement. Problems of hearsay, however, do not arise – the purpose of adducing this statement is not to prove the *truth* of its contents, but merely to show that the statement was made. It is, therefore, original evidence: *R v Chapman* (1969).

As similar fact evidence, is this evidence admissible? The test is that of probative value (*R v P*) and, as stated above, the defence raised remains an important factor in deciding admissibility. This evidence amounts to evidence of L counselling or procuring an offence. (However, even if the similar fact evidence does not disclose the commission of an offence, it may still be admissible if the similar facts are inexplicable on the basis of coincidence and are of probative value: *R v Rodley* (1913). Further, it need not be merely the actual commission of the offence which is similar. Similar fact evidence can be admissible if the circumstances surrounding the offences are similar: *R v Barrington* (1981).

According to O, L merely *suggested* the killing; further, the method suggested is different. Whilst, potentially, it may be argued that these amount to 'surrounding circumstances' within *Barrington*, it is submitted that O's evidence would lack the necessary probative value, and does not go significantly beyond mere evidence of disposition.

In conclusion, of the items of evidence available, it is submitted that only the book *may* bear sufficient probative value to go beyond mere evidence of disposition. It is arguably an 'affront to common sense' to exclude this, given the underlined passages and the nature of the defence raised.

QUESTION FOUR

Charles and Douglas have been convicted of attempted burglary after their joint trial. Charles had four previous convictions for attempted burglary and Douglas a previous conviction for perjury.

The prosecution were allowed to lead evidence of the four previous convictions, where Charles had been arrested in the early hours of the morning on each occasion attempting to open a shop door with one of a bunch of keys. The prosecution's case was that on the instant occasion Charles and Douglas were trying keys in the keyhole of a shop door. Douglas testified that he was merely sheltering from the rain, saw no keys, and had he been aware of Charles' propensity to burgle shops he would not have acceded to Charles' suggestion that they shelter there. Douglas was cross-examined by the prosecutor on his previous conviction.

Charles' counsel accused the police of 'planting' the keys on him after his arrest. Charles' previous convictions were put to the jury by the prosecutor, who together with the judge commented on Charles' failure to testify.

Advise Charles and Douglas as to any grounds for appeal.

Written by editor

Skeleton Solution

• Charles: similar fact evidence; admissibility and judicial discretion; rebutting defence raised or fairly attributable. Imputations cast, cross-examination; comment on silence of accused in court.

• Douglas: election to testify; evidence against co-accused – s1(f)(iii) Criminal Evidence Act 1898, cross-examination. Section 1(f)(ii) – imputations. Evidence of good character.

Suggested Solution

The prosecution may have been allowed to lead evidence of the *circumstances* surrounding the four previous convictions of Charles for attempted burglary as similar fact evidence; but the mere fact of the convictions could not legitimately be revealed, as Charles has not given evidence directly or indirectly of his good character (thereby allowing evidence in rebuttal of bad character, including, on slender authority (*R* v *Wood & Parker* (1841)), evidence of disposition and previous misconduct, as opposed to merely evidence of bad reputation: *R* v *Rowton* (1865)). Also, Charles has not testified in his own defence, so no consideration is necessary of whether the previous convictions were put to him in cross-examination under the Criminal Evidence Act 1898. Therefore, if the judge allowed the *fact* of Charles' convictions to be put to the jury, whether in the guise of similar fact evidence or because Charles' counsel cast imputations on police witnesses, then this was improper and constitutes grounds for an appeal.

If the circumstances of the four previous occasions, leading to Charles' arrest each time, bore such a striking similarly to the circumstances forming the basis of the instant charge of attempted burglary, then the judge was right in allowing such probative evidence to be adduced by the prosecution in their evidence in chief, as tending to prove Charles' guilt (*DPP* v *Boardman* (1975)); ie if there were such a striking similarity that to withhold that evidence, albeit prejudicial, from the jury would amount to an affront to commonsense or given the way in which Charles misconducted himself on the other occasions it would be beyond the realms of coincidence if it were not his handiwork on the instant occasion (*DPP* v *Boardman*). Following *R* v *P* (1991), as the crime is in issue here, not identification, it should alternatively be argued that 'striking similarity' is not what is important, but the strength of the relationship between the previous and present offence – ie did Charles' previous commissions of burglary give him greater opportunity to commit the present offence? What happened to the keys?

Given Charles' defence that the police 'planted' the keys on him, the prosecution may be properly permitted to adduce evidence of his activities on the other occasions to rebut that defence (*R* v *Anderson* (1988)), and may reasonably anticipate, given his 'not guilty' plea despite his being found in the shop doorway, a defence of innocent association and therefore pre-empt it by rebutting evidence in chief, to prevent a successful defence plea of no case to answer (*R* v *Lunt* (1987)). Even though, in these specific situations the similar fact evidence does not need to have the same striking similarity, nevertheless it is not the fact of conviction for attempted burglaries which has relevance, but the attendant circumstances. In addition, the judge should have given consideration to the probative value and the prejudicial effect of this similar fact evidence, deliberating as to whether the former was outweighed by the latter, before deciding on its admissibility in law, or whether to exclude in his discretion if so admissible (*R* v *Butler* (1987); *R* v *Perry* (1984)).

If the judge allowed the previous convictions to be revealed to the jury because Charles' counsel cast imputations on the character of police witnesses for the prosecution by accusing them of fabricating evidence, then the judge was seriously in error, because Charles did not testify and therefore s1(f) Criminal Evidence Act 1898 did not apply. However serious and however numerous the imputations cast on witnesses for the prosecution, under the second limb of s1(f)(ii) the accused can, with leave, be cross-examined on his convictions – so by definition if he elects not to testify the cross-examination cannot take place, and the Act cannot be circumvented by the judge's allowing revelation of previous convictions by the prosecution when the accused does not give evidence.

The testimony of Douglas is to some extent favourable to Charles, ie his assertion that he saw no keys tends to support Douglas' defence of innocent association and his assertion that the keys were 'planted' on him after his arrest. This evidence of Douglas, the accomplice of Charles, would be 'tainted' because of their alleged complicity in the crime, and would have little evidential value without corroboration (*R* v *Prater* (1960)). But of much greater relevance is the fact that in the main Douglas' evidence tends to incriminate Charles, it tends to undermine Charles' defence and as such could be classed as evidence against a co-accused (s1(f)(iii) Criminal Evidence Act 1898; *Murdoch* v *Taylor* (1965)). If the judge rules that such evidence *is* evidence against a co-accused as opposed to, for example, a mere denial of guilt, then the co-accused has the right to cross-examine under s1(f)(iii) (*Murdoch* v *Taylor*). If, however, the prosecutor wishes to cross-examine under this proviso, this can only be with leave of the judge, and the judge will, exceptionally, grant such leave in his discretion (*R* v *Seigley* (1911)). The judge must weigh in the balance the prejudicial effect and probative value in deciding whether to permit such cross-examination by the prosecutor, and if he decides to permit the cross-examination must inform the jury that Douglas' conviction for perjury goes only to his credit, not to the issue of his guilt on the instant charge.

Douglas' assertion that he would not have acceded to Charles' request to shelter in the doorway is not by implication putting his character in issue; if it amounts to evidence of his general good character (which is dubious in this problem question) then rebutting evidence by the prosecutor should take the form of general bad reputation, not the disclosure to the jury (with or without leave of the judge) of one isolated conviction albeit for perjury.

11 Opinion Evidence

11.1 Introduction

11.2 Key points

11.3 Analysis of questions

11.4 Questions

11.1 Introduction

Opinion evidence is perhaps the most straightforward topic in the laws of evidence, in that there is not a great deal of complexity or incongruity in the principles involved. There have been recent statutory changes in criminal proceedings which have made hearsay opinion evidence generally admissible. Judgments in previous proceedings are capable of being regarded as the opinion of that court, therefore will be covered in this chapter.

11.2 Key points

a) General rule is that opinion evidence, whether given as direct testimony or hearsay, is inadmissible as proof of the belief held – subject to three exceptions:

  i) General reputation

   Where direct evidence is unavailable on some matter of public concern, that matter may be proved by evidence of general reputation, eg pedigree or marriage (decreasing in importance as public records are more available and their content admissible as an exception to the hearsay rule) identifying a reference to a person, eg that a defamatory statement was accepted by the public in general as referring to the plaintiff; proving character, whether good or bad; evidence of reputation in these instances is admissible in civil cases by virtue of s7 Civil Evidence Act 1995, thus obviating the need for the notice procedure under the rules issued under s2. One final example of general reputation is the public's opinion on some matter, such as information from a survey admissible in cases involving trademarks, passing off etc: *Sodastream* v *Thorn Cascade* [1982] RPC 459.

  ii) Expert opinion evidence

   The court must be satisfied as to the competence of a witness to testify as an expert, whether by recognised qualification, and/or expertise gained by experience. Such a person's evidence is essential to assist the court not only to understand specialised facts but to form correct opinions and draw the correct inferences from those facts, or general facts. A medical orderly was held not to be an expert for the purposes of a prosecution against the defendant for assault occasioning actual bodily harm: *R* v *Inch* (1990) 91 Cr App R 51. A person who is competent as an expert witness is also compellable as such: *Harmony Shipping Co* v *Saudi Europe Line* [1979] 1 WLR 1380.

   The expert evidence may be subjected to cross-examination, including cross-examination going to credit, and may be contradicted by other, usually expert, evidence, but otherwise the expert is regarded as an independent witness whose opinion evidence has substantial probative value: *R* v *Lanfear* [1968] 2 QB 77.

Expert opinion evidence is not admissible on subject matter of which the lay opinion of the court is just as valid: *R* v *Turner* [1975] QB 834, and also the case of *R* v *Weightman* (1991) Cr App R 291, where the Court of Appeal held that a psychiatrist's evidence was inadmissible where the purpose was to tell a jury how a person who was not suffering from mental disorder might react to the stresses and strains of life. The area which has given rise to most forensic and academic discussion is that of a person's state of mind. If the issue arises in relation to the reliability of the witness's evidence, then medical opinion evidence is admissible: *Toohey* v *MPC* [1965] AC 595. But if the issue is the state of mind of the accused at the time the offence was committed, then several cases highlight the difficulties the courts face. If there is no question of mental disorder, and the issue is purely the mens rea of the accused, then that is within the competence and experience of the court and therefore expert opinion evidence of a psychiatrist is not admissible because it is not necessary: *R* v *Chard* (1971) 56 Cr App R 268. However, where there is a question of mental disorder or similar conditions outside the usual experience of the court, then expert opinion evidence of psychiatrists is admissible because necessary, eg insanity, automatism, diminished responsibility. In *R* v *Smith* [1979] 1 WLR 1445, the opinion evidence of a psychiatrist was admitted to rebut a defence of automatism on a charge of murder; in *R* v *Turner* supra. In the recent case of *R* v *Toner* (1991) 93 Cr App R 382 medical evidence was admitted which related to hypoglycaemia and its possible effect upon intent (mens rea). The court could see no difference between this and medical evidence admitted as to the effect of a drug on intent. If no such medical evidence is allowed, the court said, the jury would be deprived of assistance in a field where their ordinary experience did not enable them to judge for themselves. In *R* v *Rimmer & Beech* [1983] Crim LR 250, expert opinion evidence relating to mental state was inadmissible because in effect it was tendered to prove the veracity of the statement made by the accused in his defence and thus would have tended to usurp the function of the court. These decisions are perhaps reconcilable with *Toohey* v *MPC* supra. But in *Lowery* v *R* [1974] AC 85, the opinion evidence of a psychiatrist as to the tendency of one of the two co-accused to murder for pleasure, the admissibility of which was naturally challenged by the other co-accused, was held to have been properly admitted to assist the jury to make a decision as to the veracity of the two co-accused! The decision in *Lowery* did not receive the approval of the Court of Appeal in *Turner*, but the former is a Privy Council decision, which should, and no doubt in due course will, be overruled by the House of Lords.

The common law rule prohibiting expert opinion evidence on the ultimate issue has been abrogated in civil trials by s3 Civil Evidence Act 1972 which provides for the admissibility of expert evidence on any 'relevant matter', stated in s3(3) to include 'an issue in the proceedings in question'. In criminal trials the issue of diminished responsibility on a charge of murder can be, and often is, the subject of expert opinion evidence – and often the expert will be asked the question: 'Do you think the accused was suffering from diminished responsibility?', despite the fact that that constitutes the ultimate issue in deciding guilt of murder or manslaughter. Lord Parker CJ gave this as an example of the inroads into the common law prohibition in criminal trials: see *DPP* v *A and BC Chewing Gum* [1968] 1 QB 159 at p164. It is generally accepted that the principle in s3 Civil Evidence Act 1972 now applies also in criminal cases subject to the discretion of the judge to exclude such evidence where the expert witness would be effectively usurping the function of the jury.

Where the expert bases his opinion on facts, he cannot thus make those facts evidence unless he has first-hand knowledge of them (*R* v *Abadom* [1983] 1 All ER 364) and in any situation where the expert is giving opinion evidence with an underlying factual basis, then those facts must be proved by admissible evidence of the expert himself as a witness of fact, or of some other competent witness. To save time and costs in calling the assistants of expert witnesses, counsel should maximise the use of admissions or written statements to prove facts on which the expert's opinion is based: *R* v *Jackson* [1996] 2 Cr App R 420. The proper time to fill such 'evidential gaps' was after the first reading of the expert's statement.

An expert witness must approach his task seriously and any expert witness who does not should not be surprised if the court strongly censures him. The duties and responsibilities of expert witnesses in civil cases were clearly spelt out by Cresswell J in *National Justice Compania Naviera SA* v *Prudential Assurance Co Ltd (Ikarian Reefer)* [1995] 1 Lloyd's Rep 455. Despite this important clarification for expert witnesses of their role, there are still not infrequent instances of expert witnesses falling well short of what is required of them. See also *Autospin (Oil Seals) Ltd* v *Beehive Spinning (A Firm)* (1995) The Times 9 August.

Expert opinion hearsay evidence is admissible in civil cases under the Civil Evidence Act 1972. In criminal cases hearsay was restricted to statements of facts until s30 Criminal Justice Act 1988 provided for the admissibility of expert reports as hearsay, with leave of the court.

Disclosure of expert evidence pre-trial in criminal proceedings was provided for under s81 Police and Criminal Evidence Act 1984, under which Crown Courts Rules could be issued. Under the Act, the Crown Court (Advance Notice of Expert Evidence) Rules 1987 require that, following committal for trial, if either prosecution or defence proposes to adduce expert evidence of fact or opinion at the trial, then the other party must be furnished with that detailed expert evidence as soon as practicable. If a party fails to furnish details as required, then the expert evidence can only be adduced with leave of the court.

This requirement of disclosure has existed for some time in civil proceedings; RSC Ord 38, rules 36 to 44, issued under s2 Civil Evidence Act 1972, govern such pre-trial disclosure, whether the expert evidence be in the form of hearsay or direct testimony. Although the court may give leave to adduce despite non-compliance with the rules, Ord 38, r36 provides that expert evidence should not be adduced at the civil trial unless the party seeking to adduce has applied to the court to determine whether a direction should be given, and has complied with any such direction, or has complied with automatic directions under Ord 25, r8. Medical negligence cases are not, as was thought earlier, in any special category: *Naylor* v *Preston Area Health Authority* [1987] 1 WLR 958. Ord 38, r38 makes provision for the court to order a 'without prejudice' meeting of experts pre-trial to clarify the issues in dispute. Once an expert evidence report has been disclosed for the purpose of any contemplated civil proceedings, that report cannot be excluded from the evidence at the trial merely because the party originally seeking to adduce it has decided against using it or against calling the expert in question to testify (Ord 38, r42).

iii) *R* v *Clare*; *R* v *Peach* (1995) The Times 4 April is a good illustration of the law of evidence having to evolve in order to keep pace with technological developments. It seems to sanction a new category of witness – the 'expert ad hoc' – who can give opinion evidence after becoming qualified to do so by virtue of sustained study of one given matter. The case concerned intensive frame by frame study of video evidence and comparison with still photos, by a police constable, and the conclusions he drew from that study. It is likely, however, that the mantle of an expert ad hoc will not be bestowed too readily, and it will be necessary to show considerable application by the purported expert ad hoc to convince the court to allow his/her evidence.

iv) Non-expert opinion evidence

Section 3(2) Civil Evidence Act 1972 provides for opinion evidence of non-expert witnesses to be admissible to convey to the civil court relevant facts perceived by them as evidence of what they perceived. It is considered that this sub-section restates the common law, and is therefore applicable also to criminal proceedings. Admissibility is confined to areas of general experience and competence of the lay person, for example evidence as to identity of a person or document etc; evidence as to physical or mental condition of a person, eg that a person had been drinking heavily, but *not* that he was so drunk as to be unfit to drive through drink: *R* v *Davies* [1962] 1 WLR 1111; evidence as to the speed of a motor vehicle (but see Chapter 5.2 as to corroboration), or as to age or value other than in relation to antiques when expert opinion evidence is essential. In the case of *R* v *Simbodyal* (1991) The Times 10 October the Court of Appeal made it clear that a judge would be vulnerable to proper criticism if he appeared to be acting as a handwriting expert by comparing the notes himself.

b) *Judgments in previous proceedings*

A judgment in any proceedings is in the nature of specialised opinion – ie the opinion of the court as to whether a party has discharged the general burden of proof to the appropriate standard.

At common law the rule in *Hollington* v *Hewthorn* [1943] KB 587 stipulated that a previous judgment was inadmissible in subsequent civil proceedings as evidence of the facts on which it was based. The rule has been held to apply in subsequent criminal proceedings: *R* v *Spinks* [1982] 1 All ER 587. As regards conviction in earlier criminal proceedings of the defendant in subsequent civil proceedings, s11 Civil Evidence Act 1968 not only makes the fact of the conviction admissible but renders it conclusive of the commission of that relevant offence unless the contrary is proved. It is the fact of conviction which is crucial, not the sentence, and therefore even if a pardon is given the conviction still subsists: *R* v *Foster* [1984] 3 WLR 401. The burden of proof on the civil defendant seeking to prove 'the contrary' when a conviction is proved against him is to the civil standard; ie proof on a balance of probabilities, which, given the standard of proof in his earlier prosecution, will be an uphill task: *Hunter* v *Chief Constable of the West Midlands* [1981] 3 All ER 727. A plaintiff in civil proceedings must include in his pleadings a statement of his intention to rely on s11 Civil Evidence Act 1968, together with the particulars of the conviction and the issue in the civil proceedings to which the conviction is relevant (RSC Ord 18, r7).

In s12 Civil Evidence Act 1968 there is a similar provision in relation to previous findings in matrimonial proceedings of adultery or paternity – the adultery or paternity shall be treated as conclusively proved unless the contrary is proved. (Again, the standard, as with s11 convictions, is the civil standard of balance of probabilities.)

In criminal proceedings, where proof of guilt of a person (including the accused) is admissible because relevant to an issue in those criminal proceedings, then the conviction of that person can be proved under s74 Police and Criminal Evidence Act 1984, and he shall then be taken to have committed the offence unless the contrary is proved. A relevant issue in criminal proceedings for handling is whether the goods were stolen, which may be shown by proof under s74 of conviction of the thief. The Court of Appeal has stated that s74 should be used sparingly, particularly in the case of joint trials for eg conspiracy, and should not be used where the evidence implicates the accused: *R* v *Robertson & Golder* [1987] 3 All ER 231. Problems arise under s74(1) and (2) where two or more defendants have been jointly charged, and one or more pleads guilty, leaving the other pleading not guilty. If it is alleged that the remaining defendant was very closely linked with what are now previous convictions of the other people, the jury is likely to infer that this defendant is guilty also. In such cases, the judge could exclude the convictions under s78 Police and Criminal Evidence Act 1984, if the prosecution counsel intended to rely on the convictions of the other(s) not merely to prevent mystification of the jury, but as evidence of the guilt of the appellant – *R* v *Kempster* (1990) 90 Cr App R 14; *R* v *Mattison* [1990] Crim LR 117. Where a person has a legal burden of disproving the commission of an offence by virtue of s74, the standard is the civil one only.

11.3 Analysis of questions

Opinion evidence tends to appear as part of an examination question, usually one issue of several in a problem question which will often deal also with hearsay statements of fact. Given the emergence of hypnosis, lie-detectors, truth drugs in forensic science, opinion is an area which could well expand, and become more complex and thus more 'exam-worthy'.

11.4 Questions

QUESTION ONE

Potbelly is charged with causing the death of Cleopatra by reckless driving.

The driver of the car which caused Cleopatra's death did not stop and Potbelly's defence is an alibi.

Advise on the admissibility of the following:

a) PC Bojak says he got to the scene to find Cleopatra lying on the road, and she said, 'It was a red Ferrari ... doing eighty.' She then died. Potbelly has a red Ferrari.

b) PC Bodie says he was at an identification parade when Doyle identified Potbelly as the driver but Doyle has now gone abroad.

c) Evidence of a psychiatrist, Quincy, who has examined Potbelly, that Potbelly is highly disturbed, an individual who is capable of behaving in a manner calculated to injure people around him.

d) A 'parking ticket' issued by a traffic warden to the owner of a Ferrari bearing the same number as Potbelly's car. The ticket had been found near the scene of the accident.

Adapted from University of London LLB Examination
(for External Students) Evidence June 1983 Q6

Skeleton Solution

a) • Hearsay – dying declaration – res gestae.

• Non-expert evidence as to speed.

b) • Previous inconsistent statement – exception with identification.

• Hearsay rule – exception to rule.

c) • Expert opinion evidence – admissibility – competence of jury to decide for itself.

d) • Inadmissible hearsay – *Rice* versus *Lydon* – traffic warden as witness in court.

Suggested Solution

a) In cases of murder or manslaughter, a dying declaration by the victim, under a settled and hopeless expectation of death, is admissible as to the cause and circumstances of the death (*R* v *Woodcock* (1789)). This exception to the rule against hearsay appears to be confined to the two offences mentioned (see *R* v *Hutchinson* (1822) and *R* v *Newton and Carpenter* (1859)) but arguably extends to cover all cases where the death is the subject of the charge and accordingly could apply in the instant case of causing death by reckless driving. Alternatively, it should be argued that Cleopatra's statement formed part of the res gestae. The judge must be satisfied that the statement was so clearly made in circumstances of spontaneity or involvement in the event that the possibility of concoction or fabrication can be disregarded (*Ratten* v *R* (1972); *R* v *Andrews* (1987)). If Cleopatra's statement is admissible, it is evidence of the truth of the facts contained in it. Part of her statement relates to the speed of the car. Non-expert opinion evidence as to speed is admissible being regarded as a matter within ordinary human experience, and in this case corroboration is not imperative, as the offence is not one of exceeding a speed limit.

b) At common law, former consistent statements are generally inadmissible. One recognised exception is evidence of prior identification admissible both by the identifying witness and by other witnesses who saw the identification being made (unless the evidence contradicts the evidence of the identifying witness). Thus in *R* v *Osbourne & Virtue* (1973) where the identifying witness was unable to remember having picked anyone out of the ID parade, the Court of Appeal held that a police officer, who saw the identification being made, could testify as to the person identified. The court held the same in the case of *R* v *McCay* (1990). On one view these cases should be confined to their facts. On a wider view it may be argued that since the evidence was not admitted as an exception to the rule on prior consistent statements (there was no evidence of identification in court with which the police officer's evidence could be consistent), it was admitted as an exception to the hearsay rule, ie to prove the truth of an out-of-court statement by conduct. Accepting this argument, PC Bodie may give evidence of Doyle's identification of Potbelly. However, in *Osbourne & Virtue*, the court made no reference to the hearsay problem, and the case has been much criticised on this basis. In *McCay*, the court seemed to believe it fell within the res gestae exception, but this goes against old authority. Furthermore, in *Sparks* v *R* (1964), Lord Morris held that there is no rule which permits the giving of hearsay evidence merely because it relates to identity, and that for hearsay to be admissible it must come within a recognised exception.

c) Expert opinion evidence is admissible on subjects demanding special knowledge and competence where in its absence the court would be unable to reach a proper conclusion (*Folkes* v *Chadd & Ors* (1782); also *R* v *Weightman* (1991)). However, such evidence is inadmissible if the lay opinion of the tribunal of fact is equally valid on the subject in question. Thus if Quincey's evidence is designed to show Potbelly intended the offence, and there is no question of mental illness, the matter is properly regarded to be within the competence of the jury (*R* v *Chard* (1971)). In *R* v *Toner* (1991) mental illness had been caused, it seems, by the hypoglycaemia, and so expert medical evidence was admissible as regards its effect on intent. By contrast, matters of insanity are regarded as proper subjects of expert opinion evidence. In the case of *Lowery* v *R* (1974) the Privy Council allowed one co-defendant to adduce psychiatric evidence to show that the other was of a character and disposition likely to have committed the offence. However, in that case, it was clear from all the circumstances that one or other or both of the co-defendants must have committed the offence. It is submitted that *Lowery* be confined to its own facts given the judgment in *R* v *Turner* (1975). In the instant, case, the evidence is not only inadmissible character evidence but also outside the boundaries of admissible expert opinion evidence.

d) The parking ticket is prima facie inadmissible hearsay, being a statement, in writing, made by a person outside court, and tendered for the purpose of proving the facts contained in it, ie that Potbelly's car was within the vicinity of the accident on the day in question (presumably). By analogy with *R* v *Rice* (1963), a much criticised case, it could be argued that the parking ticket, like the airline ticket bearing a traveller's name, is admissible evidence that a car with the same number as Potbelly's was within the vicinity of the accident. It is submitted that *Rice* should not be followed *R* v *Lydon* (1987). Although it was held in that case that the ticket did not speak its contents, the ticket was valueless as a piece of real evidence without regard to the truth of its contents. To allow a ticket in evidence so that an inference can be drawn as to the truth of its contents is, in effect, to do what is prohibited by the rule against hearsay. One practical solution, in the instant case, would be to call as a witness the traffic warden in question who could refresh his or her memory by reference to the parking ticket. It may be safely assumed that the statements in the ticket were made by the warden and were contemporaneous to the events to which they related.

QUESTION TWO

Caligula is charged with procuring Livilla, a severely subnormal woman, to have unlawful sexual intercourse with a number of men contrary to s9 of the Sexual Offences Act, knowing that she was severely subnormal. The Crown wish to put the following items of evidence at his trial:

a) A certificate of the Director of St Mary's Mental Health Institute that Livilla was an inmate of the Institute and that she was severely subnormal.

b) The evidence of her mother that Livilla was incapable of reading and writing and was subnormal.

c) The evidence of Phoebe, another subnormal girl, that she had been asked by Caligula to come to a party where she could 'earn lots of money from rich businessmen'.

Adapted from University of London LLB Examination
(for External Students) Evidence June 1984 Q5

Skeleton Solution

a) Hearsay – documentary hearsay – s23 Criminal Justice Act 1988 – expert opinion.

b) Opinion evidence – outside experience of jury – subnormality – incompetence with reading and writing.

c) Competence – evidence of previous bad character of accused – probative value and prejudicial effect.

Suggested Solution

a) It is for the prosecution to prove every element of the offence charged. In this case that includes proving that Livilla was subnormal. The certificate of the Director of St Mary's Mental Health Institute seems a sensible way of proving her subnormality, but since it is by no means certain that Caligula will accept the certificate the law requires the Director himself to give evidence in person. The hearsay rule will prima facie exclude the certificate but it could be admitted under the provisions of s23 Criminal Justice Act 1988, given that one of the requirements in s23(2) is satisfied, and the court gives leave, having considered the factors in s25. If the certificate contains elements of expert opinion as to severe subnormality, this is admissible as hearsay under s30, again with leave of the court, and subject to the conditions in s30(3).

b) Opinion evidence is only admissible in a criminal case if the jury is not in a position to decide an issue without hearing someone else's opinion – in other words if the matter on which opinion evidence is given is outside the normal experience and knowledge of the jury (see *R* v *Turner* (1975) and *R* v *Weightman* (1991), where the court would not allow in psychiatrist's evidence about a person's reaction to stress and strains of life, where there was no mental illness, although she may have an abnormal personality. But subnormality and abnormality are two different things).

The mother's opinion on the issue of subnormality is inadmissible. A lay witness is not allowed to give his or her opinion on an issue which is an issue for the jury. It is for the jury to decide whether Livilla is subnormal, not for her mother, and so her opinion on this matter is inadmissible. She is not an expert, as far as we know, and so her opinion is of no assistance and is inadmissible (*M'Naghten's Case* (1843)).

The mother's evidence of Livilla's inability to read and write would be admissible. This is not opinion evidence, but is evidence of facts perceived by the mother. We can assume that she had seen and knows her daughter well enough to know whether she can read and write and would not be giving an opinion, but would be stating a fact which she herself has seen. It is possible, though it seems unlikely, that the mother was only saying her daughter could not read and write because she was in the Institute and had not perceived these facts for herself. If that is the case, her evidence on the matter would be inadmissible.

The prosecution could try to rely on the case of *R* v *Davies* (1962) where the Courts Martial Appeal Court held that a witness to a motor accident could give evidence that in his opinion a driver had taken drink. Provided he also stated the grounds on which he comes to the conclusion, such a statement is quite proper. The Crown could argue that the mother could give evidence of what she perceived, using the term 'subnormal' to describe her daughter's behaviour. It is submitted though, that the *Davies* case should not be stretched so as to allow such evidence, because the mother could give evidence of what she saw of her daughter's condition without needing to use the word 'subnormal' to describe Livilla accurately and clearly.

c) The evidence of Phoebe will not be at all admissible unless the judge is satisfied that she is a competent witness. A person who is mentally ill may give evidence if the judge is satisfied that he or she understands the oath and is able to give evidence without the mental illness making it impossible for the witness to recall events (*R* v *Hill* (1851)). Even if Phoebe is competent, her evidence is unlikely to be ruled admissible. Evidence of previous misconduct of the accused is inadmissible as evidence of his guilt unless it is so probative of guilt that this probative value outweighs its prejudicial effect. This test, laid down in *Boardman* v *DPP* (1974), means that the evidence of Phoebe must prove Caligula's guilt on the charge with regard to Livilla, to such an extent that the jury will not be acting unfairly to the accused if they jump to the conclusion that because he made such an offer to Phoebe, so he must have done to Livilla.

There seems to be nothing particularly strange about the offence charged which could be seen to make it strikingly similar to the offer made to Phoebe. Both 'victims' are mentally subnormal, but that of itself does not show such an underlying link or unity or system to make the evidence of Phoebe positively probative that the offence charged was committed. But following the case of *R* v *P* (1991) what matters more is what is in issue – identification, or the crime itself?

QUESTION THREE

Albert, Charles and Douglas are charged with armed robbery of a sub-post office and murder of the postmaster. Discuss the admissibility of the following:

a) medical evidence in the form of a psychiatrist's report in support of Albert's defence of diminished responsibility;

b) Charles having testified that he was unaware that Albert was armed, and had he known would not have been involved, psychiatric evidence that Charles is of a passive disposition and that psychopaths, such as Albert appears to be, are prone to violence and to lying;

c) evidence of Hinton, a priest, that Douglas is a regular churchgoer and a pillar of society who could not possibly commit any crime at all, let alone a grave crime of violence;

d) previous convictions of Charles and Douglas for armed robberies of sub-post offices.

Written by editor

Skeleton Solution

• Expert opinion evidence; ultimate issue; hearsay – admissibility.

• Expert opinion; factual basis; pure hypothesis; competence of jury; s1(f)(iii) Criminal Evidence Act 1898.

• Character evidence – status of character witness – evidence of general reputation, and evidence in rebuttal at common law and under s1(f)(ii) Criminal Evidence Act 1898.

• Similar fact evidence.

Suggested Solution

If Albert's plea is diminished responsibility, then he is admitting that he unlawfully killed the postmaster but running a defence which if successful will lead to his conviction for manslaughter rather than murder. The burden of proving diminished responsibility must be discharged by Albert – discharge of an evidential burden will not suffice (s2(2) Homicide Act

1957). As diminished responsibility bears on mental disorder of the accused, expert opinion evidence is admissible given that this is a matter not within the realm of the ordinary juryman's competence and experience (eg *R* v *Smith* (1979)). Given that the psychiatrist examined and questioned Albert and from that factual basis formed his opinion that Albert suffered from diminished responsibility, the evidence is admissible as expert opinion testimony of the psychiatrist (*R* v *Bradshaw* (1986)). Where the medical evidence with diminished responsibility is unequivocal and uncontradicted, the trial judge should direct the jury to accept it if there are no other circumstances to consider. Where, however, such other circumstances exist, the aforesaid medical evidence should be assessed in the light of those other circumstances – *R* v *Sanders* (1991) CA. If the underlying facts are not proved by admissible evidence – which can be percipient evidence of the psychiatrist or some other witness – then the opinion, formed on inadmissible hearsay rather than facts, would be inadmissible (*R* v *Bradshaw* and *R* v *Abadom* (1983)).

The Crown Court (Advance Notice of Expert Evidence) Rules 1987, issued under s81 Police and Criminal Evidence Act 1984, require reciprocal disclosure of expert evidence prior to a trial on indictment. Albert's counsel should therefore disclose to the prosecution, as soon as practicable after Albert's committal for trial (Rule 3), the expert evidence which the defence intend to adduce. Failure to comply is not fatal, but admissibility is then in the discretion of the trial judge (Rule 5). Given that Albert's counsel wishes to adduce a psychiatrist's report, although this is hearsay, it is now admissible subject to the Advance Notice Rules above, with leave of the court (s30 Criminal Justice Act 1988) if the psychiatrist is not to be called to give oral evidence. In deciding whether to grant leave to the report's being admitted in evidence without the psychiatrist attending as a witness, the court must have regard to factors such as the contents of the report and any unfairness to the accused (s30(3) CJA 1988).

On the facts of this murder trial, the diminished responsibility of Albert is going to be an 'ultimate issue'. The common law rule prohibiting opinion evidence on the ultimate issue has been repealed in civil cases (s3 Civil Evidence Act 1972), and it is considered that it no longer applies in criminal cases (*DPP* v *A & BC Chewing Gum* (1986)). Given the nature of the expert opinion evidence to be adduced, and its relevance to the ultimate issue, it is highly probable that the psychiatrist will have to attend and give oral testimony, being subjected to cross-examination. As he is a competent witness, he is compellable (*Harmony Shipping Co* v *Saudi Europe Line* (1979)).

The psychiatric evidence as to Charles's 'passive disposition' is of dubious admissibility, as such passivity (not bearing on mental disorder) is within the jury's sphere of competence and therefore expert evidence is unnecessary in helping them to form their own opinion (*R* v *Turner* (1975) and *R* v *Weightman* (1991). The opinion as to Albert's propensity to violence and mendacity appears to be pure hypothesis from the wording of the question – 'such as Albert appears to be' etc – and as such would be inadmissible. If there is factual evidence of Albert's psychopathy, then expert opinion evidence *may* be admissible as to the common traits of psychopaths, but contradictory opinion evidence could then be adduced on what in itself is, or should not be, an issue lending itself to expert opinion evidence. In *Lowery* v *R* (1974) opinion evidence of an expert was admitted apparently to tend to prove the veracity of one of two co-accused, but the decision was criticised in *Turner*, and the admissibility of the opinion of the psychiatrist in the case now under review appears to be less supportable than that in *Lowery*.

Charles's testimony would tend to undermine a defence by Albert of alibi or that he was unarmed etc, thereby causing Charles to lose his shield under s1(f)(iii) CEA 1898 and giving

Albert's counsel the right to cross-examine Charles on his previous convictions (*Murdoch* v *Taylor* (1965)). But, given that Albert's defence is in essence that he was present, committed homicide with mens rea for murder but because of his arrested or retarded development etc ought to be convicted of manslaughter, Charles's testimony does not undermine that defence, is not favourable to the prosecution and is not therefore 'evidence against any other person charged in the same proceedings'. Therefore Charles's evidence should not result in his previous convictions being revealed in cross-examination.

Douglas's calling a character witness to state what Hinton said amounts to his adducing evidence of his good character, not just of general reputation but of specific acts and disposition. Such evidence is strictly inadmissible (*R* v *Rowton* (1865); *R* v *Redgrave* (1981)). However, if evidence of good character is adduced on behalf of the accused, then the prosecution may lead evidence of bad character in rebuttal but this must be merely evidence of bad reputation, not specific acts or convictions or disposition etc. However, if Douglas elects to testify after Hinton has given this evidence, then with leave of the judge the prosecutor may cross-examine Douglas on his previous convictions, not to prove his guilt but to attack his credibility (s1(f)(ii) Criminal Evidence Act 1898).

In the case of both Charles and Douglas, their previous armed robberies may bear such a striking similarity to the one which is the subject of the instant charge that the circumstances of those robberies (not purely the previous convictions) may be given in evidence by the prosecutor to prove their guilt, under the doctrine of similar fact evidence (*DPP* v *Boardman* (1975)). Whether there is such a similarity or any other kind of probative relationship is a question of law for the judge who must weigh the probative value against the prejudicial effect.

12 Public Policy

12.1 Introduction

There have been substantial developments in the past decade in this area of evidence, with the courts having to resolve the conflict between the public interest in the proper administration of justice and the public, or national, interest in safeguarding national security and related matters of state and the efficient functioning of the public service. Where the former interest prevails, then there will be full disclosure of all relevant evidence (eg at pre-trial discovery stage of civil litigation). Where the latter prevails, then the protected or sensitive information will be withheld from the court (ie excluded because of 'public interest immunity').

12.2 Key points

a) *Historical background and development*

In *Duncan* v *Cammell Laird* [1942] AC 624 the House of Lords held that the jury had no discretion to order disclosure of documents when a Minister certified that they should be withheld in the interests of national security or the efficient functioning of the public service. The decision was followed despite criticism of the rigidity of the rule and the fact that exclusion on the grounds of public interest immunity was in the hands of the Executive and could easily be abused. In *Conway* v *Rimmer* [1968] AC 910 the House of Lords reviewed its earlier decision and decided that where there is a claim of public interest immunity, the decision whether to exclude is ultimately that of the judiciary, not the executive. There were some reservations as to the position of 'class' documents, eg Cabinet papers, but in subsequent cases it was stated that, whatever the nature of the document, whatever the reason given for non-disclosure, the judges (if appropriate after private scrutiny of the documents) will decide whether public interest immunity shall obtain: *Burmah Oil* v *Bank of England* [1980] AC 1090; *Air Canada* v *Secretary of State for Trade (No 2)* [1983] 2 AC 394.

b) *Extent of public interest immunity*

The extent of non-disclosure on the grounds of public interest immunity was discussed at length, and with some conflicting opinions, in *D* v *NSPCC* [1978] AC 171, where their Lordships accepted that the list of categories of public interest is not closed – but its development will be by extending its ambit by reference to pre-existing, judicially recognised, public interests. In that case their Lordships, by reference to the long-established public interest in excluding the identity of police informers, extended the scope of public interest immunity to the NSPCC in regard to its efficient functioning being dependent, like the police, on information imparted in confidence.

i) Existing, recognised, categories

These can be summarised as:

- State security

  Duncan v *Cammell Laird* exemplifies this.

- International relations

  The public policy element figures strongly in sensitive areas of English foreign policy, such as territorial disputes with other countries: *Buttes Gas* v *Hammer (No 3)* [1981] 1 QB 223.

- Detection and prevention of crime

  The public interest in withholding evidence which would identify police informants has been recognised since, at the latest, 1794 (*R* v *Hardy* (1794) 24 State Trials 199). (Consider the analogy in *D* v *NSPCC*.) The public interest is obviously not only in the detection of crime but also in its prevention, consequently it is not only the identity of informants which will be withheld but also methods used by police such as surveillance tactics and locations used, and sophisticated forensic methodology *R* v *Rankine* [1986] 2 All ER 566; *R* v *Brown and Daley* (1988) 87 Cr App R 52; *R* v *Johnson* [1989] 1 All ER 121. Where disclosure is requested by the defence to assist in establishing the innocence of the accused, then the judge must consider whether non-disclosure on this ground of public interest immunity will lead to injustice to the accused: cf *R* v *Brown and Daley* and *R* v *Johnson* supra. In the recent case of *R* v *Agar* (1990) 90 Cr App R 318, the defence counsel argued that the police informant had caused the defendant to arrive whilst they were searching the informant's house for drugs, and that the drugs were planted on the defendant by the police. On appeal, it was held that although there was a clear and well-established rule that the identity of police informants should be kept secret, there was even stronger public interest here in allowing the appellant to put forward a tenable case in its best light.

- Efficient functioning of public service

  This extends not just to government departments, but to the police, to local government and to other bodies (eg NSPCC – *D* v *NSPCC* above; Gaming Board – *Rogers* v *Home Secretary* [1973] AC 388). In the case of the police, in the recent case of *Sharples* v *Halford* (1991) The Times 9 October, it was held that police disciplinary files were the subject of public interest immunity. The trend is to restrict this head of public interest immunity to bodies performing a statutory function, and to restrain a proliferation of agencies claiming the immunity merely on the grounds of confidentiality or candour: *Science Research Council* v *Nassé* [1980] AC 1028, per Lord Scarman at p1087.

- Confidentiality

  Confidentiality of some communication or relationship is not in itself a reason for non-disclosure, but it is often a vital factor in a claim of public interest immunity. Often where confidentiality in respect of sources of information is an issue, there is a blurring of the distinction between public policy and private privilege (see chapter 13). In *British Steel Corporation* v *Granada TV* [1982] AC 1096 the House of Lords recognised that in deciding whether to order the disclosure of the identity of an informant and thus to induce a breach of confidentiality, the courts do have some discretion – but obviously it is very much the function of the person receiving the information which is the crucial factor, eg a police officer as opposed to a journalist.

In the recent case of *Brown* v *Matthews* [1990] 2 All ER 155, the Court of Appeal held that a court welfare report did not fall within that category of documents which in the public interest could not be disclosed except for the purposes for which it came into existence. Instead, the court may give leave for the report to be used in other proceedings if, after evaluating and balancing the confidentiality of the report against the need for the contents of the report to be put into evidence if there was to be a fair trial, the court decided that in this particular case, the interests of justice required the reports to be released. In other words, the Court Welfare Officer's report could be disclosed at the discretion of the court which had ordered the report.

It was also held in the case of *W* v *Edgell* [1990] 2 WLR 471, that a psychiatrist's report was not protected against disclosure.

Although a journalist who refuses to disclose his source of information is often said to be claiming journalistic, or media, privilege, the use of the word 'privilege' is almost as misleading as when public interest immunity was referred to as 'Crown privilege'. However, one distinction made between public policy and private privilege is that of waiver. If a matter is accepted as being the subject of public interest immunity, then it is not permissible for a witness to waive that 'right' to withhold evidence; but in the realm of privilege a witness may claim the privilege or may decide to waive the privilege and apprise the court of the evidence or the source of the information. In the case of journalistic privilege, s10 Contempt of Court Act 1981, governs the protection from disclosure of sources of information; on balance, this is an area of privilege rather than of public interest immunity, so will be dealt with in the next Chapter.

12.3 Analysis of questions

Questions on public policy reasons for non-disclosure, ie public interest immunity, do not appear with unfailing regularity; when they do appear they tend to be essay questions and quite often combined with private privilege, or occasionally some other area of evidence. The essay questions require a sound knowledge, plus, importantly, a critical awareness of the underlying principles and conflicts; but given that, they are often more 'self-contained' and give the knowledgeable student a better opportunity to achieve a good mark, than questions in many other more complex areas of Evidence.

12.4 Questions

QUESTION ONE

'It is universally recognised that ... there are two kinds of public interest which may clash. There is the public interest that harm shall not be done to the nation or the public service by disclosure of certain documents, and there is the public interest that the administration of justice is to be done.' (Lord Reid in *Conway* v *Rimmer*)

Discuss critically the principles upon which the courts attempt to resolve this conflict.

University of London LLB Examination
(for External Students) Evidence June 1992 Q1

General Comment

This question requires a discussion of the principles which govern the court's examination of claims of 'public interest'. You should examine the criteria which the courts use when faced with an assertion of 'public interest'.

Skeleton Solution

- Types of public interest.
- National security.
- Investigation of crime.
- Confidential/personal statements.
- *Duncan* v *Cammell Laird & Co* criteria.
- *Conway* v *Rimmer* criteria.
- Public interest v proper administration of justice.
- Contents claim v class claim.

Suggested Solution

A claim or assertion of 'public interest' is often raised in order to prevent disclosure of documents which would otherwise have to be disclosed. The courts, when faced with a claim of 'public interest' immunity from disclosure, have to perform a balancing act between the interests of the state in non-disclosure of potentially damaging documents and the proper administration of justice which requires the production of documents which a party has in its possession, custody or power which relate to an issue in dispute between the parties to litigation.

Privilege from the duty to disclose documents is a right which a party has. However, that party must assert its right to withhold a document from disclosure. Refusing to disclose a document on the grounds of public interest immunity or public policy is a duty as well as a right (as stated by Lord Simon in the case of *Rogers* v *Home Secretary* (1973). The court must protect documents which are privileged or immune from disclosure because of the 'public interest' and it is also under a duty to ensure that such documents are not disclosed.

The case of *Duncan* v *Cammell Laird & Co Ltd* (1942) was one of the first cases which dealt with the vexed problem of 'public interest' immunity. It concerned the sinking of the submarine Thetis.

Thirty-nine lives were lost when the Thetis sank. The plaintiffs sued Cammel Laird in negligence (Cammel Laird built the Thetis). The plaintiffs sought discovery of the contract between the defendant and the Government for the construction of the Thetis. The Board of Admiralty objected to the production of the contract on the grounds of public interest. The court upheld the Admiralty's objection.

Lord Simon, who gave the leading judgment in the case, held that where a government minister objects to the disclosure of documents on the grounds that the disclosure would damage, for example, the country's defence, the court could not go beyond that objection. Such objection would bind the courts. It was clear from Lord Simon's judgment that the Executive would be able to determine what types of documents were privileged from production. In effect the court subverted its power of enquiry to the Executive.

The ruling in *Duncan* was criticised on many occasions. Devlin J in the case of *Ellis* v *Home*

Office (1953) expressed considerable dissatisfaction with the ruling in *Duncan*. Devlin J was concerned with the most worrying aspect of the effect of *Duncan*, that justice would not be seen to be done. Devlin's worries were addressed by the House of Lords in the case of *Conway* v *Rimmer* (1968).

In *Conway* the House of Lords cast considerable doubt on the reasoning behind the decision in *Duncan*. It was held that the question whether evidence should be withheld from disclosure on the grounds of public interest was a question for the court only. The House decided that a government minister's decision was not binding on the courts. Although great weight would be placed on a minister's opinion the final decision was for the courts.

The House of Lords specifically addressed the question of 'class' and 'contents' claims in relation to public interest immunity. It was held that documents which are alleged to be immune from disclosure because of the class which they fall in would be examined fully and they would not be privileged from production just because they fall within a specified class. The House criticised the argument that whole classes of documents should be withheld just because it might inhibit freedom of expression within public service. In relation to 'contents' claims the court said that it would be rare to order disclosure of such a document, the argument being that they were protected from disclosure because their contents would be damaging. In 'class' claims the real question for the court will be whether withholding of such documents would be really necessary for the functioning of the public service.

The underlying reasoning in *Conway* was that ultimately the decision whether a document should be disclosed lies with the court and not the executive. This reasoning was followed in *Burmah Oil Co Ltd* v *Bank of England* (1980) where it was held that no class of document would ever be absolutely immune from production. In the case of *Air Canada* v *Secretary of State for Trade (No 2)* (1983) the House of Lords re-asserted that disclosure of high level government documents could be ordered. The question for the court in the Air Canada case was whether the documents were helpful evidentially. It seems that the court will only withhold such documents if they cannot assist the proceedings. Lord Fraser expressed the view that even Cabinet minutes are not immune from disclosure. However, he did state that they were entitled to the highest protection.

It is quite clear from the authorities that it is not only government bodies or authorities which are entitled to rely on public interest for withholding documents. In the case of *D* v *NSPCC* (1978) the House of Lords rejected the plaintiff's application for discovery of documents which could prove the identity of an NSPCC informant. The House acknowledged the importance of the NSPCC's work and the public interest in allowing the free, unimpeded flow of information. Lord Hailsham accepted that the categories of public interest are not closed.

The main categories of public interest are:

a) National security, diplomatic relations and international comity.

b) Information for the detection of crime.

c) Confidential and personal statements.

It is well established that information and documents can be withheld on the grounds of national security; diplomatic relations and international comity. The reasoning behind this is that the public interest requires the promotion of these matters. Furthermore, the public interest requires that police informers be protected; the public has a vested interest in the supply of information which can assist in the detection of crime. For example, a witness cannot be asked to name a police informer: see *R* v *Taroy* (1794). However, if a defendant can show that disclosure of an informer's name can assist in establishing innocence then disclosure will be allowed: see *R* v *Hennessey* (1978).

In relation to confidential relationships, disclosure will not be ordered as it can threaten the very existence of the confidential relationship. Such relationships include that as between priest and parishioner, doctor and patient and journalist and source. The leading case on this matter is *Science Research Council* v *Nassé* (1980) where it was held that the important test is whether discovery is necessary for disposing fairly of the proceedings. If it is necessary then the court will order discovery but the court will consider whether there are other means by which the evidence can be disclosed.

Accordingly, when issues of public interest arise, the court performs a 'balancing act' between the public interest in keeping documents disclosed and the public interest in justice being done and being seen to be done. By retaining a power to review claims of public interest the court can ensure that claims are tested in accordance with law and legal principles. One of the most alarming aspects of the decision in Duncan was that the Executive could usurp the function of the courts. However, the result of Conway is that, in principle, the Executive's powers have been curtailed and the courts have ensured that its pre-eminence in such matters is asserted.

QUESTION TWO

'Exclusion of evidence on the ground of public policy as a matter of law has only one thing in common with the exclusion of evidence which is illegally obtained as a matter of discretion: the absence of any coherent policy rationale underlying the case law.'

Discuss.

University of London LLB Examination
(for External Students) Evidence June 1987 Q3

Skeleton Solution

- Categories of case covered by public policy – state secrets – minor state secrets, identity of police informants, identity of other informants.
- Exclusion of evidence under s78 Police and Criminal Evidence Act 1984 – disciplinary and reliability approach of courts.
- Public interest in protection of civil liberties.

Suggested Solution

The exclusion of evidence on the ground of public policy is sometimes referred to as Crown privilege, public interest privilege or public interest immunity. Evidence will be excluded on grounds of public policy as a matter of law where it is deemed not to be in the public interest to allow it to be given. The privilege arises in relation to four different types or sources of information: (a) state secrets; (b) minor state interests; (c) identity of informants to the police; and (d) identity of other informants.

State secrets comprise, in general terms, matters involving the armed forces and the intelligence services. The courts have always been reluctant to allow any information to be given where the government has indicated that it should be kept secret. The policy behind this is that it is not for the courts but for government to take decisions about defence of the realm, which includes decisions about how much information should be made public of military and intelligence operations. The equation of the public interest with the interests of the government of the day is always criticised by the party of opposition, but once that party takes over in government it is quite content to use the equation in its own interest.

There are certain classes of document which the courts used to say are always privileged, for example cabinet minutes (*Conway* v *Rimmer* (1968)), but the tendency today is to examine each claim for immunity on its merits *Burmah Oil Co* v *Bank of England* (1980)). Where state secrets are involved the courts will not allow their repetition in court save in the most exceptional circumstances (*Burmah Oil Co* v *Bank of England*; *Air Canada* v *Secretary of State for Trade (No 2)* (1983)). The court will have received a certificate from a minister or senior civil servant setting out the reason why immunity is claimed and will hear the other party's outline reasons why the document should be disclosed and a balance must be struck. Either the nature of the information or its source will be a good enough reason for non-disclosure in a state-secrets case, or if the court is in some doubt about whether the information really is a secret then it may have a look at the document to see for itself, although it is reluctant to use this right.

The protection of minor state interests can be cited as a reason for withholding documents and these include matters of the internal operation of government departments. In such cases the court will rarely say that the information in the documents is of a type which should not be disclosed but may justify immunity by citing the type of document as being a type which should not be disclosed. It is usually where third parties have given the information in confidence that the court will uphold a claim to immunity (*Alfred Crompton Amusement Machines Ltd* v *Customs and Excise Commissioners* (1974)), but in the absence of involvement of innocent third parties there is no reluctance to order disclosure even where the government has said it is contrary to the public interest, provided that the nature of the document or of the information is such that the court is able to say that it cannot harm the nation's interests to order disclosure. There are cases which suggest that many internal government reports can be withheld (*Re Joseph Hargreaves* (1900); *Ellis* v *Home Office* (1953); *Broome* v *Broome* (1955)) but their authority is doubted by Cross, and since the court will now always balance the public interest in keeping them secret against the public interest in allowing a party full access to documents he needs in litigation (*Ellis* v *Home Office*), they cannot be treated as authoritative.

It is a cardinal rule that the police do not have to disclose the identity of informants. This rule has stood since well before *Marks* v *Beyfus* (1890) and cannot be challenged now, save in the most exceptional circumstances, for example in the case of *R* v *Agar* (1990). Recently the Court of Appeal has shown on a further three occasions that it is prepared to investigate whether the withholding of the informant's identity is in the public interest (*Neilson* v *Laugharne* (1981); *Hehir* v *Commissioner of Police for the Metropolis* (1982); *Peach* v *Commissioner of Police for the Metropolis* (1986)).

Two reasons have been given for this rule, firstly that sources of information may dry up and secondly that information given to the police is given in confidence and the confidence should be respected. There is, it seems, little evidence to support the first reason; but the second is persuasive. Today the court will attempt to balance the public interests cited above, but when deciding the strength of the public interest in keeping the information secret it will take into account the desirability of retaining confidence.

Informing public bodies other than the police of certain types of wrongdoing is likely to be done in confidence in the same way as information give to the police is given in confidence, but the rule appears to be that there can be no privilege arising out of confidentiality alone. Public interest immunity can arise where the recipient of the information has a statutory function to perform, but not otherwise (*D* v *NSPCC* (1978)). The apparent justification is that the scope of public interest immunity must be limited and that there can be no public interest in maintaining secrecy unless the purpose of giving the information is to start investigations.

It is clear that the courts will always try to balance the public interest in keeping matters secret against the public interest in allowing a litigant access to all information which he may need in litigation. The different types of information and the different sources from which it may come mean that different factors will be weighed when the balancing operation is done. In the recent case of *Brown* v *Matthews* (1990), the public interest in keeping a court welfare report secret was said to have to be weighed against the need for the contents of the report to be put into evidence if there was to be a fair trial. Nevertheless, it is also clear that until 1979 the balancing operation was not universally recognised and there are many cases giving different reasons for upholding or rejecting a claim of public interest immunity.

The exclusion of evidence obtained by illegal means is a matter for the discretion of the court under s78 of the Police and Criminal Evidence Act 1984. Prior to the enactment of that statutory discretion the courts had built up a complex body of law from which it was clear that a discretion existed in some circumstances but far from clear what those circumstances were. The rationale lying behind the exclusion of interest obtained by illegal means has never been clearly explained. In recent cases on the exclusionary discretion under s78, the accent has been on the 'unfairness' of admitting evidence improperly obtained, but the courts vacillate between a 'disciplinary' and 'reliability' approach (*R* v *Mason* (1987); *R* v *Alladice* (1987); *DPP* v *Marshall* (1988) and *R* v *Quinn* (1990)). Illegally, or improperly, obtained evidence (other than confessions) is admissible under English law; whether it will be excluded in any particular case depends on whether admissibility would result in unfairness, and/or whether the prejudicial effect of the evidence outweighs its probative value – but this is a matter of discretion rather than law.

One thing which is now clear about the exclusion of evidence obtained illegally is that the courts adopt the balancing operation applicable to claims of public interest immunity; they balance the public interest in using relevant probative evidence against the public interest in the protection of civil liberties (*R* v *Samuel* (1988)). Indeed it is important to note that once evidence has been obtained illegally, there is a discretion and not a duty to exclude it, and this, of course, differs from the position in true cases of public interest immunity where exclusion is a matter of law not discretion once the criteria for exclusion have been laid down.

QUESTION THREE

'The categories of public interest are not closed and must alter from time to time whether by restriction or extension as social conditions and social legislation develop.' (Lord Hailsham in *D* v *NSPCC*).

Discuss in relation to the law of evidence.

University of London Examination
(for External Students) Law of Evidence June 1993 Q2

General Comment

This is a wide open question which appears with some frequency. Here is chance to make some interesting jurisprudential statements about the relationship between policy and principle and/or the role of the judiciary in restraining self-interested decisions by government bodies (jurisprudence is not confined to jurisprudence!). It is important to give the history of the idea, arising from what was formerly known as 'Crown privilege' and then proceeding through *Duncan* v *Cammell Laird* and *Conway* v *Rimmer*; from then on it is over to you: the extensions are fairly easily noted (eg to the NSPCC) but the rationale, not easy to extract from the cases, is not.

Skeleton Solution

- Meaning of 'Crown privilege'.
- *Duncan* v *Cammell Laird*.
- The 'balancing act of the judge'.
- *D* v *NSPCC* and *Conway* v *Rimmer*.
- The idea of the minister's certificate in the light of the overall public interest.
- The subsequent developments (*Air Canada*, and others).
- The special extension in relation to crime.
- Subsequent analogous bodies.
- The confidentiality category of 'the public interest'.

Suggested Solution

Public interest privilege was originally termed 'Crown privilege' and was defined as having been the absolute right of the Crown to object to producing documents in court on the ground that it would be against the public interest to do so. The claim, made in an affidavit by a minister of the Crown, would prevent the court from looking at those documents; that principle was firmly established in *Duncan* v *Cammell Laird* (1942). Today, the phrase is regarded as a misleading misnomer (see, for example, Lord Simon in *R* v *Lewes JJ* (1973)) and although a minister of the crown is often the most appropriate person to assert the public interest, it is open to *any* interested person to raise the question; indeed, the trial judge himself may raise it. In *D* v *NSPCC* (1978), for example, Lord Simon concluded that the state could not be restricted to the Crown and the departments of central government but included the whole organisation of all the legal institutions concerned with civil rule and government. Formerly, it was considered that only the organs of central government could assert the privilege. In *D* v *NSPCC*, for example, it was extended to the National Society for the Prevention of Cruelty to Children.

If a party to litigation claims that certain documents are privileged from disclosure on the grounds of public policy, the court must hold the balance between that public interest and the public interest in the disclosure of the documents to ensure the proper administration of justice. This test was adopted in *Conway* v *Rimmer* (1968), where the House of Lords rejected their previous ruling in *Duncan* v *Cammell Laird* that the minister's certificate was conclusive and binding on the court. Although there is an argument that a minister is better placed to assess the public interest, there is also an argument about abuse of power (ever more important these days); ministers could assess (even unconsciously) the public interest to be that which equated with the party or government in power. *Conway* v *Rimmer* represented a welcome reform by ending the possibility of ministerial misuse of power by requests for immunity in cases where the alleged public interest was barely discernible yet non-disclosure of the documents could have resulted in a partial or complete denial of justice to the parties.

The judge may, therefore, now question ministerial assertions that documents be withheld and may balance against this the importance of the documents to the litigation and justice, and the importance of the litigation to the parties, provided that the party seeking disclosure has shown that the information is likely to help his own case or damage his adversary's in the sense that there is a reasonable probability, not a mere speculative belief, that it will do so (see, for example, *Air Canada* v *Secretary of State for Trade (No 2)* (1983)). That this method of judging a claim of privilege on the grounds of public policy represents a fair balance between the competing public interests may be shown by contrasting *Burmah Oil* v *Bank of England* (1980) and *Williams* v *Home Office* (1981). In the former case, an inspection of documents relating to the formulation of government economic policy, it was held that they contained nothing of sufficient evidential value to order their disclosure. By contrast, in *Williams*, a case involving the rights of the citizen and the liberty of the subject, on inspection of the documents, disclosure was ordered. The public interest in justice prevailed over the fact that disclosure could lead to ill-informed criticism of the Home Office.

It should be noted that there is a more inflexible rule in relation to information for the detection of crime. The rule, subject to few exceptions, is that in public prosecutions, and in civil proceedings arising from them, no questions may be asked and no evidence given, which would reveal the identity of an informant whose information led to the prosecution (*Marks* v *Beyfus* (1890)). The realistic and sensible basis for this rule is the danger that if disclosure were permitted, informants would be deterred from coming forward to help the police for fear of reprisal. This rule has been extended, by way of analogy, to persons supplying information to other bodies (See, for example, *R* v *Lewes JJ*, *D* v *NSPCC*, *Alfred Crompton Amusement Machines Ltd* v *Customs and Excise Commissioners* (1974)).

In each of these cases, the decision against disclosure was based upon the danger of the sources drying up (which would in turn lead to an impairment of the efficiency of those parts of the public service in question, ie, the Gaming Board, the NSPCC and the Inland Revenue). The fact that such information is given in confidence is not in itself sufficient to create public interest immunity, but it is a material factor to be taken into account in deciding the privilege claim. It is for this reason that the above cases may be legitimately reconciled with the other confidentially cases (for example, *Science Research Council* v *Nassé* (1980) and *BSC* v *Granada Television Ltd* (1982)). In *R* v *Agar* (1990), it was made clear, however, that the public interest in keeping the identity of an informant a secret had to be balanced against the public interest in seeing that a defendant is well able to defend his case in criminal proceedings. It is clear that the immunity of the press from revealing its sources of information should be regarded as being in the public interest, given its importance for the democratic nature of our institutions (see *On Liberty* by John Stuart Mill, for example), even more so than the efficient functioning of the public service, and that the freedom of the press depends upon immunity.

QUESTION FOUR

'Confidentiality is not a separate head of privilege, but it may be a very material consideration to bear in mind when privilege is claimed on the ground of public interest.' (Lord Cross in *Alfred Crompton Amusement Machines Ltd* v *Commissioners of Customs and Excise (No 2)*).

Discuss.

University of London LLB Examination
(for External Students) Evidence June 1990 Q2

Skeleton Solution

• Balance of interests with public interest immunity.

• 'High' grade to 'low' grade documents – confidentiality less relevant.

• Confidentiality more relevant with public agencies, and police informants.

• Journalistic privilege – s10 Contempt of Court Act 1981.

Suggested Solution

There are three main situations in which evidence can be withheld on grounds of privilege. Broadly, they are first, where by giving the evidence a witness exposes himself to the possibility of criminal proceedings (the privilege against self-incrimination), second, evidence of communications between party to proceedings and his lawyer or by a third party with either (legal professional privilege) and third, privilege arising on grounds of public interest (public interest immunity).

Confidentiality does not therefore of itself feature as a basis for exclusion. That said, it is true that confidentiality plays a substantial role in excluding evidence on grounds of public interest. This role will now examined.

Until comparatively recent times, establishing a claim to privilege on grounds of public interest was a relatively simple business. The minister or other political head of the organ of State claiming a privilege would submit a certificate and the courts regarded that certificate as final. This approach was approved by the House of Lords in *Duncan* v *Cammell Laird* (1942). The approach changed with the subsequent decision of the House of Lords in *Conway* v *Rimmer* (1968). That case established that the minister's view of the public interest was not conclusive and that the courts have a residual power to decide where that interest lies. It is in the evaluation that confidentiality plays a leading, though not necessarily explicit, part.

The approach adopted depends upon the type of document for which immunity is claimed. It has become the practice since *Duncan* v *Cammell Laird* for a claim of public interest privilege to be made on a contents or class basis. In the former case, the claim is that the particular document in question should not be disclosed in the public interest. It is clear from *Conway* v *Rimmer* that such a claim is very unlikely to be interfered with by the courts. Accordingly, the basis of the claim is unlikely to be investigated though it is readily apparent that the underlying reason for the claim for privilege and the reason for upholding it is the requirement of confidentiality for highly sensitive documents. For a class claim (where a claim is made on the basis that the document falls within a class of documents which should be withheld from production in the public interest) the role of confidentiality is even more evident. For class claims relative to 'high grade' documents such as Cabinet papers, privilege is very likely, subject to inspection of the relevant documents by the court, to be upheld and the usual basis is the sensitive nature of the material and the consequent need for confidentiality. This much is clear from *Conway* v *Rimmer* and subsequent authorities including *Burmah Oil* v *Bank of England* (1980) and *Air Canada* v *Secretary of State for Trade (No 2)* (1983). On the other hand, for lower grade documents or routine reports, a class claim based on confidentiality arising from the assertion that officials would feel inhibited from expressing their views if they thought that the information was to be disclosed (the 'candour' principle) is unlikely to be successful. The House of Lords in *Conway* v *Rimmer* made this clear and the courts have since rejected such claims consistently if based on this premise.

There are, however, circumstances where confidentiality in respect of routine information will found a successful claim for privilege in the public interest. These arise where disclosure might result in the drying up of information on which a public agency depends for undertaking work in the public interest. The *Alfred Crompton* case (1974) referred to in the question and *D* v *NSPCC* (1978) are examples. In the latter case, an order for disclosure of the identity of the individual who supplied information to the NSPCC about alleged cruelty to a child was refused. The information was routine but if disclosed people would be dissuaded from volunteering information to the NSPCC. If that happened, the work of the NSPCC in protecting children, manifestly in the public interest, would be seriously impeded. Similar principles can be seen in exclusion of evidence of the identity of police informers which can also be claimed under public interest privilege. *Marks* v *Beyfus* (1890) is authority for that proposition. The principle has been extended in *R* v *Rankine* (1986) to premises from which police conduct surveillance, although *R* v *Johnson* (1989) makes clear that the need for confidentiality must be made out on the evidence; such evidence should include the attitude of the occupier of the premises to be identified. Disclosure may also be ordered if it is necessary to establish an accused's innocence – *R* v *Agar* (1990).

The final area of public interest which requires comment arises in the context of the role of confidentiality in journalistic information. This is now subject to statutory intervention in the form of s10 of the Contempt of Court Act 1981. Under that section, journalistic sources are provided with protection in the public interest unless it is established to the satisfaction of the court that disclosure is necessary in the interests of justice, national security or the prevention of disorder or crime. The requirement for confidentiality in the public interest is nowhere stated in the section, but it is clear from the common law which preceded it and from *Secretary of State for Defence* v *Guardian Newspapers* (1984) that the protection of journalistic information by reason of confidentiality in the public interest forms its basis. Indeed, that is perhaps obvious because in the absence of such protection sources might well be reluctant to come forward to the media and the public would thereby be deprived of information which may be a matter of legitimate concern to them.

13 Privilege

13.1 Introduction

As with public policy in the previous chapter, privilege is an area where relevant evidence is capable of admissibility but is excluded (or may be excluded) by some extrinsic rule which denies the court the benefit of that evidence. One bald distinction between public interest immunity and privilege is that in the case of the latter the person in whom the privilege vests may waive it and thus allow the court to hear the evidence, whereas in the case of the former the decision as to disclosure of the evidence is for the court, not the witness or party. Further, evidence which is privileged may nevertheless be put before the court in some circumstances in secondary as opposed to primary form, but if evidence is the subject of public interest immunity, then the immunity cannot be circumvented by adducing secondary evidence. In this area the law is continually developing, particularly in regard to journalistic, or media, privilege.

13.2 Key points

There are four main heads under which privilege falls to be considered, ie self-incrimination privilege; legal professional privilege; 'without prejudice' communications; journalistic privilege. This fourth head highlights the blurring of the distinction between privilege and public policy which often occurs when there is a claim for non-disclosure of evidence. In all cases of privilege, however, what must be borne in mind is that although a witness is both competent and compellable, to testify does not mean to answer every question put – privilege may be claimed, and if claimed successfully no inferences may be drawn from the refusal to answer questions.

a) *Self-incrimination privilege*

Any witness may refuse to answer a question (in examination in chief or in cross-examination) if the answer would tend to expose him to a criminal charge, penalty or, in criminal proceedings only, a forfeiture. It is for the court to decide whether there is a likelihood of any such consequence: *BSC* v *Granada TV* [1982] AC 1096. Self incrimination includes incrimination of one's spouse, but whether it includes incrimination of one's employer, principal etc has not been decided: *RTZ Corporation* v *Westinghouse Electric Corporation* [1978] AC 547. Without doubt an out-of-court admission by a servant etc is not capable of amounting at common law to an admission against the interest of the employer: *Burr* v *Ware RDC* [1939] 2 All ER 688, therefore it would seem to follow that until there is some statutory intervention a servant cannot claim a right not to answer a question tending to incriminate his employer, because such a question should not be put – but this reasoning cannot be employed to agents of principals, directors of companies etc.

If a witness is wrongly compelled to answer a question where the answer tends to expose him to criminal proceedings, then the answer is treated as an inadmissible confession. The privilege is not available to an accused in respect of the charge he faces, whether the question be put in cross-examination during the trial or on the *voir dire* – but the accused who testifies can refuse to answer questions where the answer would tend to expose him to other criminal proceedings. The privilege is under some attack in civil actions, see Lord Templeman in *AT & T Istel* v *Tully* [1992] 3 All ER 523 at 530.

b) *Legal professional privilege*

This covers both communications between lawyer and client regarding legal advice, and communications between client and/or lawyer and other persons where the 'dominant purpose' is to seek advice, opinion etc preparatory to contemplated or pending legal proceedings. In *Ventouris* v *Mountain* (1991) The Independent 4 March the Court of Appeal held that legal professional privilege could not attach to original documents which did not come into existence for the purposes of the litigation, but were already in existence before litigation was contemplated or commenced.

i) Lawyer-client communications

These are privileged (the privilege is in the client, who may therefore waive it) whether or not proceedings are pending, provided the purpose was to obtain, or give legal advice. Other communications made between lawyer and client, although not specifically seeking or giving legal advice, are similarly protected from disclosure, given they are part of the ongoing relationship: *Balabel* v *Air-India* [1988] 2 All ER 246. The lawyer need not be a solicitor or barrister, ie could be an unqualified employee, or in matters relating to conveyancing could be a licensed conveyancer: s33 Administration of Justice Act 1985.

The privilege does not attach to communications made to assist the client to commit crimes or to defraud, whether or not the lawyer is aware of the client's motive for seeking advice: *R* v *Cox and Railton* (1884) 14 QBD 153. But a distinction must be drawn between communications made to facilitate, or assist in, commission of crime or tort giving rise to the instant proceedings (no privilege) and those which relate to other wrongdoing even though relevant in the instant proceedings: *R* v *Crown Court at Snaresbrook, ex parte DPP* [1988] 1 All ER 315. Also, for the purpose of s10 of the Police and Criminal Evidence Act 1984, if items are held for the furtherance of some criminal purpose it is irrelevant whether the person holding the items is aware of the criminal purpose or not: *Francis & Francis* v *Central Criminal Court* [1988] 3 All ER 775. No privilege attaches, per *Cox and Railton*, supra. The definition of 'furthering a criminal purpose' is restricted to some extent so that it does not extend to every unlawful scheme; for example, it does not apply to a conveyance carried out without consideration designed to defeat creditors – *Re Konigsberg* [1989] 3 All ER 289. In order to determine whether documents fall within s10(2) Police and Criminal Evidence Act 1984, the court has the power to inspect the documents – *R* v *Governor of Pentonville Prison, ex parte Osman* [1989] 3 All ER 701.

Legal professional privilege will not usually apply to communications, otherwise privileged, the production of which can assist in the defence of an accused person: *R* v *Barton* [1973] 1 WLR 115. But the court must consider the conflicting interests of respecting legal professional confidences and promoting the proper administration of justice: *R* v *Ataou* [1988] 2 All ER 321.

Where privilege attaches to a communication it attaches to the original only. If the communication falls into the hands of a third party who makes a copy, or if an oral communication is overheard, then a witness may give that secondary evidence of the communication: *Calcraft* v *Guest* [1898] 1 QB 759; *R* v *Tompkins* (1977) 67 Cr App R 181.

Where the party in whom the privilege vests is aware of the fact that the other party intends to adduce secondary evidence he may seek an injunction restraining the disclosure of the privileged information, and it is immaterial whether the other party obtained the material by some unfair means or fortuitously: *Lord Ashburton* v *Pape* [1913] 2 Ch 469; *Guinness Peat Properties* v *Fitzroy Robinson* [1987] 2 All ER 716. The case of *Webster* v *James Chapman* [1989] 3 All ER 939 said that where protection of confidential information was sought the court was required to exercise its discretion by balancing the legitimate interests of the plaintiff in seeking to keep the confidential information suppressed, and the legitimate interests of the defendant in seeking to make use of it. In carrying out that balancing exercise the circumstances in which the information came into the hands of the defendant, the issues in the action, the relevance of the document and whether the document would in one way or another have to be disclosed, were all highly relevant. In *Derby & Co Ltd* v *Weldon (No 8)* [1990] 3 All ER 762, the court held that where privileged documents came into the hands of the other side, inadvertently, and the other side must have realised a mistake had been made, the court had the power to intervene and order the other side to return all copies of the privileged documents and to grant an injunction to stop them using the information contained in or derived from documents. An injunction is an equitable remedy and therefore discretionary; it has been held that where privileged documents were filched in the courtroom they could not be used: *ITC Film Distributors* v *Video Exchange* [1982] Ch 431. It has also been held that no injunction will be granted to restrain the prosecution from adducing secondary evidence of privileged communications which have inadvertently fallen into their possession: *Butler* v *Board of Trade* [1971] Ch 680.

The person in whom the privilege vests, ie the client, may waive the privilege; an express waiver results in the lawyer having to answer any questions put to him about the communications in question. Alternatively, the client may, when testifying, impliedly waive the privilege by giving evidence about the content of such communications. Similarly, where a plaintiff alleged a letter had been deliberately concealed from him by his former solicitors (M and O), he was held to have waived the legal professional privilege in respect of documents going to the issues in that case. The plaintiff K had brought proceedings against W, his solicitor subsequent to M and O, who in turn sought discovery of documents (papers and letters which had passed between the plaintiff and his former solicitors M and O in previous related proceedings) and pleaded limitation. Discovery of these documents was crucial to the limitation issue, as the plaintiff claimed that he was not aware, and could not with due diligence have been aware earlier of the letter giving rise to the current proceedings. By claiming that the letter in question had been deliberately concealed from him, the plaintiff had waived the privilege in respect of solicitor/client material relating to that issue: *Kershaw* v *Whelan* [1996] 1 WLR 358.

The client may also impliedly waive privilege by including a privileged document in the list exchanged between parties. If this has happened, the court should then conduct a balancing exercise to see whether or not the other side should be allowed to use this document (*Webster* v *James Chapman* (above)); but, if the other side must have realised the mistake, the court should order the return of the document and grant an injunction to stop the use of the information (*Derby & Co Ltd* v *Weldon (No 8)* (above)).

ii) Communications with third parties

Similar principles apply to those applicable to lawyer–client communications. However, for privilege to attach, communications with third parties must have been made in contemplation of litigation, eg seeking expert's opinion. There may be several purposes to be served by lawyer or client communicating with a third party, but if the communication is to be privileged under this head, the *dominant* purpose must be preparation for anticipated litigation: *Waugh* v *British Railways Board* [1981] 1 QB 736; cf *Peach* v *Commissioner of Police for the Metropolis* [1986] 2 All ER 129.

c) *Without prejudice communications*

Because one of the major objectives of civil procedure is settlement without resort to litigation, parties to a prospective or potential civil suit, and their lawyers, must be able to negotiate and make offers of settlement or compromise without the fear of such communications being admitted in evidence against them – as admissions of liability – if the attempts at settlement fail and litigation ensues. To remove such fear of disclosure in court if negotiations break down, privilege attaches to such 'without prejudice' communications.

This privilege is in many respects more valuable than legal professional privilege:

i) it is a *joint* privilege of both the parties, and their lawyers;

ii) waiver must be by *both* parties to be effective;

iii) the communication cannot be proved by secondary evidence.

Communications do not necessarily have to be headed 'without prejudice' for the privilege to attach; conversely the phrase 'without prejudice' on a communication does not automatically vest privilege in it – ultimately any dispute as to privilege will be resolved by the court: *South Shropshire District Council* v *Amos* [1987] 1 All ER 340; *Buckinghamshire County Council* v *Moran* [1989] 3 WLR 152.

A privilege similar to that attaching to such 'without prejudice' communications attaches (by analogy) to communications made in the course of attempts at matrimonial reconciliation. These may be communications between the spouses, or communications between spouse and conciliator. The conciliator may be someone such as a marriage guidance counsellor, probation officer, priest, doctor or any other individual who is invited to assist in reconciliation: *Theodoropoulas* v *Theodoropoulas* [1964] P 311; *Mole* v *Mole* [1951] P 21 and see Lord Simon's statement regarding the public policy underlying this privilege in *D* v *NSPCC* [1978] AC 171 at p236.

d) *Journalistic privilege*

Sometimes dealt with as part of public interest immunity, but it may be waived by the journalist who decides to disclose his sources, therefore, although to some extent 'straddling' public policy and private privilege, it seems to be correctly placed in the latter area of non-disclosure.

A journalist may decline to answer questions which would result in disclosure of his source of information contained in a publication – but this privilege is not without restriction. There are conflicting interests, viz:

i)   freedom of the press, and the public's right to know;

ii) interests of administration of justice; prevention of crime;

iii) efficient functioning of the press if sources are open to disclosure and therefore may dry up (drawing an analogy with police and their sources).

Section 10 of the Contempt of Court Act 1981 recognises that sources of information may be privileged, *unless* disclosure is necessary 'in the interests of justice or national security or for the prevention of disorder or crime'.

Where disclosure is sought, the burden of proving that it is necessary for one of the four specified reasons is on the party seeking such disclosure: *Secretary of State for Defence* v *Guardian Newspapers* [1984] 3 All ER 601. As regards the definition of 'necessary in the interests of justice', in the case of *X Ltd* v *Morgan-Grampian Ltd* [1990] 2 WLR 1000 the House of Lords said it should not just mean administration of justice in legal proceedings. It should mean that persons should be enabled to exercise important legal rights and to protect themselves from serious legal wrongs whether or not court proceedings will be necessary to do this. As regards 'prevention of crime' as a reason for disclosure of the source of information, the party seeking disclosure does not need to specify any particular crime which will be prevented, but merely satisfy the court that disclosure is necessary to prevent criminal activity generally – which substantially erodes the privilege: *Re an Inquiry under the Company Securities (Insider Dealing) Act 1985* [1988] 1 All ER 203. However, there must be sufficient evidence to satisfy the court that disclosure is *necessary* for the prevention of crime: *X* v *Y* [1988] 2 All ER 648, otherwise, if the burden of proof is not discharged by the party seeking disclosure, the privilege of the journalist prevails.

13.3 Analysis of questions

Privilege tends to arise quite regularly, often in conjunction with public interest immunity or with documentary evidence, especially documentary hearsay. Occasionally essay questions are set dealing with some area of privilege, eg self-incrimination privilege, therefore requiring knowledge of the right to silence and inadmissible confessions, but very often it is the blurred distinction between privilege and public interest immunity which is the pivotal point of essay questions in this area.

13.4 Questions

QUESTION ONE

'Because the extent of rules of privilege is to deprive the tribunal of relevant evidence, powerful arguments are required to justify their existence.' (Cross).

What are the 'powerful arguments' which justify legal professional privilege and 'without prejudice' privilege? Are they convincing?

University of London LLB Examination
(for External Students) Law of Evidence June 1995 Q3

General Comment

It is necessary here to deal with the limits of each type of privilege, illustrating to what extent the privilege attaches and who has the privilege. This will show just what is denied to the tribunal, and to what extent this can be overcome in other ways. The answer should conclude by looking at the advantages to the parties and the legal system generally provided by the privileges.

Skeleton Solution

Legal professional privilege – describe its scope with emphasis on the narrowness of application, illegality exception, etc.

Describe ways of using overlapping evidence, secondary evidence, etc.

Give arguments justifying legal professional privilege, and extend these to without prejudice privilege.

Conclude by illustrating overwhelming advantages of having the privileges, protection of parties, preventing unnecessary and oppressive litigation.

Suggested Solution

Legal professional privilege may be described as that privilege against disclosure that the law provides to certain communications between client and lawyer, and between either of them and third parties. Communications between client and lawyer are privileged in so far as they concern the obtaining, giving and receiving of legal advice. Whether or not litigation is contemplated or proceeding, such communications are privileged against disclosure (*Wheeler* v *Le Marchant* (1881)). This extends to oral, as well as written, communications and the essence of it is that the communication must be intended to be confidential so that no privilege attaches if the presence of others or the context indicates non-confidentiality.

The case law shows many unsuccesful attempts to raise privilege, often in quite unusual circumstances. In *Re Konigsberg (A Bankrupt)* (1989) an attempt was made by a wife to prevent disclosure of an affidavit made by a solicitor who formerly acted for wife and husband. The affidavit had been sworn for the purposes of the husband's trustee in bankruptcy, and privilege was refused because the trustee, effectively, stood in the husband's shoes as the owner of the privilege, jointly with the wife, joint clients not being entitled to maintain the privilege against each other or to waive the benefit of privilege for the other.

The other form of legal professional privilege concerns communications between a client or his lawyer and third parties in circumstances where the dominant purpose of the communication is pending or contemplated litigation (*Waugh* v *British Railways Board* 1980)). This dominant purpose requirement is fairly strictly observed and has defeated many claims of privilege, such as in *Waugh* itself and *Neilson* v *Laugharne* (1981), although in the latter case other privilege was available. Nevertheless, the privilege can extend to in-house communications as in *Waugh* and *Alfred Crompton Amusement Machines Ltd* v *Customs and Excise Commissioners (No 2)* (1974). The whole point of the privilege is that it protects the privacy of the confidential and vulnerable parts of the client-lawyer communication, and other communications as necessary, in a litigation situation, such as *R* v *R* (1994) where the evidence of an expert defence witness on DNA was held to be a proper subject for privilege. The privilege does not protect materials which did not come into existence for a privileged purpose as in *Harmony Shipping Co SA* v *Saudi Europe Line Ltd* (1979), where an original unprivileged document was supplied to a handwriting expert within the context of privileged correspondence by one party. He was allowed to give his opinion in examination by the other side; in effect there was an overlap between evidence that he could properly give and matters protected by his own client's privilege.

The privilege cannot be abused by a client knowingly entering into communication with his lawyer as part of a fraud or a design involving clear illegality (*R* v *Cox & Railton* (1884)). Copies of privileged documents which come into the possession of the other party without impropriety appear to be completely admissible as secondary evidence on the authority of *Calcraft* v *Guest* (1898), although it may be possible to injunct this before the admission (*Ashburton* v *Pape* (1913)). The privilege is that of the client, and the obvious rationale of the privilege is to secure the candour about admissions and concessions that can only come about in confidential communication. If such matters were open to discovery they would undoubtedly lead to great difficulties in preparing cases and might well influence the judgment of the tribunal itself. This latter point is highlighted by 'without prejudice' correspondence and its growing use. Such correspondence, in which matters of negotiation or attempts to settle are discussed, is of the greatest value in preventing unnecessary litigation. The essence of the privilege is that, regardless of whether the correspondence is headed 'without prejudice' or not, provided that there is a clear understanding that this is an attempt to settle, the correspondence is not to be further used if it is unsuccessful in achieving settlement out of court. This clearly removes the constraints imposed by the possibility of the correspondence appearing before a court and of inferences being drawn. The maximum of flexibility has been introduced by the widespread acceptance and use of the Calderbank letter (*Calderbank* v *C* (1976)), which expressly retains the right to refer to the correspondence on the limited question of costs. Such letters are a vital tool where payments into court are not appropriate or possible. They can be examined by the court to determine the question whether an agreement has actually been concluded (*Tomlin* v *Standard Telephone and Cables Ltd* (1969)), the privilege having ended when the need for it ended. On balance, the range of relevant evidence denied to the courts by legal professional privilege that cannot be obtained by other means is surprisingly small. The relevant evidence that is kept from the courts by 'without prejudice' correspondence is considerable, but is often rendered unnecessary, along with the litigation of the question, by reason of the settlements reached. The arguments for both types of privilege are thoroughly convincing and justify the retention of both.

QUESTION TWO

'The law relating to privilege is in need of substantial reform.'

Discuss.

University of London LLB Examination
(for External Students) Evidence June 1989 Q7

Skeleton Solution

- Private privilege generally, and distinctive nature of public interest immunity.
- Exclusion of evidence under three main heads: self-incrimination privilege; legal professional privilege; 'without prejudice' communications.
- Arguments for reform of the law.

Suggested Solution

For evidence to be admissible it must firstly be legally relevant to the issue before the court and, given that high degree of relevance, it must not infringe any of the exclusionary rules which, for varying reasons, forbid the admission of evidence or permit a party or witness to refuse to give evidence on some issue. Evidence which is relevant may be excluded by the laws of evidence where public policy so dictates – ie the concept of 'public interest immunity' – or, alternatively, a party or a witness may be permitted to claim a privilege whereby he is not compelled to give evidence despite its relevance and reliability because there are recognised extrinsic factors which outweigh the public interest in the court's being apprised of all relevant facts in order to reach the proper conclusion.

The basic difference between 'public interest immunity' and 'privilege' is that in the case of the former the courts decide as a matter of law (and policy) whether the evidence, albeit relevant, must be excluded, in the case of the latter the party or witness may claim the privilege (in which case the court will decide on the issue of exclusion) or may waive any potential privilege, thus relieving the court of the duty to deliberate and to adjudicate on disclosure.

The successful claiming of privilege means that the court must decide the issue before it without the benefit of all the relevant facts; this, however, is fairly commonplace in the adversarial or accusatorial system in English courts where a number of exclusionary rules deprive the court of the entirety of relevant material (the hearsay rule in criminal cases is a prime example).

One general, but important, point to bear in mind is that where a person whether witness or party claims privilege, no inferences adverse to that person can be drawn (*Wentworth* v *Lloyd* (1864)).

There are three main heads of privilege:

a) *Self-incrimination privilege*

This is based on the law's encouragement of witnesses to testify without fear of being forced to choose between incriminating themselves and committing perjury and, more importantly perhaps, on the unwillingness of the law to force any person (whether a witness or a party in civil or criminal proceedings) to give evidence which will be self-incriminatory (*Blunt* v *Park Lane Hotel* (1942)). It is for the judge to decide whether there is a real as opposed to fanciful risk of criminal proceedings if the question is answered by the witness (*R* v *Boyes* (1861)). If the evidence against the witness is already so strong that proceedings will be taken whether or not the witness answers the question, then any claim of privilege will fail (*RTZ Corpn* v *Westinghouse* (1978)).

If a witness is wrongly denied the self-incrimination privilege and thus compelled to answer the question, his response, in any subsequent criminal proceedings against him, is on the same footing as an inadmissible confession and therefore cannot be used (*R* v *Garbett* (1847)). This, however, is not a great safeguard since the response will be an admission of guilt of that crime. Therefore, although that response cannot be used in subsequent proceedings, it alerts the police to the fact that the witness committed that offence and a subsequent interview could well elicit an admissible confession which could be used without any reference to the earlier proceedings or the denial of the self-incrimination privilege. Apart from that weakness, value judgments must be made when the privilege is claimed, ie is there a *real* likelihood of subsequent criminal proceedings? Are those proceedings, should they be instituted, for an offence the triviality of which is outweighed by the need to have the relevant evidence put before the court in the instant case? Given the wide margin for error by the judge, either the repugnance of enforced self-incrimination or the proper administration of justice by the admission of relevant evidence should be the one determinant. Additionally there is alarming uncertainty as to whether the privilege can be claimed by directors, agents or employees of a corporate body on behalf of the corporate body (*RTZ Corpn* v *Westinghouse*).

Finally, the privilege can be claimed in respect of the witness' spouse, but perhaps incongruously in 1989, not in respect of a co-habitant or 'common law' spouse.

b)   *Legal professional privilege*

This privilege covers two sorts of communications: (i) communications between client and legal adviser for the purpose of obtaining or giving legal advice; and (ii) those between client or lawyer and third parties (eg experts) where the dominant purpose is preparing for contemplated or imminent legal proceedings. The rationale of this privilege is said to be that the lawyer-client relationship would be unworkable if communications were liable to compulsory disclosure by the courts (*Waugh* v *British Railways Board* (1980)).

As regards lawyer-client communications under (i) above they are privileged from disclosure even though there was no prospect of litigation, provided the purpose was requesting or giving legal advice. Provided there was no question of the advice being sought or given to facilitate fraud (*R* v *Cox and Railton* (1884) but see *R* v *Crown Court at Snaresbrook, ex parte DPP* (1988)), the communication will not be disclosed in court unless the client waives the privilege. But the privilege will be overriden by the public interest in avoiding the conviction of an innocent accused person. In *R* v *Barton* (1973) it was held that no privilege attached to lawyer-client communications where their production in court could help the defence of an accused person. Obviously there is in this situation a degree of conjecture on the part of the judge in resolving the conflict between legal professional privilege and public policy regarding the administration of justice. The problem of resolution of these conflicting interests is highlighted in the case of *R* v *Ataou* (1988) (where the judge did not even avert his mind to the competing interest!).

As distinct from matters of public interest immunity or 'without prejudice' communications (infra), when legal professional privilege attaches to original documents or conversations, then these communications may be proved by secondary evidence (*Calcraft* v *Guest* (1898)). Therefore, overheard privileged conversations, duplicates of privileged documents etc may be admitted in court whether this secondary evidence has been obtained fortuitously or by some wrongful act. Where the possession of the secondary evidence becomes known to the party in whom the privilege vests, then an injunction may be obtained to prevent its disclosure, but an injunction is discretionary (*Lord Ashburton* v *Pape* (1913); *Calcraft* v *Guest*) and whatever the circumstances is not retroactive (*ITC* v *Video Exchange* (1982)). The case of *Derby & Co Ltd* v *Weldon (No 8)* (1990) suggests that where a privileged document falls into the hands of the other side by mistake, and that side must have realised the mistake, the court should exercise its discretion to prevent the information being used by that side.

An illogical distinction has been made between privileged documents stolen inside the court and those stolen elsewhere – secondary evidence of the former is not admissible; secondary evidence of the latter is admissible, subject to a speedy application for an injunction (*ITC* v *Video Exchange*).

A further illogicality is the distinction made in *Butler* v *Board of Trade* (1971) where it was held that in the case of a prosecution there can be no question of an injunction prohibiting the adducing of secondary evidence of privileged material. It was stated that public policy dictated that decision but it has since been quite strongly criticised (in *Goddard* v *Nationwide Building Society* (1986)).

Again, therefore, in the realm of legal professional privilege there abound incongruities and anomalies. Reform is long overdue to clarify the extent to which legal professional privilege attaches to primary and secondary communications in both civil and criminal proceedings. So much uncertainty and irreconcilability has been created by appellate court decisions that it may require the intervention of Parliament to clarify the law.

c) *'Without prejudice' communications*

Where attempts are being made by parties to settle their differences without litigation, then public policy dictates that there should be joint privilege attaching to such negotiations, ie they cannot be disclosed in subsequent litigation unless *both* parties agree (*La Roche* v *Armstrong* (1922); *Rush & Tompkins* v *GLC* (1988)). Unlike the illogicality in legal professional privilege, secondary evidence of the communication is not admissible because the rationale of the privilege is to encourage uninhibited negotiation, settlement, and avoidance of litigation.

The fact that the phrase 'without prejudice' is not specifically used is immaterial provided a genuine attempt was being made to settle a dispute (*Chocoladefabriken Lindt* v *The Nestlé Co Ltd* (1978)). Conversely, merely heading a document or communication 'without privilege' does not *ipso facto* render it privileged; it is for the court to determine whether it amounted to a genuine attempt to resolve a dispute without resort to litigation (*South Shropshire District Council* v *Amos* (1987)).

In this area of attempted settlements which also covers genuine attempts at matrimonial reconciliation (see *D* v *NSPCC* (1978)) the content of communications may be protected from disclosure, for sound reasons of public policy in civil law where one of the major objectives is the settlement of disputes without recourse to litigation. In this area also there is less need for reform of the law than in the other two areas of privilege discussed.

QUESTION THREE

'The rationale of legal professional privilege is inseparable from the adversarial system of litigation which would become unworkable if no document could ever be kept from an opponent.' (Cross).

Discuss.

University of London LLB Examination
(for External Students) Law of Evidence June 1994 Q2

General Comment

Legal professional privilege is a fairly discrete topic. However, to answer this question fully, it is obvious that the student requires knowledge of the adversarial/inquisitorial systems (although no great detail is needed!). Again, knowledge of possible alternative means of preventing disclosure (public interest immunity?) will be useful. Above all, the importance of the privilege within the context of the adversarial system, and generally, should be discussed.

Skeleton Solution

- Brief explanation of adversarial (inquisitorial) system.
- Brief explanation of the privilege (lawyer/client/third party).
- The exceptions to the privilege.
- Discussion:
  - Is the privilege still of importance. having considered the established exceptions?
  - Are there other means of preventing disclosure – eg, public interest immunity?
  - Are there other reasons for the importance of the privilege?

Suggested Solution

Clearly, it is in a party's interests to have all relevant facts which support his or her case before the court. However, in almost every case there will be a number of facts which may *detract* from a party's case, and which a party will therefore not wish to be disclosed. Legal professional privilege provides parties with a method of restricting the disclosure of *communications* of such facts.

As the quotation suggests, legal professional privilege (henceforward 'LPP') can be seen to be of greater importance in an adversarial system (where parties pit their evidence and arguments against each other), than in an inquisitorial system where the judge has the investigative role of sifting through the evidence. In the former system, the competitive atmosphere encourages parties to 'keep their cards close to their chest'.

Before considering whether the adversarial system would be unworkable without LPP it is useful to consider, in brief, what it entails. LPP acts to prevent disclosure of two types of communication:

i) Communications between lawyer and client: as long as the communication is for the purposes of the giving or receiving of legal advice, it is covered (*Greenhough* v *Gaskell* (1833)).

ii) Communications by either lawyer or client with third parties: such communications are privileged only if their dominant purpose is for use in anticipated or pending litigation (*Waugh* v *BRB* (1980)).

Is the adversarial system unworkable without LPP? This question is usefully addressed by considering the exceptions to the privilege.

LPP covers *communications* not facts. Thus, instructions to and from a lawyer are covered. But if a pre-existing document is shown to a lawyer it can be argued that the contents of this document are not subject to privilege (*Brown* v *Foster* (1857)). Equally, evidence perceived by a lawyer about the client (eg his mental state) is not privileged since it is a *fact* not a communication (*Jones* v *Godrich* (1845)).

The privilege is that of the client, not the lawyer; hence it may be waived by the client at any time (but not by the lawyer, who must assert it at all times). Once waived, the privilege is lost and cannot then be re-asserted by the client or the lawyer (*Lillicrap* v *Nalder & Sons* (1993)).

Legal advice sought to facilitate the commission of crime is *not* privileged (*R* v *Cox & Railton* (1884)). This applies whether or not the lawyer is aware of the purpose of the advice; however it the lawyer merely responds by warning the client that the conduct may lead to a prosecution, then the privilege remains intact (*Butler* v *Board of Trade* (1971)).

Evidence to prove innocence is not privileged – this is because the privilege gives way to the public interest in the avoidance of conviction of the innocent. Thus, if documents help to further the defence of an accused, no privilege will attach to them (*R* v *Barton* (1973)).

Legal professional privilege permits certain parties to refuse to give evidence (ie client/lawyer/certain third parties). If documents fall into the hands of persons other than the above, these persons may produce (indeed may be compelled to produce) the documents (*Calcraft* v *Guest* (1898)). This is true even if the documents are obtained by improper means (*R* v *Tompkins* (1977)) (although subject of course to other rules of evidence). However, injunctions may be granted against a party holding secondary evidence of documents if they have not as yet been used in litigation (*Lord Ashburton* v *Pape* (1913)).

In an action commenced by writ, parties must, before trial, disclose a written statement of the oral evidence of fact which they intend to adduce at trial. Failure to comply will result in that party being prevented from adducing the evidence without the leave of the judge (RSC O.38 r2A). This in effect removes the privilege in *civil* proceedings with regard to facts contained in communications, which the party wishes to adduce at trial via oral testimony.

From the above, it is clear that exceptions to LPP do exist. However, and particularly in the criminal sphere, these exceptions cannot be said to be so far-reaching as to have emasculated LPP.

As long as general confidentiality remains unprotected by the law of public interest immunity (*D* v *NSPCC* (1978)), LPP remains of great importance in a legal system under which parties are posited as adversaries. However, it is submitted that the true importance of LPP is not confined to adversarial systems of litigation. It's real importance lies in the fact that it encourages parties to state facts within their knowledge to their legal representatives, with fullness and honesty, without fear of being compelled to disclose them at a later date (per Lord Wilberforce in *Waugh* v *BRB* (1980)). Without this assurance, it is submitted, any system of litigation becomes unworkable.

QUESTION FOUR

Mrs Windfall is suing the Rest in Peace Hospital Company (RIPH) for negligently causing the death of her husband, during an operation in which the drug Happydreams had been administered by Dr Corpsemaker, one of the hospital's doctors, to Mr Windfall. Consider the issues in the law of evidence relating to the following items of evidence:

a) A research paper by Dr Ironlegs, in which he warns of the danger of administering Happydreams where a patient's heart rate is above a particular level. The paper is published in the medical journal 'Bones and Skeletons'. Dr Ironlegs is unavailable to give evidence in the case.

b) Two computerised documents produced by advanced computers at St Lucifer's hospital and St Juda's hospital recording the effects of administering Happydreams to two patients during an operation. The computer had controlled the administration of the drug during each operation according to a programme fed into it by research scientists. In each case the computer recorded the amount of the drug fed into the patient and the resultant change in heart rate.

c)   The record of a disciplinary enquiry against Dr Corpsemaker in which the hospital's Board had found him guilty of negligence. The report had been forwarded to RIPH's internal lawyers in the event that the hospital was sued or prosecuted, and the hospital have refused to give discovery of the document.

d)   The conviction of Corpsemaker for recklessly causing death on a previous occasion at another hospital.

Adapted from University of London LLB Examination
(for External Students) Evidence June 1987 Q6

Skeleton Solution

a)   • Relevance of article – documentary hearsay – s2 Civil Evidence Act 1968 – notice procedure.

b)   • Relevance – admissibility under s5 Civil Evidence Act 1968 – conditions.

c)   • Legal professional privilege – dominant purpose test.

d)   • Relevance – similar fact evidence.

     • Relevance to vicarious liability of hospital,

Suggested Solution

It is not known on what basis the Rest in Peace Hospital is being sued in negligence. It is most likely that the claim depends upon proof of the negligence of Dr Corpsemaker, for which the hospital is vicariously liable, although part (iv) indicates that there may be a claim that the hospital was primarily liable for employing Dr Corpsemaker at all.

a)   *The research paper*

The research paper could be of relevance in one of two ways, either because Dr Corpsemaker did not read it and therefore acted negligently or because he did not act according to its advice. In either case it would be necessary to prove that what it said was correct. If it is alleged that Dr Corpsemaker was negligent in not reading it then the question arises whether that caused any damage because if, in fact, the article was nonsense and would properly have been ignored then his failure to read it would not have caused any damage. If, on the other hand, the allegation is that Dr Corpsemaker, although having read it, should have followed the advice of the article then the question arises whether he acted with due care by not checking Mr Windfall's blood pressure first.

In civil proceedings documentary hearsay evidence is admissible if either it is first hand hearsay or it is second hand hearsay contained in a documentary record. In addition notice should have been served of Mrs Windfall's intention to adduce it.

It is submitted that the research paper contains first hand hearsay evidence of the truth of its contents. The maker of the assertions contained within it was Dr Ironlegs and although it would have passed through the hands of the printers they would not be making a separate statement themselves. Therefore the article as published would still have been Dr Ironlegs's statement and would be admissible under s2(1) of the Civil Evidence Act 1968. Necessarily the article would contain elements of opinion but these would be admissible because s1 Civil Evidence Act 1972 extends the 1968 Act so as to allow hearsay evidence of opinion as well as of statements of fact.

To an extent the article may contain restatements of research of people other than Dr Ironlegs. If it did then statements in it about that other research would be inadmissible because Dr Ironlegs would not be able to give direct oral evidence of their truth (*The Ymnos* (1981)).

Before the article could be used, however, it would be necessary for Mrs Windfall to give notice to the hospital in compliance with RSC O38 rr21 and 22. In outline, this requires her to give notice of her intention to use the hearsay evidence, attaching a copy of it to the notice. We are told that Dr Ironlegs is unavailable to give evidence, but not the reason for his unavailability. If it is because he is dead, overseas, unfit or cannot be found then such a reason should be given for his proposed non attendance.

b) *The computer print-outs*

There is a question of the relevance of the evidence of what happened to two other patients. It is not necessarily the case that what happened to them would always happen to a patient to whom Happydreams is administered. In the absence of any further information on the matter it will be assumed that this evidence is relevant.

Computer print-outs in civil cases are only admissible if they fall within the strict rules of admissibility contained in s5 of the 1968 Act. Section 5 requires, firstly, that the statement produced by the computer is one of which direct oral evidence would be admissible. The statement upon which Mrs Windfall will wish to rely is the statement about the change in heart rate occurring after the administration of Happydreams. This is something about which direct oral evidence would be admissible if there were anyone with direct knowledge of it. Therefore, provided the appropriate notice is served (RSC Ord 38 rr21 and 24) and the strict conditions relating to use of the computer are complied with (s5 Civil Evidence Act 1968) the print-out would be admissible as evidence of what happened to those other patients. The trial judge would be entitled to draw any reasonable inference from the print-outs, for example the need to check assiduously the patient's heart rate (s6 Civil Evidence Act 1968).

c) *The disciplinary report*

The hospital would be entitled to refuse to disclose the report if the dominant purpose of compiling it was for the furtherance of pending or contemplated litigation (*Waugh* v *British Railways Board* (1980)). It appears that this was not so, and that the dominant purpose was for disciplinary purposes within the hospital itself. A party cannot protect a report simply by passing it to his lawyers, it is the purpose for which it is compiled which counts for the purposes of privilege and not the purpose to which it is put after it is compiled (*Neilson* v *Laugharne* (1981); *Guinness Peat* v *Fitzroy Robinson* (1987); *Ventouris* v *Mountain* (1991)).

d) *Dr Corpsemaker's conviction*

Unless the conviction of Dr Corpsemaker for causing death at the other hospital shows that he acted negligently on this occasion it would not be admissible. The admissibility of similar fact evidence in civil cases is more easily achieved than in criminal cases, but it is still necessary for it to be probative of the issue on which it is adduced (*Mood Music* v *De Wolfe* (1976)). As far as can be gathered from the information given, there is nothing about the conviction which proves negligence in relation to Mr Windfall.

Evidence of the conviction could be relevant not in relation to whether Dr Corpsemaker was negligent in treating Mr Windfall, but in relation to whether the hospital was negligent in employing Dr Corpsemaker in the first place. The liability of the hospital in such a claim would be primary not vicarious. In the absence of any information about the way in which Dr Corpsemaker killed the other patient it cannot be said whether the hospital was negligent in employing him to administer Happydreams to Mr Windfall.

14 Proof without Evidence

14.1 Introduction

In some circumstances a court may be satisfied that facts are established without requiring them to be proved by relevant evidence. In some cases the facts may be established with virtually no evidence, eg the facts are formally admitted or judicially noticed; in others the facts are presumed in favour of the party alleging them and therefore may be established by less evidence than would otherwise be required. These three exceptional areas, therefore, are formal admissions, judicial notice, and presumptions.

14.2 Key points

a) *Formal admissions*

Where a fact is formally admitted for the purpose of the proceedings, then no proof is necessary as that fact is no longer in issue between the parties.

In civil cases, formal admissions may be made at various pre-trial stages or at trial. Such formal admissions bind those making them only for the purpose of those proceedings, but in those proceedings are conclusive of the facts which are admitted.

In criminal cases, provision is made for formal admissions by s10 Criminal Justice Act 1967. If such admissions are made otherwise than in court they must comply with the requirements of s10(2) as to their form. Formal admissions in court may be made orally by counsel: *R* v *Lewis* [1989] Crim LR 61. Formal admissions may be withdrawn, but only with leave of the court: s10(4).

Whether in civil or criminal proceedings, formal admissions, which are conclusive, must be distinguished from informal admissions and confessions which are by no means conclusive but rather may be rejected as inadmissible after the party against whom they are tendered has adduced rebutting evidence – or in the case of confessions, the criminal court of its own motion may put the prosecution to proof of admissibility.

b) *Judicial notice*

In both civil and criminal cases the court will acknowledge the truth of some facts without any need for proof. This creates no problems in civil cases, but in criminal cases there is the problem, when the judge takes judicial notice of a fact, as to how the jury ought to be directed; it appears to be accepted that although in the jury's realm of fact rather than the judge's realm of law, the judge must nevertheless direct the jury to take the fact as proved: *R* v *Simpson* [1983] 1 WLR 1494; cf *Gibson* v *Wales* [1983] 1 WLR 393.

Judicial notice may be taken of notorious facts, or may be taken after reference.

i)   Notoriety

Where the fact is a matter of common knowledge (universally, or in the case of magistrates it may be locally) which is so notorious as not to be open to any serious dispute, then judicial notice will be taken of it without reference to any source. Classic examples of a miriad of such facts include a fortnight being too short a period for human gestation, criminals leading unhappy lives, postcards being correspondence which may be read by anyone.

ii)   Notice after reference

The party seeking such judicial notice of a fact must provide any required source of reference. Most of these cases of judicial notice relate to political matters, such as the existence of a state of war; the meaning of the classification 'secret' on a government document; the extent of territorial sovereignty (and therefore jurisdiction of English courts). Others have involved professional practice, eg that of the Ordnance Survey (in interpreting map references), and readily demonstrable public facts, eg the meaning of words in common usage, or geographical facts, where reference may be made to dictionaries, maps etc.

Problems arise where judicial notice is taken after receiving evidence, and where personal knowledge of the judge is involved. In the classic case of *McQuaker* v *Goddard* [1940] 1 KB 687, the judge consulted books and heard evidence on the issue before taking judicial notice of the fact that a camel was a domestic animal. This is on the borderline of judicial notice/proof by evidence, but can be justified as being the former given that it is confined to constant facts which are therefore not determined by the special facts of any case. The problem of the extent to which a judge can utilise his personal knowledge has spawned a lot of case law, yet the basic distinction is between the judge's properly applying his general knowledge of the subject matter to his understanding, and evaluation, of the evidence which has been adduced, and his improperly using his personal knowledge in place of evidence adduced. But in this latter situation a distinction must be drawn between judges and on the other hand magistrates and jurors whose local knowledge may be of something so notorious in the locality that judicial notice may be taken rather than evidence: *Ingram* v *Percival* [1969] 1 QB 548.

c)   *Presumptions*

When a presumption operates, then the court either must, or may, come to the conclusion which the presumption points to, unless there is evidence (or sufficient evidence) to the contrary. All true presumptions are rebuttable by evidence to the contrary; there are two so-called 'irrebuttable presumptions', ie that a child under ten cannot commit an offence, and that a boy under 14 is incapable of any offence which involves proof of his commission of sexual intercourse. These are not presumptions, but rules of substantive law. In addition there are presumptions which do not depend on proof of a basic fact, but are rather rules governing the incidence of the evidential and legal burdens of proof, and to some extent the standard in criminal cases; for example the presumption of sanity and of innocence – the former dictates that the defence has a legal burden of proving a defence of insanity or insane automatism and the latter dictates that the prosecution must prove beyond reasonable doubt every element of the offence charged and any other fact in issue such as the admissibility of a confession.

Further presumptions of fact need not detain the student of evidence for long – they are merely commonly recurring examples of circumstantial evidence, ie illustrations of evidence relevant to the facts in issue. For example, if a party destroys or conceals evidence the court may infer that the evidence was unfavourable to his case; or the 'presumption of continuance', to the effect that any proven state of affairs may be assumed to have continued for some time, the duration depending on all the circumstances (examples being the question of the speed of a vehicle at a specific time and the continued existence of a person proved to be alive at some earlier time than that in question); and the inference which the court *may* draw as to whether the natural and probable consequences of an act of the accused were intended or foreseen by him.

All the above are often classed as not being 'true presumptions', in that rules of substantive law, rules governing the incidence of the burdens of proof, and pieces of circumstantial evidence, do not amount to presumptions in the true sense. 'True' presumptions are said to be rebuttable presumptions of law, ie on proof of a basic fact the presumption arises, and in the absence of sufficient evidence in rebuttal the prescribed conclusion *must* be drawn by the court. How much evidence is required in rebuttal determines whether the presumption is persuasive or evidential; conversely, whether the rebuttable presumption of law is persuasive or evidential dictates whether the party seeking to rebut must discharge a legal burden of proof or merely an evidential burden. If the appropriate burden is not discharged the court *must* draw the prescribed conclusion; if the burden is discharged the presumption is rebutted and the issue must be proved by admissible evidence without the aid, or hindrance, of the presumption.

The most frequently recurring, and therefore examinable, rebuttable presumptions of law are marriage, legitimacy, death, regularity, *res ipsa loquitur*.

i) Presumption of marriage

On proof of a marriage ceremony, the law presumes the formal validity of the marriage: *Piers* v *Piers* (1849) 2 HL Cas 331. The presumption is persuasive in civil cases, but only evidential in criminal cases when the prosecution bears the legal burden of proving validity. The law will also assume the essential validity of the marriage – ie that the parties had the capacity to marry (16 years old and not already validly married). This presumption of essential validity appears to be persuasive in civil cases, but the standard of proof in rebuttal, albeit the civil standard, is lower than that imposed in respect of rebuttal of the presumption of formal validity: *Re Peete, Peete* v *Crompton* [1952] 2 All ER 599. On proof of cohabitation, a presumption arises that the couple were living together as lawful spouses. In civil proceedings this presumption of marriage is persuasive: *Re Taylor* [1961] 1 WLR 9, but when relied on by the prosecution, proof of cohabitation does not even raise an evidentiary presumption unless coupled with production of a marriage certificate: *R* v *Birtles* (1911) 6 Cr App R 177.

ii) Presumption of legitimacy

On proof of the basic fact that a child was born, or conceived, in wedlock, it is presumed that he is the legitimate issue of the spouses. In civil proceedings, the presumption is persuasive – to the civil standard of proof: s26 Family Law Reform Act 1969. In criminal proceedings, eg a charge of incest by the accused with a child born to or conceived by his wife during the subsistence of their marriage, the presumption can only be evidential. On general criminal law principles, the accused merely has to raise a reasonable doubt as to an element of the offence to ensure an acquittal, therefore evidence sufficient to raise such a doubt as to the legitimacy of the daughter must suffice, as opposed to proving illegitimacy in a civil dispute over paternity, custody, access, maintenance, etc.

iii) Presumption of death

The rebuttable presumption of death arises on proof of basic facts which were stipulated in *Chard* v *Chard* [1956] P 259, ie there were persons likely to have heard of the person whose death is an issue, but they have not heard of him for at least seven years immediately preceding the proceedings and all due, appropriate, enquiries have been made, then the person will be presumed to have died at some time within the seven year period of silence and absence. The presumption is evidential only. There is conflict, however, as to whether, without evidence in rebuttal, death will be assumed to have occurred at some time during the seven years immediately preceding the hearing, or whether death can be assumed at the end of the seven year period of continuous silence and absence and at all times thereafter. Whichever view prevails, if a specific date of death must be established (for purposes of succession etc), then evidence must be adduced to prove the actual time of death.

iv) Presumption of regularity

On proof of the basic fact that some person acted as the holder of a public office (eg judge, magistrate, police constable) it is presumed that he was duly appointed. It is presumed that devices which are usually efficient (eg speedometers of police vehicles, intoximeters, radar speed meters, radar guns) were working properly at the relevant time. On proof of necessary business transactions being carried out, it is presumed that they were carried out in the correct sequence. The presumption is evidential only, but in criminal proceedings the defence *must* adduce evidence to discharge the evidential burden borne by them on proof of the basic fact; it is not enough merely to challenge the regularity: see *Hill* v *Baxter* [1958] 1 QB 277 re discharge of evidential burden by defence.

v) Res ipsa loquitur

On proof by the plaintiff in a negligence action that the accident which caused his injuries is one which in the normal course of events would not occur without negligence on the part of the person in control of the relevant operation, and that he, the plaintiff, cannot prove it was caused by the defendant's negligence, then the plaintiff may seek assistance from the principle *res ipsa loquitur*, ie 'the thing speaks for itself'. Given that, in the circumstances of the accident, the sole control by the defendant or his employees, and the ignorance of the plaintiff as to the defendant's conduct is proved, then it may be presumed that the accident was caused by the defendant's negligence (primary or vicarious). But whether the presumption is merely one of fact, or whether it is an evidential, or a persuasive, presumption of law is open to debate as the law is far from clear. If a presumption of fact, then in the absence of evidence from the defendant, the court *may* reach the conclusion prescribed by the presumption but does not have to. If the presumption is an evidential presumption of law, then it is rebutted if the defendant adduces evidence consistent equally with negligence and pure accident. If the presumption is persuasive, the defendant must disprove negligence. There are authorities in support of all three contentions, but this could be the result of the wide variance in the basic facts which give rise to the presumption in the reported cases.

vi) Conflicting presumptions

Where there are two presumptions in conflict in the proceedings, then if they are of equal effect (eg both are persuasive presumptions) the court may decide that they cancel each other and the parties must discharge their burdens of proof by admissible evidence only: *Monckton* v *Tarr* (1930) 23 BWCC 504. Alternatively, the court may take account of public policy considerations in determining which presumption prevails: *Taylor* v *Taylor* [1965] 1 All ER 872. The classic case of *R* v *Willshire* (1881) 6 QBD 366 on conflicting presumptions can be interpreted as being purely a case of deciding which party had to discharge a legal, as opposed to evidential, burden of proof; but where presumptions arise they will have a bearing by their nature, on the incidence of the legal and/or evidential burden.

14.3 Analysis of questions

Once the student has mastered the classification of 'true' presumptions, then the rules are not very complex. Given an understanding of the burdens of proof, a student is then well equipped to deal with questions in this area, where, perhaps above all, essay questions are 'self-contained'. Judicial notice and formal admissions rarely appear, even as part of a question.

14.4 Questions

QUESTION ONE

Monica and Clint were married in California in 1960.

In 1965 Clint goes off to Vietnam with the Marines. In 1966 Monica hears that he was reported missing. In 1975 she gives up waiting for him to return and comes to England where she meets and marries Ogilvy in 1977. One of Clint's old Vietnam friends, Matt, turns up in London, visits Monica and Ogilvy and he says that he could swear he saw Clint in a village in Vietnam in 1971, where he was living with a Vietnamese girl.

In 1983 Monica sues Ogilvy for divorce and Ogilvy's defence is that their marriage is a nullity because in 1977 Monica was still married to Clint. Matt is a mercenary in Africa and can no longer be traced. Monica has some evidence that Clint might have been married previously to Jane in 1955 and that Jane is still alive.

Advise Monica.

University of London LLB Examination
(for External Students) Evidence June 1983 Q3

Skeleton Solution

- Presumption of validity of marriage – standard of proof needed with evidence in rebuttal.
- 1960 marriage validity – 1977 marriage validity – presumption of death.
- Where two presumptions apply – ordinary rules of burden and standard of proof.

Suggested Solution

Beginning with the marriage of M and C in California in 1960, it will be presumed that they were validly married and that they had the necessary capacity to marry on proof of the primary fact that they went through a ceremony of marriage. The presumption of marriage is a very strong presumption, rebuttable only by strong evidence. Lord Cottenham LC in *Piers* v *Piers* (1849) held that the presumption is not lightly to be repelled and required evidence, going beyond a mere balance of probability, which is strong, distinct, satisfactory and conclusive. In *Mahadervan* v *Mahadervan* (1964), it was held that the court must be satisfied beyond reasonable doubt in order for the presumption to be rebutted. However, later in *Blyth* v *Blyth* (1966), the House of Lords seem to suggest that the standard of proof in matrimonial matters is the ordinary civil standard. Whatever the true position, it is submitted that the evidence in rebuttal is required to be cogent. Evidence of a valid prior marriage may suffice (*Gatty & Gatty* v *Attorney-General* (1951)) unless that marriage itself cannot be shown conclusively to have been valid (*Taylor* v *Taylor* (1967)). Accordingly M may here argue that the persuasive presumption of validity of the marriage of 1960 is rebutted by evidence of a valid prior marriage, that between C and J in 1955. The conclusion would be that her marriage to O in 1977 is valid. However, the weak link in this argument is the doubt that surrounds the alleged marriage of 1955. It is submitted that M will fail to show conclusively the validity of the 1955 marriage and will therefore fail to rebut the presumption of validity in relation to the marriage of 1960. Nor may she argue that the presumption is inapplicable to a foreign marriage (that of 1960) in order to prevent the invalidation of the subsequent English marriage (that of 1977). In *Mahadervan* v *Mahadervan* it was held that a presumption in favour of validity carried as much weight in relation to a foreign marriage as to an English one. In this respect the nationality of the marriages in question is irrelevant.

If the above reasoning is correct, the 1960 marriage will be held to be valid, the subsequent marriage of 1977 invalid. However, M may argue the validity of the 1977 marriage on the basis that at that time C was dead. If there is no acceptable affirmative evidence that a person was alive at some time during a continuous period of seven years or more and if it can be proved (a) that there are persons who would be likely to have heard of him over that period, (b) that those persons have not heard of him, and (c) that all due enquiries have been made appropriate to the circumstances, that person may be presumed to have died at some time within that period (*Chard* v *Chard* (1956)). It is no bar to M employing the presumption that she wishes to show that C was dead at the date of her marriage to O (1977) as opposed to the date of the present trial. In *Chipchase* v *Chipchase* (1939) it was assumed that the presumption could apply retrospectively, ie at some date prior to the date of the trial. However, even assuming that M satisfied the first and the third conditions, of *Chard* v *Chard* (supra), there is evidence here that C was heard of in 1971, by M. This would interrupt the continuous period of seven years, which must have begun in 1966 when C was reported missing, after only five years. Does evidence of the alleged sighting of C in 1971 suffice to rebut the presumption? It seems clear from *Prudential Assurance Co* v *Edmonds* (1877) that the presumption of death is evidential, ie it casts a burden of adducing evidence on the party against whom it operates (in our case, O). If O gives evidence of the sighting of C in 1971, this may rebut the presumption. However, whether this evidence is reliable is a question for the judge as trier of fact. One important factor concerning reliability is that M is unavailable to give evidence or to have his evidence challenged in cross-examination. Even assuming that M were to succeed in showing that C died at some stage between 1966 and 1977, in reliance on the presumption of death, and that the 1977 marriage was therefore valid, this conclusion would conflict with that based on the presumption of the validity of the marriage of 1960. In this situation, where two presumptions apply but produce different conclusions, the ordinary rules for burden and standard of proof apply without resort to any presumptions (*R* v *Wiltshire CCR* (1881)) ie the presumptions cancel each other out. On this basis it is submitted that the weight of the evidence suggests that the marriage of 1960 was valid, that C was alive in 1977 and that the marriage of that date was accordingly invalid.

QUESTION TWO

'Every writer of sufficient intelligence to appreciate the difficulties of the subject matter has approached the topic of presumptions with a sense of hopelessness and left it with a feeling of despair.' (Morgan)

Why are presumptions so difficult to analyse and classify?

University of London LLB Examination
(for External Students) Evidence June 1985 Q3

Skeleton Solution

- Introduction – different effects of presumptions – scope of discussion.
- The general context – definition of terms – stages of a trial.
- Traditional classification, introduction – irrebuttable presumptions of law.
- Rebuttable presumptions of law – two types – new names – Lord Denning and Lord Bridge – two types .
- Presumptions of fact – definition – Lord Denning and Lord Bridge – distinction between evidential and factual presumptions – permissive presumptions.
- Criminal cases – burden placed on accused.
- Conclusion – reasons for confusion.

Suggested Solution

a) *Introduction*

The area of presumptions has given rise to a great deal of division of terminology and of conceptual thinking. These differences among many eminent academic and practising lawyers has come about because of the three-part role of presumptions in English law. Presumptions sometimes alter the normal rules on burden of proof, for policy reasons; at other times they allow the proof of fact 'A' to be the result of proving fact 'B'; at other times they act simply to direct the mind of the trier of fact towards possible inferences which may be drawn from the evidence adduced. Indeed at time a presumption may do all three of these things. This complex role can only be understood if the rules on burden of proof are borne in mind, together with the procedure at each stage of a trial. These will be discussed in section (b) below.

There are many different presumptions and many policy reasons behind those presumptions. As conceptions of public policy change, so the effect of presumptions will change; this makes the task of classification all the more difficult. It is proposed to deal with the traditional, or orthodox, classification and to show how each old category has been altered in terminology by recent commentators. The following discussion will be in relation to civil cases only, when covering basic principles; the rules applicable to criminal cases will be dealt with separately.

b) *The general context*

Although there is a considerable variation in terminology in the area of burdens of proof, this answer will use that favoured by Cross (*Cross on Evidence* (8th edition, 1995)). In other words the burden of proving an issue will be referred to as the legal burden of proof; the onus of raising an issue not already raised will be called the evidential burden; the risk of not calling evidence on an issue which one's opponent has already raised is the tactical burden; and the overall burden of persuading the court to find in one's favour will be called the ultimate burden.

It must be remembered that burdens and standards of proof are irrelevant unless the trier of fact or law actually has to make a decision. Throughout the calling of evidence it is naive to assume that the trier of fact takes each piece of evidence in turn and considers whether the case has been proved – that decision is only taken at the end of the case, when all the evidence has been called, so that everything can be seen in context. There are only three stages of a trial at which burdens are important. The first is at the end of the plaintiff's case, when the judge has to decide whether the evidential burden on the plaintiff has been discharged, in other words whether he has called evidence from which a reasonable jury could find for him (the rare case where the defendant has the right to begin works on the same principle). The second is when all evidence has been called and the judge has to consider whether sufficient evidence has been called on each issue for that issue to need to be decided. The third stage comes immediately after the second and is when the trier of fact (usually the judge in a civil case) has to decide whether the ultimate burden has been satisfied. At the first two stages questions of the discharge of evidential burdens arise, at the final stage it is the legal burden on each issue which is important.

c) *The traditional classification – introduction*

The traditional classification on presumptions is into three categories, ie irrebuttable presumptions of law, rebuttable presumptions of law and presumptions of fact. Irrebuttable presumptions of law are not true presumptions at all (this is one of the few statements on this topic with which all commentators agree!). Rather they are rules of law put into presumptive form. For example s50 Children and Young Persons Act 1933 (as amended by s16(1) Children and Young Persons Act 1963) states that 'it shall be conclusively presumed that no child under the age of ten years can be guilty of any offence'. This could be amended by the omission of the first six words so as to be the same rule, but not in presumptive form: 'no child under the age of ten years can be guilty of an offence'. Clearly nothing is added, or lost, by stating the rule in terms of a presumption, but it is not really a presumption at all. Therefore irrebuttable presumptions of law will not be discussed further.

d) *Rebuttable presumptions of law*

Rebuttable presumptions of law all follow the same logical form. On proof of fact 'A', fact 'B' is presumed to be true. The traditional classification of presumptions does not further divide these presumptions, but as has been pointed out many times there are two types of rebuttable presumption of law. The first type is the presumption which says that on proof of fact 'A' fact 'B' shall be taken to be true unless it is proved that fact 'B' is not true. The other type is the presumption which says that on proof of fact 'A' fact 'B' shall be taken to be true unless sufficient evidence is raised to throw doubt on whether fact 'B' really is true. The distinction can be illustrated by the following example:

A child is born to Mrs X while she is married to Mr X. Mr X leaves Mrs X and refuses to pay any maintenance for the child, because he claims he is not the father. Mrs X sues for maintenance.

There is a presumption that a child born in wedlock is the child of the mother's husband (*Banbury Peerage Case* (1811)). Theoretically this presumption could be rebutted by Mr X (the defendant) proving that he was not the father, or by him adducing evidence which showed a 50–50 chance of him not being the father. Since the burden of proving the right to maintenance will be on Mrs X (the plaintiff), so if Mr X could show an equal chance of him not being the father then he would have prevented Mrs X proving on balance of probabilities that she was entitled to maintenance money from him. So the presumption could require proof to the contrary or it could require the defendant merely to prevent the plaintiff proving her case, without proving his case himself. In fact the presumption of legitimacy places a legal burden on the party rebutting the presumption (see now s26 Family Law Reform Act 1969). But the theoretical position of rebuttable presumption is clear – they are of two types.

This failure of the traditional classification to distinguish between the two types of rebuttable presumption of law led to various attempts to adopt a two-part classification.

Lord Denning called the presumptions which put a legal burden on the rebutter 'compelling presumptions' ((1945) 61 MLR 379; see also Carter, *Cases and Statutes on Evidence* (2nd edition, 1990, pp78–79) though the more common terminology is 'persuasive presumptions' (*Cross on Evidence* (8th edition, 1995)); Heydon, *Evidence Cases and Statutes* (2nd edition, 1984, p43)). This new title is useful in that it distinguishes such presumptions from those which impose a lesser burden on the rebutter. But it has not gone without criticism. Lord Bridge ((1949) 12 MLR 272) has argued that the classification of such rules as presumptions is all wrong. He pointed out that these compelling or persuasive presumptions are rules of law which determine that a certain result must follow from the proof of certain facts. In the example given above, on proof by Mrs X of birth in wedlock the law stipulates that legitimacy must be found unless there is proof to the contrary. Lord Bridge's argument was that this is not a presumption at all, it is a rule of law dressed up as a presumption. It is certainly true that there is little difference between a common law rule that says the burden of proving illegitimacy is on the defendant once the plaintiff has proved birth in wedlock. Each of the rules is really in the same form – on the happening of a certain event, certain consequences follow; on the happening of the start of the case the ultimate burden is on the plaintiff, on the happening of proof of birth in wedlock the legal burden of proving illegitimacy is on the defendant. Each rule can be put into the same pattern. Therefore the question arises whether it is right to classify 'compelling' or 'persuasive' presumptions as presumptions. Lord Bridge argued that one should bear in mind the stages of the trial at which the issue of legitimacy will arise. The plaintiff must produce evidence on which a reasonable jury could find birth in wedlock; then the defendant has to prove illegitimacy. No question of presumption arises, he argued; there are two distinct issues – has the plaintiff prove birth in wedlock, has the defendant proved illegitimacy? It is submitted that Lord Bridge's approach does not properly explain the concept of the persuasive presumption. It is certainly true that the effect of the 'presumptions' is to state a rule of law, that the defendant bears the burden of proving illegitimacy; but that burden only arises once the basis for it has been established by the plaintiff. If the plaintiff calls no evidence relating to birth in wedlock, then her case would be rejected on the defendant making a submission of no case. It is artificial to separate the cases where a presumption places a legal burden of proof on the rebutter and those where only an evidential burden is placed on him, by arguing that the former category is not a presumption but is a rule of law. Both are presumptions and both presumptions arise because the law says they arise. In both cases the trier of fact must draw a certain conclusion unless some evidence is called to the contrary. The only difference between the two is the amount of evidence required to rebut the presumption.

The classification of the second type of rebuttable presumption of law is not subject to the same difficulties. This second category – the presumption that on proof of fact 'A', the trier of fact must conclude fact 'B' unless the other party can balance the probability of 'B' being true and being not true – has been defined by Cross as the 'evidential presumption' (*Cross on Evidence* (8th edition, 1995)) but Lord Bridge simply called these 'presumptions'; this being the result of his basic thesis that there is only one sort of presumption, all other things which are called presumptions being defined using other terminology (12 MLR 272, 279).

The effect of an evidential presumption, as mentioned above, is to place a burden on the rebutter to adduce sufficient evidence to prevent the proponent from proving his case. In other words a tactical burden is placed on the rebutter.

Evidential presumptions may be of two types. The first type reflects common sense by requiring fact 'B' to be presumed on the proof of fact 'A' even though as a matter of common sense the natural conclusion is that fact 'B' is true; the second type gives additional weight to fact 'A that common sense would always indicate. For example, the common law presumption of regularity states that if a person acts in an office for which certain formal qualifications are needed it is to be presumed that he has those qualifications (*Berryman* v *Wise* (1791)). As a matter of common sense proof that a man sat as a judge at the Old Bailey would be clear proof that he was qualified to do so; after all, if he were not qualified then he would have been found out. In such a case there is no need for there to be any legal presumption, the trier of fact would draw the required conclusion anyway. But, it could be that the use of a church for a wedding ceremony would not, necessarily, be construed by a reasonable man to be proof that it was properly licensed for weddings; nonetheless the presumption of regularity applies so that the trier of fact must find that it was licensed unless the opponent on the issue can show that there was an equal chance of the church not being licensed (*R* v *Cresswell* (1876)). Despite these two types of evidential presumptions, there seems to be no need to divide them into separate categories of presumptions because they both work in the same way. They both place a tactical burden on the opponent of the issue once the proponent has proved the basic facts.

There has, though, been some difference of terminology in that Lord Denning did not give evidential presumptions a separate name, but classed them together with presumptions of fact, as 'provisional' presumptions. This analysis will be discussed below, when dealing with presumptions of fact.

e)   *Presumptions of fact*

The traditional presumption of fact has two aspects. The first is that there are some inferences which a trier of fact will draw because common sense tells him to. For example, if evidence is given that a man walking alongside a golf course was hit by a golf ball the trier of fact will conclude, in the absence of other evidence, that the ball came from the golf course. The second aspect of presumptions of fact is that there are certain issues of fact which arise regularly in trials and the courts have stated that the jury is entitled to draw certain conclusions in those cases. For example, there is a presumption of continuance of life, which states that a life is presumed to continue for a reasonable time. This is a commonsense inference from proof of the fact that someone is alive and well, but arises so frequently that the appellate courts have from time to time identified it as a presumption (*R* v *Lumley* (1869)). It is interesting to note that it has been said that presumptions of fact only arise in this second sense of the commonly recurring fact. The argument here seems to be that some presumptions of fact are recognised by the appellate courts so often that it would be an error of law by the trial judge if he failed to make a direction that the presumption can be made.

Furthermore, it must be noted that Lord Denning called presumptions of fact 'provisional' presumptions, on the basis that they put a tactical burden on the opponent of the issue, and this tactical burden can be satisfied by calling evidence which throws doubt on the truth of the presumed fact. In other words, the presumption will only be drawn when the proponent's evidence is called and may be displaced before the final decision has to be made; it is provisional not permanent. He seemed to group evidential presumptions (presumptions of law placing a tactical burden on the rebutter) and presumptions of fact together in that they both place a tactical burden only on the rebutter. But, as Lord Bridge pointed out, evidential presumptions must be drawn as a matter of law, whereas factual presumptions are permissive only, they may be drawn (12 MLR 272, 278–279). It is submitted, with respect, that Lord Denning failed to appreciate the true effect of the evidential and factual presumptions. Both presumptions only arise at the end of the case; they help the discharge of the legal burden on an issue, by allowing the trier of fact to draw an inference from the evidence presented. But what if no evidence is given by the defendant, must he necessarily fail? Is there a difference between the evidential and factual presumptions? It is submitted that there is a difference. In order to appreciate the difference it is necessary to go back to basics and consider the essence of a presumption.

All presumptions can be written in the same form: on proof of fact 'A' fact 'B' is proved. There are two elements – the proof of fact 'A'; and the proof of fact 'B'. In the case of a conclusive or irrebuttable presumption of law it is not possible to call evidence disproving fact 'B', once fact 'A' has been established. For example, it is not possible to prove that a 13 year old boy committed rape (*R* v *Waite* (1892)). But it is possible to call evidence that the boy in question was over 13 at the time of the alleged rape. In other words, although the presumption cannot be rebutted, it is possible to prevent the presumption arising in the first place.

Applying that principle to evidential and factual presumptions, the trier of fact could always conclude that the evidence called is not strong enough to prove that a certain man sat as a judge at the Old Bailey. If the trier of fact is not satisfied that he sat, then no presumption as to his qualifications must be drawn. Similarly, if the judge is asked to presume that a 35 year old man was likely to live for a further ten years, the judge may find on the evidence presented that the man was not 35 at the time alleged. In both cases the failure to prove the basic fact means that the presumed fact is not proved. But the converse case shows the difference between evidential and factual presumption. Say the judge is satisfied that the man in the first case sat at the Old Bailey, or that the man in the second case was aged 35 at the relevant time; in the first case if the party who wishes to dispute the man's qualifications calls no evidence then, as a matter of law, the trial judge would have to find that the man in question was qualified to sit. In other words once the basic fact is established the presumed fact *must* be found to be true. In the second case, though, even if the trial judge is satisfied that the man in question was 35 and in good health at the relevant time he would still be free to find that he would not be expected to live for a further ten years if, for example, there was a war on and the man was likely to be conscripted for dangerous duties. The second case illustrates that the trier of fact *may* draw a presumption once the basic facts are proved, but does not have to as a matter of law; whereas when dealing with evidential presumptions the presumed fact must be found to be true in the absence of rebutting evidence, once the basic fact is established. Therefore, it is submitted, Lord Denning was wrong to argue that there is no difference between evidential presumptions and presumptions of fact.

There is a further difficulty in the area of presumptions of fact, in that certain rules of law state that the trier of fact may draw a certain conclusion on the proof of certain basic facts. These instances are different from evidential presumptions in that the trier of fact is not bound to find the presumed fact once the basic fact is true and they are different from presumptions of fact in that the law stipulates that the conclusion may be drawn from the basic fact, rather than that being the result of applying commonsense. For example, if an employer has issued an employee with a timetable which directs him to drive from one place to another in an unreasonably short time, then by virtue of s78A Road Traffic Regulations Act 1967, the timetable 'may be produced as prima facie evidence' of incitement to commit a speeding offence. There is no requirement that the jury must find the employer guilty in the absence of proof or evidence to the contrary. The effect of this sort of statutory provision is clear if the stages of the trial mentioned in section (b) above are remembered. The prosecution must make out a prima facie case, fit to be left to the jury. If they cannot do so then the accused may make a submission of no case, which would lead to his acquittal. Section 78A provides that the evidential burden on the prosecution will be satisfied by the timetable being adduced. In other words, the trier of law must draw the presumption that there is a case to answer, even though the trier of fact would be free to reject the timetable as being insufficient evidence to found a conviction.

Such a statutory presumption is not classified by most writers. Lord Denning did not mention them, nor Lord Bridge, nor Cross, nor Heydon, nor Nokes. Carter has labelled them 'permissive' presumptions because the trier of fact is permitted but not obliged, to conclude that there was incitement once the timetable has been adduced (*Cases and Statutes* (2nd edition, 1990, p77)).

f) *Criminal cases*

Although the occasional criminal example has been given above, the general rules stated are only applicable to civil cases. This point is not always appreciated. The reason for it is simple. In a civil case there is no conceptual difficulty in placing a legal burden of proof on the defendant once the plaintiff has adduced some evidence on an issue (nor on the plaintiff if the defendant raises the issue). But in a criminal case the accused only bears a legal burden in two instances – if he wishes to prove insanity (*M'Naghten's Case* (1843)) and where a statute requires him to prove his defence (*R v Carr-Briant* (1943); *R v Edwards* (1975)). In all other cases the burden on him can be evidential only. Therefore if the prosecution wishes to rely on a presumption, the accused never has to disprove the presumed fact.

g) *Conclusion*

It can be seen from the above discussion that presumptions cover many areas of the law and have been subject to many differences in analysis. It is submitted that the difficulty of analysis and classification is caused by six main factors. Firstly, the failure to distinguish between criminal and civil cases has caused confusion to those who have attempted to set out rules of presumption applicable across the board. Secondly the use of the word presumption can cause a reaction, as with Lord Bridge, that a presumption is a conclusion drawn from the proof of basic facts and anything which does not fit into that model must be called something else – even if it has been called a presumption by other writers for many years. Thirdly, it is not always fully appreciated that some presumptions place a legal burden on the party rebutting and sometimes merely a tactical burden. In this area more than any other the terminology of writers tends to confuse. Williams talked of evidential presumptions because of his definition of the evidential burden; others define that burden as the tactical burden, but retain the term 'evidential presumption', the potential for confusion then is clear. Fourthly, the place of presumptions of fact is changing. The so-called doctrine of recent possession (someone found in possession of stolen goods shortly after they were stolen may be presumed to have come by them dishonestly) has been classified as a presumption of law (*R* v *Hepworth & Fearnley* (1955)) but the Court of Appeal has recently made it clear that it is a presumption of fact only (*R* v *Ball* (1983)). Similar confusion has been caused with the presumption that a man intends the natural and probable consequences of his acts; this started out as a presumption of fact (*R* v *Steane* (1947)), was turned into a presumption of law (*DPP* v *Smith* (1961)) and is now a presumption of fact again (s8 Criminal Justice Act 1967). This sort of change makes the use of older definitions of presumptions dangerous. Fifthly, presumptions of law are random rules affecting the way cases are proved and the way burdens of proof are distributed. The lack of any system of policy behind the presumptions misleads some commentators to attempt to over-simplify the categories. It is submitted that Lord Denning's classification of certain presumptions as 'provisional' falls within this point. Sixthly, the use by the judges of the term 'shifting of the burden of proof' is so widespread, and in many instances so misconceived, that one is tempted to look for a presumption to justify the supposed shift. For example, the 'doctrine' of res ipsa loquitur is treated as a presumption of fact in all parts of the world, where it is recognised that if the only logical inference to draw from the facts proved is that there was negligence then that conclusion must be drawn. But nowhere other than this country has consistently held that the doctrine creates a persuasive presumption placing a legal burden of proof on the rebutter. The confusion has been caused by inexact use of burden of proof terminology.

It is interesting to note that of all the major works on evidence only Carter has pointed out the true effect of what he calls 'permissive' presumptions – rules of law which allow the trier of law no right to reject a piece of evidence as insufficiently probative to be left to the trier of fact. But, even he does not make the point that such a presumption is useless by itself. To use the example given above, s78A Road Traffic Regulations Act 1967 allows the prosecution of an employer for incitement to exceed the speed limit, to use a timetable issued by the employer as evidence against him. This prevents the trial judge withdrawing the case from the jury for lack of evidence on the issue of incitement, but if the case is one where the judge would be minded to withdraw the case for lack of evidence and the jury convicts, then surely the convicted employer would have a ground for appeal in the same way that any appeal should be allowed where the evidence against the accused should, at common law, have been ruled to be insufficient. This new category of presumption, therefore, also has its problems. It only need be relied on if there is no other evidence against the employer, but in that case any conviction could well be perverse. By dressing-up s78A as a presumption there is every possibility that it will be given more significance than it deserves.

Finally, it cannot be stated that the existence of so many classifications and names of presumptions is of any real use unless and until the courts start to put one terminology or another into practice. Although Lord Denning introduced his own terminology and analysis in several cases (eg *Emmanuel* v *Emmanuel* (1946); *Huyton-with-Roby UDC* v *Hunter* (1955)) such usage has not been uniform. The source of confusion in the absence of judicial guidance is clear once the many sources of the word 'presumption' have been seen.

QUESTION THREE

a) What place has judicial notice in the context of our trial system?

b) How much use may a judge or magistrate make of his or her personal knowledge?

University of London LLB Examination
(for External Students) Evidence June 1985 Q4

Skeleton Solution

- The place of judicial notice, introduction – defining the problem.
- Judicial notice of facts – notice without inquiry – notice after inquiry.
- Judicial notice of law – scope of rule – rationale.
- Theory of judicial notice – two principles – policy – function of judge place of judicial notice.
- Personal knowledge, introduction – definition of the problem.
- Knowledge of the law – tacit notice.
- Knowledge of fact – introduction.
- Judge's personal knowledge of fact – limited scope of use – practical considerations.
- Magistrates' personal knowledge – knowledge of local matters – expert knowledge – difference in treatment of judge and justices.

Suggested Solution

a) *The place of judicial notice*

    i) Introduction

        The principle that questions of fact are for the jury and questions of law for the judge is so well established that no authority need be cited in its support. There is, though, a significant area where the judge decides questions of fact and directs the jury to reach a decision in accordance with his direction. This is the area of judicial notice. In this answer the place of judicial notice will be examined from three angles. Firstly will be considered the extent to which a judge in a criminal case may decide issues of fact. The second perspective will involve discussion of the way matters of law are proved. Thirdly will be examined whether there is any consistent theory as to the proper place for judicial notice.

    ii) Judicial notice of facts

        There are some facts of such common knowledge that it is thought improper to leave the jury any scope for diversion from accepted wisdom. (This discussion will assume that there is a judge and jury, for the sake of convenience.) For example, the Court of

Common Pleas once held that it was right for a judge to direct a jury that rain falls (*Fay v Prentice* (1845)). To allow the jury the possibility of disagreeing in such a case may be harmless in that it could be said with some confidence that no jury would disagree. Nonetheless, just to be sure, no evidence is allowed to go to the jury to give them cause for doubt.

Clearly this is a usurpation of the function of the jury by the trial judge. He directs them that an issue of fact must be decided in a certain way. As has already been mentioned, there is no harm in this in such an obvious case. But the right of the judge to direct the jury on questions of fact goes beyond cases where the fact is obvious to anyone. There are some facts of which judicial notice will be taken even though the trial judge may not have been able to state the fact without help from a work of reference. In such cases he is said to take notice after inquiry (*Cross on Evidence* (8th edition, 1995)). For example in *Duff Development Co v Government of Kelantan* (1924) the House of Lords held that judicial notice should be taken of the fact that Kelantan was a sovereign state once the Secretary of State for the Colonies had certified that this was so. There is a clear policy element to such a decision, namely that the courts should not reach decisions which might upset the comity of nations. Notice after inquiry is not limited to such cases, though, it applies also to questions of fact which arise frequently and so should be decided in a consistent manner by the courts. To leave such questions to juries may lead to embarrassing conflicts of decisions. For example, in *Davey v Harrow Corporation* (1958) the Court of Appeal stated that judicial notice could be taken of the practice of the Ordnance Survey, primarily to prevent different juries reaching different decisions where similar points of the interpretation of maps arise.

iii) Judicial notice of law

It is no usurpation of the function of the jury for a trial judge to direct them on the law, because that is his exclusive province. It is frequently said that everyone is presumed to know the law (the closes thing we have to be an authority on this is *Bilbie v Lumley* (1802)). To expect every trial judge to know the full contents of every statute and precedent is, obviously, quite unreasonable, though. Therefore the judge is allowed to 'refresh his memory' by references to statutes, precedents and works of authority. The formal rules of admissibility of evidence do not apply to legal argument, because the judge does not hear 'evidence'. Rather he refers to various authorities in order to remind himself of what he is seemed to know already.

Judicial notice is taken of English law, but not of other jurisdictions, except in certain special circumstances (for which see Nokes, 'The Limits of Judicial Notice' (1958) 74 LQR 59, 61–62). Judicial notice is also taken of the contents of statutes (s3 Interpretation Act 1978 and s4(2) European Communities Act 1972 for the taking of judicial notice of the contents of the Community Treaties) and of general customs (*Brandao v Barnett* (1846)). In some instances even local customs have been the proper subject of judicial notice; for example the local custom that markets in the City of London are market overt for the sale of goods, but not for their purchase by the shopkeeper (*Hargreave v Spink* (1892)).

The rationale behind all these cases seems to be that the judge must decide questions of law in a way which allows for accuracy of decision and consistency from case to case (see Carter, *Cases and Statutes on Evidence* (2nd edition, 1990, pp123–125)). To impose rules of evidence on the adduction of law reports, for example, would exclude them as hearsay (subject to civil cases where the statutory exceptions, ss2 and 4 Civil Evidence Act 1968, apply). Such a result would be absurdly inconvenient, so by making questions of law the subject of judicial notice this inconvenience can be circumvented.

iv) Theory of judicial notice

It will be seen from the above discussion that there are three common areas within which the rules of judicial notice apply. Firstly to questions of fact which are known to all; secondly to questions of fact which need to be decided uniformly from case to case, but which need inquiry to be established; and thirdly questions of law which are within the judge's exclusive domain. The question arises whether there is a consistent policy behind all three areas.

It is often asserted that the underlying principle of the rules of judicial notice is that 'notorious' matters should not be the subject of dispute, instead they should be recognised as notorious and applied the same in every case (see, for example, *Phipson on Evidence* (14th edition, 1990, paras 2–21)). This theory is supported to an extent by the history of judicial notice (Nokes, 74 LQR 59, 63–70), but there are, in fact, two distinct principles which are applied. The first is that for reasons of policy certain facts should not be challenged by evidence. An example is given above in the *Duff Development Co* case and this principle also explains such cases as *Fay* v *Prentice*. The other principle, which applies to the taking of judicial notice of questions of law, is that the function of the judge to decide questions of law should not be hampered by technical arguments over the admissibility of reference works.

The place of judicial notice in the trial system, therefore, is to provide a degree of consistency of decision to everyday questions of fact and to allow judges to reach decisions on questions of law in the most effective way. Judicial notice can thus be seen as a set of rules providing for the saving of time and the increase of efficiency in the courts.

b) *Personal knowledge of judge or magistrate*

i) Introduction

The above discussion of judicial notice divides the subject into two parts – notice of fact and notice of law. This distinction is maintained in the rules relating to the use which may be made of personal knowledge by a judge or magistrate.

ii) Personal knowledge of law

If a judge has to decide a question of law he will not always need to be referred to statutes or authorities. Some areas of the law will be well known to him and his memory of these will not need to be refreshed. Clearly it would be unsatisfactory for a judge to have to be referred to statutes and authorities every time, therefore he is allowed to rely on his personal knowledge of the law. Cross has pointed out that some reliance on personal knowledge is inevitable in the decision by a judge or jury of any issue (*Cross on Evidence* (8th edition, 1995)). For example, if a judge has to decide whether a particular house is covered by the Rent and Housing Acts provisions which give tenants statutory rights against their landlord, he would not have to be referred to a dictionary in order to know what 'dwelling' means because he will already know what it means. In every case where a legal point arises it will be discussed in English, the judge relies on his personal knowledge of the English language in order to understand the argument. This is what Cross called a 'tacit' application of judicial notice.

iii) Personal knowledge of fact

The decision of questions of fact by a judge raises different principles, though. In criminal cases it is, of course, the function of the jury to consider questions of fact, subject to directions of fact of which judicial notice has been taken. In civil cases the virtual extinction of the jury means that the judge has to decide both law and fact. The judge when deciding questions of fact is in essentially the same position as a jury or a bench of magistrates. It is not yet clear whether judges and magistrates are in the same position when it comes to the use of personal knowledge in the reaching of a decision of fact.

iv) Judge's knowledge of fact

It is clear that a judge may rely on his personal knowledge of matters of general, or common, knowledge. The problem arises when he had to deal with an issue on which he has local knowledge. Is he allowed to rely on that local knowledge?

The start of the discussion must be the normal rule that questions of fact must be decided according to the evidence called, the trier of fact being entitled to draw any legitimate logical inference from that evidence. If, for example, the question arises whether the defendant trespassed on the plaintiff's land and the plaintiff calls evidence that the defendant was seen entered the land by climbing over a particular gate, and the defendant calls no evidence in rebuttal; then it would appear that the judge would have no option but to find for the plaintiff.

The position is made difficult if the judge knows that the gate is twenty feet high and covered from top to bottom in barbed wire. Is he allowed to rely on this knowledge and use it as the basis of rejecting the evidence called by the plaintiff? The old position was that the trier of fact, whether judge or jury, was not allowed to rely on personal local knowledge (*R* v *Sutton* (1816)). But this was altered gradually, so that in 1841 the trier of fact was allowed to make limited reference to his personal knowledge, and over 100 years later the general rule was stated that personal knowledge of notorious local matters could be relied on provided it was properly used and reasonably applied (*Reynolds* v *Llanelly Associated Tinplate* (1948)). The rule laid down is very wide and vague, indeed this was accepted by the judge who decided the *Reynolds* case. The position of the trained judge does not appear to have altered since 1948. Therefore it can be said, albeit tentatively, that a judge may rely on his personal knowledge of notorious local facts when it is proper and reasonable so to do. The test of when it is proper and reasonable is, necessarily, wide because much would depend on the availability of cogent evidence to prove the point and on whether time and expense would be saved by the judge relying on his knowledge rather than hearing such evidence. In the example give above, therefore, the trial judge would only be allowed to rely on his personal knowledge of the state of the gate if it was a matter which was notorious in the locality.

It may be useful to add that many County Court actions are heard by local judges who, it seems, must from time to time rely on their personal knowledge of the area. But the judges in such cases will not usually give detailed judgments, so the reliance on personal knowledge may be greater in practice than the Court of Appeal has ever had the opportunity to appreciate.

Certainly in principle, there is little to commend any distinction between a professional judge acting as a trier of fact and any other tribunal; nonetheless, such a distinction is drawn, as will now be shown.

v) Magistrates' knowledge of fact

It has been stated above that magistrates are treated differently to professional judges in the respect that they may rely on personal knowledge to a greater extent. Two recent Divisional Court decisions uphold a distinction between magistrates and judges.

In *Ingram* v *Percival* (1969) it was held that local magistrates were entitled to rely on their own knowledge of the tidal limits of local waters. In *Wetherall* v *Harrison* (1976) the Divisional Court held that a magistrate was allowed to rely on his professional knowledge as a doctor when considering a medical defence put forward by the accused. The reasoning in both cases was similar and was that magistrates are local justices untrained in the law; as such their local expertise should be used to the advantage of the administration of justice, as should any other specialist knowledge which they have to offer. In *Wetherall* v *Harrison* the position of the professional judge and the lay magistrate was said to be different because the professional judge is trained to put certain matters out of his mind, whereas the layman was not. Manchester (42 MLR 22, 28) has argued that there was no authority to support this distinction between the use by the different tribunals of personal knowledge. Perhaps it is not fair to counter this with the trite argument that there is never an authority for any proposition until the first authority is created. His point is that the Divisional Court when drawing this distinction assumed that it should be drawn, without sufficiently citing reasons why it should be drawn.

The position of magistrates, therefore, can be summarised in two propositions. Firstly, they may rely on their knowledge of local matters and are not limited, as are judges, to local matters which are 'notorious' (note: there is a signal failure in the authorities to define 'notorious', see 74 LQR 59, 59–70). Secondly they may rely on their professional knowledge in assessing the weight to give evidence called. The first principle has been criticised on the ground that no adequate reason has been given why the distinction should be drawn. Indeed it is hard to see why one trier of fact should be in any different position to any other. Perhaps the rule does not apply very often in practice, though. If evidence is called as to the circumstances of the case then there will be little scope for the justices to rely on their local knowledge. In *Ingram* v *Percival* they only relied on their own knowledge because no evidence had been called on the extent of the tidal waters. It may be that such a position will only rarely arise, usually evidence would be called. The trained judge, unlike the lay magistrates, would be able to direct the parties towards the lack of evidence if he feels that there is a relevant matter which requires to be proved. Perhaps this is the true reason behind the distinction – ability of the trier of fact to determine whether the case is better proved by relying on personal knowledge or by requiring evidence to be called.

The second principle may, in fact, reflect less of a difference in treatment between justices and judges than Manchester suggests. He argues that *Wetherall* v *Harrison* allows justices to rely on professional knowledge to a greater extent than judges (42 MLR 22, 28). It is arguable that this is not so. A professional judge is allowed to rely on his professional instincts and experience when assessing the credibility of a witness. He would have seen and heard more witnesses in his career than any magistrate.

Inevitably he would have developed a 'feel' for when a witness is honest or untruthful. There has never been any suggestion that he cannot rely on that experience. Is this any different to the position of the lay justice who is a doctor who does not believe a witness because professional experience tells him that the story told is untrue? It is submitted that there is no difference.

QUESTION FOUR

What is the relationship between the burden of proof and presumptions? It is possible to classify presumptions by reference to their impact on the burden of proof? Give reasons.

University of London LLB Examination
(for External Students) Evidence June 1986 Q2

Skeleton Solution

- Burden of proof – two types – definition.
- Standard rule on burden of proof in civil and criminal cases – exceptions.
- Presumptions – definition – examples – effect on burden of proof.
- Challenge of basic facts or challenge of conclusion.
- Classifying presumptions according to their effect on burden of proof.

Suggested Solution

The burden of proof in any trial, civil or criminal, involves two elements, namely, the evidential burden and the legal burden. Indeed, these two burdens arise on each issue in the trial, as well as on the overall issue of which party is to win the case. The evidential burden lies on the party who has to adduce sufficient evidence to make an issue a live issue (*Cross on Evidence* (8th edition, 1995)). In other words it is the burden of raising sufficient evidence such that the issue involved could be decided in his favour. The legal burden is the burden of raising sufficient evidence to prove the issue, in other words sufficient evidence to satisfy the trier of fact that the issue in question should be decided in his favour (*Cross on Evidence* (8th edition, 1995)).

The normal rule in both civil and criminal trials is that the party who first raises an issue should prove it (*Abrath* v *North East Railway Co* (1886)); *Woolmington* v *DPP* (1935)). So, for example, if a prosecution is brought accusing a man of rape, it is for the prosecution to adduce sufficient evidence on all the elements of the offence which could satisfy a reasonable jury of the accused's guilt and it is also for the prosecution to prove guilt before it will win its case. Similarly the plaintiff in a negligence case must adduce sufficient evidence upon which a reasonable trier of fact could be satisfied that a duty of care was owed, that that duty was broken and that the damage incurred was non-remote, and must also satisfy the judge that all three elements were present.

Sometimes this normal rule is altered, however. On occasion it is for the defendant to raise an issue before the prosecution must disprove it – here the defendant bears an evidential burden and the prosecution the legal burden once that evidential burden has been satisfied. At other times the defendant bears a legal burden once the prosecution has raised an issue. At other times, still, the defendant bears both evidential and legal burdens on an issue; the most important examples of this later case are where the defendant argues insanity (*M'Naghten's Case* (1843)) and where he seeks to rely in his defence upon some exception, exemption, proviso, excuse or qualification to a statutory offence tried in the magistrates court (s101 Magistrates' Courts Act 1980 and see *R* v *Edwards* (1975)).

In civil cases it is more difficult to be precise about the incidents of the legal and evidential burdens, because, in almost all cases, the whole matter will be tried by judge alone and there is limited scope for a submission of no case to answer. The submission of no case is the stage of the criminal trial at which the prosecution has to satisfy the judge that it has adduced evidence upon which a reasonable jury could convict the accused (*R* v *Galbraith* (1981)). In civil trials the defendant's election to make a submission of no case is tantamount to a decision not to call evidence (*Alexander* v *Rayson* (1936)) and is, therefore, only rarely employed; in criminal trials, however, the submission is made in the absence of the trier of fact (the jury) and there is no bar on calling evidence afterwards in the event that the submission fails.

There is another burden which is of great practical importance, but does not form part of the strict theory of the law of evidence. Whenever one party has seen his opponent put forward evidence which could persuade a reasonable trier of fact that an issue should be decided in his (the opponent's) favour, the party has a choice, he could sit back and call no evidence, hoping that in fact the trier of fact will not be persuaded, or he could put forward evidence himself so as to counteract the effect of the evidence already adduced. When the evidence against him is strong he knows that he is almost certain to lose unless he calls evidence, and it is not uncommon for it to be said that in such circumstances he bears a tactical burden – he does not have to prove anything and the issue has already been raised, but if he does not call evidence to rebut the evidence already called then his tactics will have failed because he will lose his case (*Cross on Evidence* (8th edition, 1995)).

A presumption is a device by which one party may be aided in the task of satisfying a burden. The basic position is that the judge or jury approaches each issue with an open mind and in the absence of evidence which would satisfy a reasonable man that the issue concerned is made out, that mind will not be swayed to decide in favour of the party bearing the burden. But, presumptions come to the assistance of the party bearing the burden by allowing, or requiring, the judge or jury to decide that the burden is satisfied once certain prescribed evidence has been adduced, even though that evidence may not satisfy the judge or jury in the absence of the presumption. For example, once it has been proved that a person has not been heard of for seven years by those who would normally be expected to hear from him and reasonable enquiries have been made to ascertain his whereabouts, it will be presumed that he is dead (*Chard* v *Chard* (1956)). Of course it is by no means the case that such a person will be dead, he may just have disappeared from circulation, and therefore it may be that left alone a judge or jury may not be satisfied of his death, but the law prescribes as being conclusions which are drawn after the proof of certain basic facts. If we use the example already adverted to and assume that one party wants to prove that Mr A is dead; he could prove this by direct evidence, say, that his corpse was identified, and this will be direct proof of death; alternatively when proving the issue of death it is possible to prove the absence for seven years etc and from proof of those basic facts the conclusion will be drawn that Mr A is dead.

Generally, the nature of a presumption is that it prescribes a conclusion which could or should be drawn once the basic facts are proved, but it can be rebutted, either by proving that the basic facts are not made out or by direct evidence to contradict the conclusion which would otherwise be drawn from those basic facts. The rebuttal of presumptions may arise in one of two ways. Firstly it may be that once a presumption has been drawn it must be disproved in order to be rebutted, on the other hand it may be enough to rebut a presumption that it is shown that there was an equal chance of the conclusion drawn being untrue as there is of it being true. These are normally explained by saying that in the first type a legal burden is placed on the rebutter, whereas in the second an evidential burden only is imposed, but this explanation does not tell the full story. The true position is that sometimes a presumption must be drawn once the primary facts are proved, for example the presumption of death mentioned above – in such cases the only way in which the conclusion reached can be challenged is by challenging the basic facts. For example, if it is desired to rebut the presumption of death it will be necessary to show that the person in question is still alive, but once that has been shown the presumption simply never arises. It is not the case that the plaintiff can satisfy the judge that the three elements of the presumption are made out and then it is for the defendant to challenge that result, because the presumption can only ever be drawn after all the evidence has been heard, for plaintiff and defence. On the other hand some presumptions can be rebutted by leaving the basic facts intact and challenging the conclusion. For example, there is a presumption that a child born in wedlock is legitimate provided the husband had access to the wife at the likely time of conception (*Banbury Peerage Case* (1811)). It is quite possible for the husband to challenge the wife's evidence about access, but it is equally possible for the husband to accept the basic facts and rebut the presumption by more direct evidence of illegitimacy, for example blood group evidence which shows that he is definitely not the father. In such a case the presumption arises once the wife has called evidence on the basic facts and that evidence is not challenged, but the husband can still rebut the presumption.

Therefore, the position is that some presumptions arise only after all the relevant evidence on the fact in issue has been adduced, whereas others arise once the basic facts are proved and it is then open to rebuttal on the ground that despite the basic facts being proved the conclusion should not follow. It is in the context of this latter type of presumption that the different burdens on the rebutter arise. If it is proposed to challenge the basic facts of a presumption then all that the rebutter has to do is show that the basic facts are not proved, in other words he must show it equally likely that the basic facts are not true as that they are true. If, though, it is proposed to challenge the conclusion without challenging the basic facts, then it must be asked what is the standard of challenge required; sometimes the rebutter will have to prove that the conclusion is not merited on the facts of the case, at other times he will successfully rebut the presumption by showing that the conclusion is equally likely to be untrue as it is to be true.

Presumptions rarely have the effect of deciding the overall outcome of a trial, it is more likely that they will assist in the decision on one or more issues. But, in some cases, the only issue at trial is the very one on which the presumption assists.

It can be seen from what has been said above that a presumption may have one of five effects. A presumption may allow one party to satisfy his evidential burden on a particular issue without affecting his legal burden; or it may allow him to satisfy his legal burden on that issue and place a legal burden of disproof on his opponent; or it may allow him to satisfy his legal burden on that issue and place a burden on his opponent to show that the conclusion drawn is equally likely to be false as true; or it may allow him to satisfy his evidential burden on an issue on which he bears no legal burden; or it may allow him to satisfy his legal burden on an issue on which his opponent bears an evidential burden. There is no presumption which determines the whole outcome of a case except in cases where one issue is paramount and a presumption assists in the determination of that issue.

Following what has been said above, it becomes possible to classify presumptions according to their effect on the burden of proof. If a presumption helps a party to meet his evidential burden then it is 'permissive', though of the leading writers only Carter specifically covers this type of presumption (*Cases and Statutes on Evidence* (2nd edition, 1990, pp77–78)). No distinction is drawn between permissive presumptions where the party using the presumption bears the legal burden on the issue and where his opponent bears that burden once the presumption is drawn. If it allows a legal burden to be satisfied in the absence of proof to the contrary then a presumption may be called 'persuasive' (*Cross on Evidence* (8th edition, 1995)) or, as Lord Denning prefers 'compelling' ((1945) 61 LQR 379). If it allows a legal burden to be satisfied but can be rebutted by evidence that the conclusion is equally likely to be false as true then it is an 'evidential' presumption (*Cross on Evidence* (8th edition, 1995); Carter, *Cases and Statutes on Evidence* (2nd edition, 1990, p78)). Lord Bridge wrote of such presumptions that they should be known simply as 'presumptions' because if a legal burden is imposed on the rebutter then we are not concerned with a presumption but with a rule of law which determines that a certain result must follow the proof of certain basic fact ((1949) 12 MLR 272). Lord Bridge's classification, it is submitted, is artificial because almost all presumptions involve rules of law which give special weight to the proof of basic facts. In some cases the conclusion which is drawn on proof of the basic facts is one which common sense would dictate in any event, but in many more cases the conclusion is only drawn because the law requires it; and, in such cases, whether a legal burden of disproof is placed on the rebutter or just a burden to balance the probabilities makes no difference in as much as a rule of law is involved which gives artificial weight to the basic facts.

QUESTION FIVE

Consider whether the presumptions of legitimacy, death and marriage serve any practical purpose in the law in relation to:

a)   facilitating proof of the presumed fact;

b)   their impact on the burden of proof.

University of London LLB Examination
(for External Students) Evidence June 1987 Q4

Skeleton Solution

Definition of the three types of presumption:

a)   *Presumptions of legitimacy* – other methods of proving legitimacy – effect on burden of proof – civil and criminal cases.

b)   *Presumption of death* – alternative methods of proving that the person is alive – effect on burden of proof – evidential only.

c)   *Presumption of marriage* – practical effect of presumption – relatively easy alternative proof – effect on burden of proof.

Suggested Solution

The three presumptions mentioned in the question provide means of proving certain facts for the purpose of legal proceedings without having to call evidence which actually proves them to be true. In outline the three presumptions operate as follows. The presumption of legitimacy provides that once it is proved that a child was born to a woman who was married either at the time of conception or at the time of birth then it will be presumed that it is her husband's child (*Banbury Peerage Case* (1811)). The presumption of death provides that once it is proved that someone has been unheard of for seven years by those who are most likely to have heard of him, then he will be presumed to be dead (*Chard* v *Chard* (1956)). The presumption of marriage is more complicated since it can operate in two ways. Firstly, it will be presumed that a couple are married if it is proved that they have gone through a ceremony of marriage and that they have cohabited as man and wife (*Piers* v *Piers* (1849)). Secondly, it will be presumed that a couple are married if they cohabit as man and wife and are reputed to be married (*Sastry Velaider Aronegary* v *Sambecutty Vailalie* (1881)). Indeed the first of the two aspects of the presumption of marriage itself has two aspects in that it will be presumed that the ceremony itself was effective and that the parties had the capacity to marry.

a) *The presumption of legitimacy*

The presumption of legitimacy as outlined above operated to allow proof of paternity without the need to call medical evidence to establish that the husband could be the father. Indeed there is little evidence that can ever be used to prove that a particular man is the father of a child. Blood group evidence can prove that he is not and can prove that someone with the same blood type is the father, but it cannot go any further than that. Other more technical medical evidence could be called to establish paternity (for example so-called 'genetic fingerprint' evidence) whether the case is criminal or civil.

The effect of the presumption on the burden of proof differs according to whether the case is criminal or civil. In criminal cases where the prosecution wishes to rebut the presumption it will always bear a legal burden of proof and if the defence wishes to rebut it then an evidential burden only must be satisfied. There appears to be no authority directly to point but this results from the normal common law rules of burden and standard of proof, namely that the defence only bears a legal burden where the defence is insanity or where statute imposes such a burden.

In civil cases the presumption places a legal burden of proof on the party seeking to rebut it, whether that be plaintiff or defendant. The standard of proof in civil cases is the balance of probabilities. There is a question whether the presumption itself carries any weight, in other words whether the judge should consider the presumption itself to be evidence which points towards legitimacy, but it is thought that it does not and that its only effect is to place the burden of proof on the rebutter. If the presumption were intended to have weight as evidence then its effect would be not just to dictate who bears the burden of proof but also to increase the standard of proof required from the rebutter, yet the standard is the balance of probabilities only by virtue of s26 of the Family Law Reform Act 1969.

b) *The presumption of death*

Of the three presumptions discussed the presumption of death probably has the most widespread application in practice. It is also the most effective of the three in terms of assisting the court to reach a conclusion on a matter on which there is likely to be no evidence. A person (X) will be presumed to be dead if it can be proved: (1) that there are persons who could be expected to have heard of him; (2) that those persons have not heard of him for seven years; and (3) that reasonable steps have been taken to ascertain whether he is still alive. On proof of these three basic facts the judge must conclude that X is dead unless there is direct evidence that he is not dead. The presumption of death operates to allow for death to be presumed in many cases where it simply cannot be proved one way or the other whether X is in fact dead.

It is, of course, quite possible that X will still be alive but the possibility of this is reduced by the need to prove the first of the three basic facts outlined above. Unless it can be proved that someone is likely to have heard of him then the presumption cannot arise. If X goes abroad, declaring that he wants no further contact with his family or friends and is not heard of for seven years by them then the presumption would not arise, because as a matter of common sense as much as anything else, it is not a compelling conclusion that the reason for not hearing of him is that he is dead.

The need to prove seven years' absence does not give rise to a presumption that X died seven years from the time he was last heard of. The presumption, according to *Re Phene's Trusts* (1870) operates only to establish that X is dead at the time of the legal proceedings. There is some authority to the contrary, notably *Chipchase* v *Chipchase* (1939), but the proper view of such cases is that there was some evidence to show the time of death.

The presumption of death places an evidential burden only on the rebutting party, not a legal burden. To this extent it differs in its operation from the presumption of legitimacy. This difference also means that the effect of the presumption is the same no matter which party it operates against and no matter whether the proceedings are civil or criminal. The presumption will not, of course, be rebutted simply because some evidence is called which shows that one of the basic facts may not be made out. If that evidence is sufficiently cogent then the presumption will not arise at all because the basic fact would not be proved by the party trying to establish death, but once the judge is satisfied on all the evidence that the basic facts are proved then it is only direct evidence that X is alive which can rebut it.

In addition to the formal presumption of death which must arise on the proof of the three basic facts outlined above, the court is always entitled to presume that someone is dead as a matter of inference from other facts. For example, if someone falls from a ship into the middle of the Atlantic ocean and despite attempts to find him he is declared lost, the possibility of him still being alive a year later when nothing has been heard to suggest that he had been picked up by another vessel is remote. The court would be entitled to draw the inference that he is dead from the circumstances of his disappearance. This is not a question of a formal presumption of law being applied, but is a purely factual exercise.

c) *The presumption of marriage*

Whether two people are married can have consequences in both criminal and civil cases. Today the compulsory registration of marriages allows little scope for the presumption to arise, save in cases where there is a question over the legitimacy of the ceremony. Whether the presumption arises on proof of a ceremony and cohabitation or on proof of cohabitation and repute the effect is the same – marriage is presumed unless there is strong evidence that the parties are not legitimately married.

The proof of a ceremony of marriage gives rise to two presumptions which together form the presumption of marriage. The first is the presumption that the ceremony was conducted by an authorised person and in an authorised place. The second is that the parties had the capacity to marry, in other words that they were over 16 years of age, had any parental consent that may have been necessary and were not already married. The practical effect of the presumption is to allow the court to consider a couple to be properly married. The practical effect of the presumption is to allow the court to consider a couple to be properly married without having to investigate all sorts of matters upon which evidence may not be available. For example where a couple underwent a ceremony of marriage 40 years prior to the court proceedings it is highly unlikely that it could be discovered whether the person who married them was properly authorised, so the presumption operates to allow a common sense conclusion to be drawn by the court.

To presume marriage from cohabitation and repute, in other words to presume marriage from evidence that the couple lived together and were reputed to be married, raises rather different issues. In such cases there may be no evidence before the court that any ceremony was entered into, but the presumption still allows a common sense conclusion to be drawn from the proof of the basic facts. In practical terms cases are rare where cohabitation and repute need to be relied upon because of the registration of marriages, but such cases can still arise for example where the parties originally came from a country where there is no such registration.

It is arguable that the presumption of marriage adds little to the right of a court to draw an inference from facts which are proved to it. Perhaps the only effect of it is to prevent the court from refusing to draw the inference of marriage where evidence of the basic facts is proved on balance of probabilities but not to any higher standard.

The presumption of marriage which arises from proof of a ceremony and cohabitation operates somewhat differently to the other presumptions discussed above. This is because the presumption itself is not really concerned with marriage but with the validity of appointment and certification of places and people. The presumption is that: (1) the place in which some ceremony was carried out was licensed; (2) the person conducting it was authorised to do so; (3) the parties concerned were over 16; (4) neither party was already married; and (5) the parties had obtained any parental or other consent which was required. It is these formal matters which are presumed and once they are presumed it then follows that the ceremony was valid. There is no presumption applied directly to the marriage itself.

The effect of this presumption on the burden of proof is also somewhat difficult to state. It is often said that the party who wishes to show that the parties are not married bears a legal burden of proof. But this burden is usually a burden of proving that the basic facts are not established rather than a burden that the presumed fact is not established from the basic facts. The challenge may be made, for example, on the ground that the official who married the parties was not properly authorised or that one of the parties was already married. But that challenge goes to proof of the basic facts not of the presumed fact. In other words it prevents the basic facts being established. To put it another way, where a party to an action wishes to argue that the basic facts are not established then it is for him to prove it. The standard required is the balance of probabilities (*Blyth* v *Blyth* (1966)), but of course, the more unusual the argument being put forward the less probable it is that that argument is correct. For example if it is alleged that a ceremony carried out in a church was not valid because the church was not a proper place for the celebration of marriage then the burden will be very heavy because of the inherent unlikelihood of the allegation.

Once the basic facts of this presumption are established then the only way of rebutting the presumption of marriage is by proving that the marriage has been dissolved.

The presumption which arises out of proof of cohabitation and repute probably places a legal burden of disproof on the rebutter in civil cases. The scope for rebuttal of this presumption is greater because the basic facts can be established without having to prove any ceremony at all. Therefore the rebutter may successfully challenge the presumption by proving that the ceremony which was undergone was not valid. The effect of the cohabitation and repute presumption in many cases is to add to the other presumption of marriage. There are cases, like *R* v *Shepherd* (1904), where a ceremony has been proved and cohabitation and repute have also been proved, and the judge has held that the challenge to the validity of the ceremony had failed because the evidence of cohabitation and repute is strong.

In criminal cases, as shown above in the case of the presumption of legitimacy, nothing more than an evidential burden can be placed on the accused and nothing less than a legal burden on the prosecution, although the prosecution's task may be made easier in bigamy cases because evidence of cohabitation and repute could be an admission by the defendant(s) that they are married.

QUESTION SIX

'It is not only the adduction of *prima facie* evidence by the proponent which results in an evidential burden being cast on the opponent. The same effect may result from the operation of a presumption.' (Phipson and Elliot).

Discuss. To what extent do you agree that the operation of presumptions is based more on considerations of public policy than of logic?

University of London LLB Examination
(for External Students) Evidence June 1991 Q4

General Comment

This rather long question requires a treatment in outline of the role of evidential burden under the general law and (as the main part of the answer) the effects of common law presumptions on the burden. The latter is best dealt with by reference to the principal rebuttable presumptions of law.

Skeleton Solution

• Role of the evidential burden under the general law with particular reference to common law defences; distinction of tactical or provisional burden.

• Effect of presumptions – res ipsa loquitur; death; legitimacy; marriage. The relationship in criminal trials with the *Woolmington* principle; the diffuseness of the language used to describe the evidential effects of presumptions and the variations of approach in the case law.

Suggested Solution

A party wishing to establish his case to the requisite standard of proof in civil or criminal proceedings has two hurdles to surmount. He must first ensure that the tribunal of fact considers his story. He must then ensure that the jury act on it in his favour. The second is the discharge of the burden of proof on the party. The first is the discharge of the evidential burden – sufficient evidence to make the party's case a live issue. Sufficient in other words, for the tribunal of fact to consider his story at all.

Clearly, if a party has to discharge the burden of proof, he must get his contentions considered by the tribunal of fact in the first place. The party having the legal burden also generally has the evidential burden. To this extent, therefore, the evidential burden is of little consequence. There are, however, cases where the evidential burden can be critical. Common law defences are a case in point. The prosecution have the legal burden to establish an accused's guilt, but before a jury is entitled to consider an accused's defence of provocation (*Mancini* v *DPP*

(1942)), duress (*R* v *Gill* (1963)), self-defence (*R* v *Lobell* (1957)) and, probably, accident (*Bratty* v *Attorney General for Northern Ireland* (1963)) and alibi (*R* v *Johnson* (1961)). The evidential burden must be discharged by the accused before the jury will be entitled to consider the defence. Indeed, it would appear that any defence which is more than the denial of an essential element of the prosecution's case is subject to such a burden.

But the fact that one party puts up a case which, in the absence of contradictory evidence, he may win does not result in an evidential burden being placed on that party, unless the term is being used as a description of the need by that opponent to produce factual controverting evidence, or to neutralise the evidence by cross-examination, or lose the case. It is submitted that this is not the meaning properly ascribed to the term evidential burden in its technical sense. The requirement for an opponent to meet unfavourable evidence is sometimes called a 'tactical' or 'provisional' burden and this is a source of confusion. It is not an evidential burden.

The field of presumptions does however provide examples for which the quotation in the question is apt. These presumptions have the effect of establishing certain facts ('the presumed facts') once other facts ('the basic facts') are proved. For the purposes of discussion, the presumptions of res ipsa loquitur, death, legitimacy and marriage will be examined.

Res ipsa loquitur applies only to civil proceedings. If a state of affairs is under control of a party and an accident occurs which would not in the ordinary course of events happen in the absence of negligence, then negligence will be presumed. The evidential effect is not entirely settled, and there are cases indicating that it is really no more than a label for circumstantial evidence – or a presumption of fact (*Langham* v *Governors of Wellingborough School* (1932)). *The Kite* (1933) indicates that it is a rebuttable presumption of law casting an evidential burden on the opposing party. On the other hand, the presumption casts the legal burden on the party against whom it operates, according to *Barkway* v *South Wales Transport Executive* (1949). The most recent pronouncement from the Privy Council in *Ng Chun Pui* v *Lee Chuen Tat* (1988) follows the proposition that the maxim casts an evidential burden on the opposing party.

Under the presumption of death, the fact of death is presumed on proof of an absence of seven years or more, nothing having been heard of the absentee by persons who might have heard of him, due enquiries having been made. It is apparent from the decision of the House of Lords in *Prudential* v *Edmonds* (1877) that this presumption operates to cast an evidential burden on the party against whom it operates.

The presumption of legitimacy is less straightforward in that it is overlaid by statute, and also reveals the need to consider the position in civil and criminal cases separately.

At common law, the presumed fact – legitimacy – was established by proof of the basic facts of birth or conception in lawful wedlock. The effect of the presumption according to *Morris* v *Davies* (1837) was to place the legal burden (and not just an evidential burden) on the opposing party. Clearly, the former requirement is the important one, since to discharge the legal burden, the party must discharge the evidential burden on that issue.

But in criminal trials, the placing of the legal burden on an accused would appear to conflict with the *Woolmington* (1935) principle. The exceptions under that rule (insanity raised by defence and statutory exceptions) clearly exclude presumptions. Thus, it might be that the presumption of legitimacy if deployed by the prosecution has the maximum effect of placing an evidential burden on the accused.

Finally, with the presumption of marriage, there are three different situations to consider, formal validity, essential validity and presumption of marriage by cohabitation and repute. A marriage proved to have complied with the necessary formalities of local law is presumed to be formally valid. Likewise, the parties are presumed to have had the capacity to enter into the marriage. *Piers* v *Piers* (1849) applied *Morris* v *Davies* from which it is apparent that the evidential effect was to put the legal burden on the party against whom the presumption operated in civil trials. Essential validity is more ambiguous. *Tweny* v *Tweny* (1946) indicates that the effect is to place evidential burden on the party against whom the presumption operates, though it hardly seems very sensible to invest in two related aspects of the same presumption with different evidential effects.

On the third aspect of the presumption, a cohabiting couple reputed in the community to have been married are taken at common law to have been through a valid marriage ceremony at some time in the past. *Sastry* v *Sambecutty* (1881) is authority for the view that this places the legal burden on the opposing party, although, as with the other aspects of the presumption, the language is less than clear. This aspect, together with formal validity, must be subject to the proviso that in criminal trials, the maximum effect of the presumption when relied on by the prosecution is to place an evidential burden on the accused, for the *Woolmington* principle is otherwise infringed.

There is little doubt that public policy has played a significant part in development of presumptions. The sanctity of marriage and the stigma of illegitimacy were influential in establishing their evidential effects. It is also true that notwithstanding efforts to provide a coherent strategy for analysis of those evidential effects, satisfactory classification of them is still elusive. This is apparent from the above discussion, demonstrating, for example, seemingly different evidential effects for different aspects of the same presumption, and divergence in judicial views of the effects of the same presumption.

One explanation for this elusiveness is that they were developed to satisfy policy concerns rather than legal principle. If that is the case, establishing a coherent legal framework for the operation of presumptions may not be capable of achievement.

15 University of London LLB (External) 1996 Questions and Suggested Solutions

UNIVERSITY OF LONDON
LLB EXAMINATIONS 1996
for External Students
PARTS I AND II EXAMINATIONS (Scheme A)
THIRD AND FOURTH YEAR EXAMINATIONS (Scheme B)
GRADUATE ENTRY LEVEL II (Route A)
GRADUATE ENTRY THIRD YEAR EXAMINATIONS (Route B)

LAW OF EVIDENCE

Thursday, 13 June: 10.00 am to 1.00 pm

Answer *FOUR* of the following EIGHT questions, including at least *ONE* from Part A and *ONE* from Part B.

PART A

1   'The whole point of a lot of circumstantial evidence is to establish the accused's membership of a number of different classes of persons more likely than non-members to have done or omitted to do some act.' (Cross)

Discuss.

2   What principles or policies, if any, can you detect behind judicial allocations of the legal burden of proof in criminal cases?

3   'If there are to be any rules peculiar to hearsay evidence, the definition of hearsay for the purpose of such rules should include all that is presently within its ambit except implied assertions.' (Law Commission Consultation Paper No 138)

Discuss.

4   'The job of court and jury is to see *whether* the suspect has *committed the particular offence*.' (Llewellyn)

Have recent developments in relation to similar fact evidence made this objective more likely to be achieved?

PART B

5   David, Tim and William are charged with conspiracy to commit robbery. The case for the prosecution is that at a meeting at David's flat in London they, and another man called Peter, agreed to work as a team to commit robberies on London Underground trains. The chief witness against them is Peter, who has pleaded guilty to taking part in the conspiracy and has now agreed to give evidence for the prosecution. David does not give evidence, but his counsel puts to Peter in cross-examination that Peter has a grudge against David, who has been having an affair with Peter's wife, and is telling lies about David to get his revenge. Tim gives evidence and says that he was present at the meeting

between the four men. He says that the three others tried to persuade him to take part in their plan, but he refused and told them that God would punish them for their wickedness. William gives evidence of an alibi and calls Rebecca, who confirms his story that he spent the weekend during which the meeting is alleged to have taken place staying with her at a hotel in France.

David has three spent convictions for robbery. Tim has a recent conviction for perjury. William has no previous convictions, but he has two previous acquittals for burglary. On each occasion he gave evidence on an alibi which was supported by other witnesses. Rebecca has recent convictions for assault, theft and managing a brothel.

Discuss the evidential issues that arise.

6   Tom is charged with causing the death of Harry by reckless driving. The case for the prosecution is that Tom was driving too fast and failed to stop at a set of traffic lights which gave pedestrians the right of way. Harry was crossing the road and was hit by Tom. He died forty minutes later in an ambulance. Just before he died he said to Johnnie, a paramedic, 'You don't think I'm going to make it, do you? That driver never gave me a chance. He just drove straight at me when the lights were against him.' Shortly after the accident PC Ellis arrived at the scene. He was approached by Leo who said that he had been standing nearby and had seen everything. Leo told PC Ellis that he had seen the lights were on red to traffic when Harry was knocked down. He also said that afterwards he had spoken to Tom and that Tom had said, 'I never saw the lights at all; I was thinking about my wife. She's going to leave me after ten years of marriage.' PC Ellis made a note of his conversation with Leo and took his name and address. Leo never made a formal statement to the police. He has now left his address and cannot be traced.

Advise the prosecution on the evidential issues that arise.

7   Several antique shops had been burgled within a ten mile radius of Marlborough. One day in January DC Pierrepoint visited Quentin, a man with a long record of burglaries, and asked him to come down to the police station to help the police with their inquiries. Quentin agreed. When they arrived, Pierrepoint left Quentin to wait for several hours in a room without light or heating. At the end of that time Quentin asked to see a solicitor. Pierrepoint agreed to find one. Ten minutes later he falsely told Quentin that none was available. He then said that he was ready to start asking questions. Quentin was an alcoholic and had by then been without a drink for so long that he was beginning to feel sick. He wanted to get the interview over as soon as possible and so agreed to do without a solicitor. In the course of the interview he confessed to taking part in one of the burglaries but denied the rest. He told Pierrepoint that he would find the stolen property from the burglary in which he had taken part hidden under the floorboards of an empty house nearby. The police searched the house and the property was found where Quentin had said it would be.

Discuss the evidential issues arising.

8   a)   Philip was indicted for possession of cocaine with intent to supply. When the police lawfully searched his house they found, in addition to a quantity of cocaine, £5,650 in cash. The prosecution have relied on this discovery in support of their case. Philip admitted possession of the cocaine but said that it was solely for his personal use. Philip told the police that he always kept a large float of cash handy because he collected modern paintings and believed that artists were often more willing to sell their work

for a lower price if they could be paid in cash. Philip repeated this explanation when giving evidence in his own defence.

How should the judge direct the jury in relation to the evidence from both prosecution and defence?

b) Sam and Toby are indicted for robbery. Both have given evidence denying the offence. Sam's counsel has adduced evidence to show that Sam is a man of previous good character. Toby's counsel has not been able to adduce similar evidence in respect of his client because Toby has three recent convictions for burglary and receiving stolen goods. This information has not, however, emerged during the trial and the jury has heard nothing about Toby's character.

How should the judge direct the jury in the light of this situation?

QUESTION ONE

'The whole point of a lot of circumstantial evidence is to establish the accused's membership of a number of different classes of persons more likely than non-members to have done or omitted to do some act.' (Cross)

Discuss.

University of London LLB Examination
(for External Students) Evidence June 1996 Q1

General Comment

The quoted passage points the candidate towards those aspects of circumstantial evidence which operate by a process of accumulation of the surrounding facts and circumstances of a crime or situation from which some inference may safely be drawn as to whether a particular person or persons were likely to have been involved in that crime or situation.

Skeleton Solution

- Brief definition of circumstantial evidence.
- Examples of types of evidence that might inferentially link a person to a class of persons.
- The overlap and tensions between circumstantial evidence and the hearsay rule.
- Uses of circumstantial evidence other than to establish membership of a class.
- Conclusion as to the validity of the proposition.

Suggested Solution

Circumstantial evidence might well be defined as evidence of facts concerning the surrounding context or circumstances of a crime, from which the existence or non-existence of some fact in issue can be inferred. It is not direct evidence of the matter but a sufficient number of such inferences can combine together to give an undeniable and, in proper circumstances, overwhelming weight to the evidence in the same way that a rope of great strength can be plaited from fragile strands.

The type of evidence that, by way of inference, might link a person to membership of a class of persons can be seen in cases such as *R* v *Rice* (1963) where the issue was whether Rice had been on a particular flight from London to Manchester. Despite arguments based upon hearsay, a ticket in the name of Rice for that particular flight was admitted as evidence of surrounding circumstance from which a safe inference could properly be drawn that someone called Rice had purchased and carried that ticket on the flight. The significance of this case for the Cross proposition is that such inferences might place a person in several different classes concurrently. It could fix him in time, place, travelling singly or in company, on a particular aeroplane or perhaps in a particular seat or class of passenger if this were relevant.

Similar reasoning can be seen in *R* v *Lydon* (1986) concerning pieces of paper with the accused's forename on them close to and linked forensically with a gun found on the getaway route from a robbery. There are clearly established circumstantial classes here, first between the pieces of paper and someone called 'Sean', then between someone called 'Sean' and the gun because of a proved forensic connection between the ink used and the gun, and finally between 'Sean' and the robbery because of the inference that the gun was the one used in the crime. This could then be used to support the inferences to be drawn from identification evidence that

189

placed the accused within certain classes as to height, build and appearance but which was inconclusive on other matters.

There is clearly an overlap and a tension between this type of circumstantial evidence and the hearsay rule, and this point was argued vigorously for the defence in both of the above-mentioned cases. On analysis, it can be easily seen that the fact of a hearsay component by way of implied assertion as in *Rice* should not prevent inferences being drawn from it which are dictated, not by expediency or excessive reliance upon legalistic distinctions, but by the simple logic that a ticket in the name of Rice is more likely to have been purchased by a person of that name than otherwise.

There are uses of circumstantial evidence other than to place a person within a class of persons but these are comparatively rare, eg evidence of prior intention or preparatory acts which are more relied upon to support the inference that a person went on to do a certain act (as in *R* v *Buckley* (1873) or *R* v *Moghal* (1977)), as well as the circumstance where a person fails to make a statement where one might be reasonably expected (as in *Bessela* v *Stern* (1877)), or a failure to give answers, explanations or evidence in criminal law situations as covered by the Criminal Justice and Public Order Act 1994. In general, these must be seen as exceptional to the normal use of circumstantial evidence in that they are provided by the common law or statute to deal with very specific inferences which may or may not be drawn, and may not be relied upon for other purposes.

In conclusion, it is submitted that the proposition from Cross provides an accurate and illuminating summary of the function and use of most circumstantial evidence.

QUESTION TWO

What principles or policies, if any, can you detect behind judicial allocations of the legal burden of proof in criminal cases?

University of London LLB Examination
(for External Students) Evidence June 1996 Q2

General Comment

The question calls for a good knowledge of Lord Sankey's rule in *Woolmington* v *DPP* and the judicial glosses that have been put upon it subsequently, particularly with respect to implied statutory exceptions and the use of s101 Magistrates' Courts Act 1980. Some analysis of the difficulties involved in discharging a legal burden of proof is necessary to answer the question fully.

Skeleton Solution

- *Woolmington* v *DPP* and Lord Sankey's dictum.
- The exceptions and the opportunity for judicial allocation of burden.
- Section 101 MCA 1980: the principles and policies involved.
- Ease or difficulty of discharging the legal burden.
- Whether a true exception or part of the description of the offence?
- Applicability of s101 principles to trial on indictment.

Suggested Solution

The modern law concerning the incidence of the legal burden in criminal trials can be traced to the dictum of Lord Sankey in *Woolmington* v *DPP* (1935), the 'golden thread' argument that, subject to insanity or statutory exception, the legal burden of proving all elements will remain throughout upon the prosecution. It might be thought from this that judicial allocation of the burden is a non-event but this is far from the case. The area that provides considerable scope for judicial views is that of implied statutory exceptions stemming from the rather broad wording of s101 Magistrates' Courts Act (MCA) 1980. The provision applies to summary trials and has the effect of placing upon a defendant the burden of proving any exception, proviso, excuse or qualification that accompanies the description of the offence in any enactment relied upon by the prosecution. The policies underlying this section are the same ones that underly *Woolmington* itself, namely that for criminal liability it should never be the rule that a person is presumed to be guilty, simpliciter, until he or she can discharge a burden of proving their own innocence. In many cases it would be impossible to begin to discharge such a burden, as with a well-known liar who is accused of theft and only has his own word with which to defend himself.

Section 101 is intended to apply only to statutory offences where the prohibited situation is clearly described and the excusatory circumstance is expressly provided for. The situation is such that proving the excuse will usually be a very simple matter, such as proving the lawful authority for obstructing the highway where a person has been injured as a result, as in *Gatland* v *MPC* (1968). By contrast, the difficulties for the prosecution of discharging a burden of proof that the accused did not fit within the excusatory circumstance would be almost insuperable, usually requiring the proof of a negative. The significance of the ease or difficulty for either party in discharging the burden of proving excusatory circumstances was examined by the House of Lords in *Nimmo* v *Alexander Cowan & Sons Ltd* (1968). The case fell very close to the line and, by a three to two majority, the House held that where the wording of the statute was not clear on the point, the court was entitled to look at the relative ease of each party in proving the excuse as well as the mischief aimed at by the Act.

One very real problem for the courts comes from the situation where it is not at all clear whether there is a separable clearly excusatory part to the provision, or whether what is written is meant to describe the definition of the actus reus itself, as was the situation in the leading case of *R* v *Hunt* (1987). Here, the words in the Misuse of Drugs Act 1971, to the effect that the Act did not apply to preparations of less than 0.2 per cent morphine, were viewed by the House of Lords as not imposing a burden upon the accused to prove by way of defence, but as imposing a burden upon the Crown to prove as a constituent element of the actus reus. The point was made that the *Woolmington* dictum applied both to implied and express statutory exceptions. In view of the highly specialised and onerous problem of discharging the burden in *Hunt*, this is clearly based upon the *Woolmington* thinking.

In *Hunt*, the court confirmed the view of the Court of Appeal in *R* v *Edwards* (1975) that the same principles should apply to trials on indictment as to summary trials by s101, and the reason for this is to give a consistency of approach. This seems to apply a fortiori where the offence is clearly a regulatory one as in *R* v *Alath Construction Ltd* (1990), a case about breach of a tree-preservation order. *Hunt* also showed that any difficulties of construction should be resolved in favour of the defendant so as to place the burden upon the prosecution. This principle was illustrated in *Westminster City Council* v *Croyalgrange Ltd* (1986), where the House of Lords took the view that an exception qualified a statutory prohibition which was not, in itself, the offence charged. This allowed the court to take the position that s101 did not apply to a sex establishment licence situation and the legal burden remained upon the Crown throughout.

QUESTION THREE

'If there are to be any rules peculiar to hearsay evidence, the definition of hearsay for the purpose of such rules should include all that is presently within its ambit except implied assertions.' (Law Commission Consultation Paper No 138)

Discuss.

University of London LLB Examination
(for External Students) Evidence June 1996 Q3

General Comment

There are various ways to approach a question such as this but it is necessary to bring out the distinction between express and implied assertions to see whether such distinctions justify a different, more relaxed reception for implied assertions despite their obvious hearsay component and effect. The cases cited in the Consultation Paper No 138 provide a good framework upon which to build a discussion.

Skeleton Solution

• Brief definition/description of implied assertions.
• Survey of case law development of hearsay rule as applied to implied assertions.
• Difficulties involved in judicial analysis of whether assertion contained in evidence or not.
• Consultation Paper views and recommendations.
• Conclusion.

Suggested Solution

To understand the Law Commission's views on the hearsay rule and implied assertions it is necessary to distinguish such assertions from express assertions. Words, spoken or written, or in rare cases conduct alone, may be to such effect that inferences can be drawn from them. If the inference drawn is in the form of an assertion of fact, this will be an implied assertion such as the shouted words in *Teper* v *R* (1952) of '… your place burning and you going away from the fire' (implied assertion that shop owner was present at scene of fire), or the desperate gesturing of the dying woman in *Chandrasekera* v *R* (1937) (sign language indicating and asserting identity of assailant).

The case law on implied assertion and hearsay is fairly voluminous and seems to stem from *Wright* v *Doe d Tatham* (1837), where letters sought to be admitted to assert that the writers considered the recipient to be sane were analysed as inadmissible hearsay, through to cases such as *R* v *Harry* (1988) and *R* v *Kearley* (1992) where inferences that defendants were drug dealers were likely to have been drawn as evidence of telephone calls and personal visits by potential drug purchasers had been sought to be admitted. In *Kearley* admission of such evidence for the Crown grounded a successful appeal and defence evidence of this type was properly excluded in *Harry*. The House of Lords judgments in *Kearley* reveal the very serious difficulties in rationalising and analysing such evidence at all, as the same evidence will often be able to be rationalised on a different basis altogether, such as the airline ticket in *R* v *Rice* (1963) (circumstantial real evidence) or the phone call in *Ratten* v *R* (1972) (evidence of facts in issue – the state of affairs at the home).

It is very clear from the cases on implied assertions that the difficulties involved in considering express hearsay assertions are greatly increased when the matter becomes one of implication from absence of facts. The 'record' cases such as *R* v *Shore* (1983) and *R* v *Patel* (1981) indicate that absence of a record, where one might be expected to be found, is treated as direct evidence rather than a matter of implied assertion. This explanation is not altogether convincing and there is no doubt that these difficulties have had considerable influence on the Law Commission.

The Consultation Paper appears to be heavily influenced by the unconvincing and somewhat artificial distinctions used in the implied assertion cases, and it comes to the conclusion that any future shape of the hearsay rule ought not to include implied assertions at all, on the basis that this would prevent resort to strained judicial reasoning. The Commission has drawn support for its reasoning in the fact that many common law countries have evidence codes which expressly exclude implied assertions by defining hearsay by reference to evidence of words or acts intended by the speaker or creator to be assertive. This 'intention to assert' is suggested by the Paper as an integral and essential part of any future hearsay rule.

In conclusion, it is difficult to get away from the view that implied assertions provide enormous problems if caught by the hearsay rule, but it is also true that there are considerable possibilities for miscarriages of justice and of excessively collateral examinations if the rule does not apply to such assertions at all. The danger is of replacing long arguments on admissibility with long arguments about relevance, collateral evidence and the propriety and correctness of inferences to be drawn from such evidence. The general problems concerning hearsay outlined by Lord Reid in *Myers* v *DPP* (1965) were shown to be very much still relevant in *Kearley* and are very unlikely to go away altogether, whatever comes out of the Consultation Paper. It is submitted that it would be unwise to have a new regime which does not have at least a discretionary power to catch implied assertions within some exclusionary rule, although there may be scope for extension of other discretions such as s78 Police and Criminal Evidence Act 1984 or the common law discretion to exclude highly prejudicial evidence of relatively low probative value.

QUESTION FOUR

'The job of court and jury is to see *whether* the suspect has *committed the particular offence*.' (Llewellyn)

Have recent developments in relation to similar fact evidence made this objective more likely to be achieved?

University of London LLB Examination
(for External Students) Evidence June 1996 Q4

General Comment

It is necessary here to analyse the recent Court of Appeal and House of Lords cases to see whether the general change of emphasis in similar fact evidence cases, particularly sexual assaults, away from questions of admissibility and more towards weight of evidence, has made sustainable and safe convictions more likely or less so. An important consideration is the effect upon the judges' power to hold a voir dire and to give adequate and understandable directions to the jury.

Skeleton Solution

• Recent cases and their implications, striking similarity, collusion and distortion.
• Independence of evidence.
• Judges' power to admit or to exclude evidence.
• Considerations that might alter the balance between prosecution and defence.
• Other changes in the law of evidence bearing upon the matter.
• Conclusion.

Suggested Solution

The most recent developments in the areas of similar fact evidence have been mainly concerned with the area of sexual offences against multiple victims, usually children, where the question of cross-admissibility of their evidence under the similar fact evidence rationale has been in issue. *R* v *P* (1991) started the ball rolling with the view of the House of Lords that 'striking similarity' of evidence was not an indispensable precondition for admissibility except where identity is in issue, and that probative force was what should be looked for in such cases. This decision has considerable implications for a general widening of admissibility but, by itself, might not have had too radical an effect. The obvious problem for a judge moves from the relatively straightforward matter of a voir dire argument about admissibility to the truly formidable task of directing the jury as to the true relationship and significance of the different witnesses' evidence. It is certainly not clear that this will achieve the objective set out in Llewellyn's proposition, and it may well do the opposite. A consequence that follows this wider admissibility, as surely as night follows day, is that of the possibility for accidental or deliberate collusion between witnesses in this type of case. The real point in issue here is whether the question is one of admissibility, or whether it is one of weight and so for the jury. The point is far from easy and has given the Court of Appeal considerable food for thought in cases such as *R* v *Ananthanarayanan* (1994), *R* v *Ryder* (1994), *R* v *W* (1994) and, most recently, both the Court of Appeal and the House of Lords considered the matter in *R* v *H* (1994). In the earlier cases, the view of the Court of Appeal was, generally, that the matter was one for the judge on a question of admissibility. There was an abrupt (and not very well explained) change of tack in *R* v *H* by the Court of Appeal, to the view that the question of collusion went to probative value and was for the jury to decide rather than the judge on admissibility. The House of Lords confirmed this view by a majority decision and the thrust of the Lord Chancellor's judgment seems to be that collusion is, generally, not a matter to be considered at the stage of deciding admissibility, apart from the most exceptional cases.

This judgment has enormous implications for the judge and jury alike. If a judge believes himself bound to admit evidence in the face of quite strong evidence of possible collusion or accidental contamination, as can easily have occurred in familial situations, his difficulties in directing the jury as to the appropriate weight to attach to evidence are likely to become insuperable. The jury is likely to ask itself why the judge admitted the evidence at all, or might jump to the opposite conclusion and disregard the collusion point altogether. It is hard to escape the conclusion that a jury will find itself in very great difficulties in such cases and take the safe course of acquittal.

It may well be that one result of *R* v *H* is that more prosecutions are commenced and, paradoxically, a greater number of acquittals or successful appeals result. The point that seems to have come out of the case is that the 'independent' quality of similar fact evidence that has figured so prominently in its development seems to have been relegated to an altogether lower scale of importance. There is certainly an impression to be gained from the judgment that other recent changes in the law of evidence, such as the abrogation of formal corroboration warnings, have also been seen to abrogate the need for support between those witnesses who were formerly subject to such warnings. It is submitted that this may well have caused a significant departure from guiding principles developed over a long period and in a much wider context than multiple juvenile sexual complaint cases, which will be likely to require the House of Lords to revisit this area in the not too distant future. A possible basis for a further House of Lords appeal might be the distinction, picked up by Lord Mustill in *R* v *H*, of the difference in thinking and approach between those cases where collusion of a deliberate type might have occurred and those altogether different situations where accidental contamination or a particular pattern of questions has occurred. Another possible side effect of the cases since *R* v *P* is some resurgence of the 'special' treatment of certain types of sexual offence so condemned in *DPP* v *Boardman* (1975).

QUESTION FIVE

David, Tim and William are charged with conspiracy to commit robbery. The case for the prosecution is that at a meeting at David's flat in London they, and another man called Peter, agreed to work as a team to commit robberies on London Underground trains. The chief witness against them is Peter, who has pleaded guilty to taking part in the conspiracy and has now agreed to give evidence for the prosecution. David does not give evidence, but his counsel puts to Peter in cross-examination that Peter has a grudge against David, who has been having an affair with Peter's wife, and is telling lies about David to get his revenge. Tim gives evidence and says that he was present at the meeting between the four men. He says that the three others tried to persuade him to take part in their plan, but he refused and told them that God would punish them for their wickedness. William gives evidence of an alibi and calls Rebecca, who confirms his story that he spent the weekend during which the meeting is alleged to have taken place staying with her at a hotel in France.

David has three spent convictions for robbery. Tim has a recent conviction for perjury. William has no previous convictions, but he has two previous acquittals for burglary. On each occasion he gave evidence on an alibi which was supported by other witnesses. Rebecca has recent convictions for assault, theft and managing a brothel.

Discuss the evidential issues that arise.

University of London LLB Examination
(for External Students) Evidence June 1996 Q5

General Comment

The points involved here are mainly about character evidence and the loss of shield under s1 Criminal Evidence Act 1898, alibi evidence and the use that may properly be made of previous convictions or acquittals.

Skeleton Solution

- Peter's competence as a witness.
- David not giving evidence: s1(f)(ii) CEA 1898, *R* v *Butterwasser*.
- Common law on loss of shield.
- David's convictions and good character.
- Tim's evidence: s1(f)(iii) CEA 1898, giving 'evidence against'.
- Previous consistent statements.
- Tim's convictions and character.
- William's evidence of alibi and Rebecca's testimony.
- Rebecca's character and her previous convictions.
- Collateral evidence rule.

Suggested Solution

Peter has agreed to give evidence for the prosecution and, after pleading guilty to the conspiracy, will now be a competent witness for the prosecution and will be likely to be sentenced after the trial of David, Tim and William: *R* v *Weekes* (1982). David does not give evidence but his counsel puts to Peter that he is lying. There is not much doubt that, if David had been 'called as a witness', the nature of his defence would be such as to 'involve imputations on the character of ... witnesses for the prosecution' under s1(f)(ii) Criminal Evidence Act (CEA) 1898, so as to cause him loss of shield against questions on his past convictions or character. However, as David has not testified, and provided that his counsel has not sought to establish David's good character by cross examination or other evidence, the shield will not be lost by putting Peter's character in issue: *R* v *Butterwasser* (1948). Even if the shield were to be lost, the spent convictions should not be referred to if it is reasonably avoidable, according to the *Practice Direction* of 1975 by the then Lord Chief Justice.

If David is, except for the spent convictions, of good character, it might very well be worth his counsel putting this forward, subject to the leave of the court. This was the import of *R* v *Nye* (1982), according to the views of the Court of Appeal, but the Court would not interfere with the judge's discretion in not allowing this. A direction as to good character can be valuable for one who is co-accused with others of bad character. In accordance with the principles laid down in *R* v *Vye* (1993) this will include a 'second limb' direction that good character may go to the issue of guilt as well as credibility.

Tim's evidence is almost certain to be seen as 'evidence against' his co-accused, causing him to lose his shield under s1(f)(iii) CEA 1898. *Murdoch* v *Taylor* (1965) clearly shows that evidence that either supports the prosecution case in a material respect or undermines the defence of a co-accused is enough for s1(f)(iii) to apply. Tim's evidence clearly does both, and the court will have no discretion to prevent counsel for his co-accused cross-examining him, although it will have discretion to prevent the prosecution doing so in a proper case. Any cross-examination of Tim will only be relevant to his credit as a witness, a recent conviction for perjury being highly relevant to such a matter.

William gives evidence of an alibi. A mere denial of taking part in some joint enterprise is not sufficient to constitute 'evidence against' a co-accused for s1(f)(iii) unless it either points inevitably to the guilt of the co-accused as in *R* v *Davis* (1975), the 'cut throat' defence, or is an outright contradiction of the evidence of the co-accused as in *R* v *Varley* (1982). The

Varley point is appropriate at least in respect of Tim and also in respect of Peter who is, despite his guilty plea, 'charged in the same proceedings'. It looks as if he will lose his shield but all that we know of his character is his two acquittals, in each case on an alibi. These matters would certainly not be relevant to loss of shield under s1(f)(i) CEA 1898, as only proof of commission of or conviction for an offence is admissible. They would, however, be in line with what Lord Sankey said in *Maxwell* v *DPP* (1935), as relating to s1(f)(ii) and (iii), where the question is asked in order to elicit evidence as to statements made in trials which resulted in acquittal which tend to throw doubt upon the evidence actually being given in the instant trial. The earlier alibis might, of course, be relevant in the same way as in *Jones* v *DPP* (1962), on the basis of striking similarity of the actual alibi relied upon.

Rebecca's testimony may, as with William's own evidence, be viewed as 'evidence against' the co-accused under s1(f)(iii) but that will only lose William his shield. It cannot lose her any shield because she is not 'charged and a witness' in the proceedings so s1(f) is not concerned with her character. She is, however, like any other witness who, not being an accused, is liable to have questions put to her attack her credibility as a witness, but these questions will be governed by the collateral evidence rule as set out in *Attorney-General* v *Hitchcock* (1847). If any of the recent convictions had bearing upon her testimony in William's defence, such as dates which cast doubts upon her testimony or other matters relating to her truthfulness, previous inconsistent statements etc, questions upon those matters would probably not fall foul of the rule. This questioning would only go to her credibility. Theoretically, Rebecca's convictions may be asked about under s6 Criminal Procedure Act 1865 almost regardless of relevance but it is open to the judge to prevent questioning which sheds no light on the issues or the witness's character.

QUESTION SIX

Tom is charged with causing the death of Harry by reckless driving. The case for the prosecution is that Tom was driving too fast and failed to stop at a set of traffic lights which gave pedestrians the right of way. Harry was crossing the road and was hit by Tom. He died forty minutes later in an ambulance. Just before he died he said to Johnnie, a paramedic, 'You don't think I'm going to make it, do you? That driver never gave me a chance. He just drove straight at me when the lights were against him.' Shortly after the accident PC Ellis arrived at the scene. He was approached by Leo who said that he had been standing nearby and had seen everything. Leo told PC Ellis that he had seen the lights were on red to traffic when Harry was knocked down. He also said that afterwards he had spoken to Tom and that Tom had said, 'I never saw the lights at all; I was thinking about my wife. She's going to leave me after ten years of marriage.' PC Ellis made a note of his conversation with Leo and took his name and address. Leo never made a formal statement to the police. He has now left his address and cannot be traced.

Advise the prosecution on the evidential issues that arise.

University of London LLB Examination
(for External Students) Evidence June 1996 Q6

General Comment

This problem calls for a solid approach to the hearsay rule and the various common law and statutory exceptions appropriate to criminal trials. Some items of evidence might be rationalised under several different exceptions so a reasonably comprehensive approach is needed.

Skeleton Solution

- Brief discussion of hearsay rule.
- Johnnie's evidence: statement of a fact relevant to facts in issue – res gestae – dying declarations – possibility of s24 CJA 1988.
- PC Ellis's evidence: s24 CJA 1988 – Leo's own observations – Leo's report of Tom's words.
- Confessions/admissions and multiple hearsay.

Suggested Solution

The evidentiary issues involved here are those surrounding the application of the hearsay rule to criminal trials. The rule may be stated as being that evidence of out-of-court statements, containing assertions, may not be repeated in court for the purpose of showing the truth of an assertion even though it might be admitted for other relevant purposes.

Harry made a very clear statement to Johnnie that could be very useful to the prosecution if admitted into evidence. There are various possibilities. Assuming that Johnnie made no note of the words, he might be allowed to give evidence of Harry's statement as evidence of facts relevant to facts in issue along the lines seen in *Ratten* v *R* (1972), to show the state of affairs, ie that Harry was crossing properly, if this was in issue. The statement might also be repeatable by Johnnie under the res gestae exception relating to spontaneous utterances by persons closely involved in events, whether as participant or witness, where the statement is more or less contemporaneous with the event and where concoction or distortion can reasonably be disregarded. Provided that the matter could be brought within the guidelines given by Lord Ackner in *R* v *Andrews* (1987) covering the continuing domination of the victim's mind and the exclusion of mistake, concoction or distortion, this is probably admissible. The time gap of 40 minutes or so would not necessarily be fatal to such an admission, as the chronological strictures of *R* v *Bedingfield* (1879) have been replaced by the test of the domination of the victim's mind discussed by Lord Ackner in *R* v *Andrews*. There seems a possibility that Harry's words might be admissible as a dying declaration as to the cause of his condition along the lines in *R* v *Woodcock* (1879), such statements having been admitted in death by reckless driving charges in other jurisdictions, but it would be necessary to show Harry's 'settled hopeless expectation of death' and this is by no means certain. If Johnnie had made a note of Harry's words as part of his duties, it seems possible that the note might be admissible as a business document, created in the course of an occupation under s24 Criminal Justice Act (CJA) 1988 on the basis that Harry is dead, subject to the discretion to exclude under s25. Any such note is unlikely to have been made for the purposes of criminal investigation or proceedings so as to trigger the leave requirement of s26.

PC Ellis's evidence falls into two parts, Leo's own observations and Leo's repetition of Tom's words. The part of Leo's words which describes what he actually saw will probably be admissible as evidence of fact of which direct oral evidence by Leo would be admissible if contained in a document created by the holder of an office (PC Ellis) because of the inability to trace Leo: s23(2)(c) CJA 1988. This would be the effect of s24 CJA 1988 and would be subject to the requirement of leave under s26 because the document was clearly prepared for criminal investigation and possibly contemplated criminal proceedings. If Leo had actually signed PC Ellis's note, this would probably be admissible under s23 as Leo's 'own' document, again, subject to leave under s26 CJA 1988.

Those of Leo's words which repeat what Tom said must be treated in a different way because they are not 'evidence of any fact of which clear oral evidence by him would be admissible'. They are clearly hearsay, and Leo himself could not give evidence of them unless within some established exceptions, so ss23 and 24 will not help. Section 24 might have been of use if Leo himself had received Tom's statement in the course of trade business or as holder of an office as an intermediary, but this seems not to have been the case. Tom's words, as an informal admission, would seem to fall within the extended meaning given to confessions by s82(1) Police and Criminal Evidence Act (PACE) 1984, 'whether made to a person in authority or not ...' and the general exception to the hearsay rule given by the common law to confessions is continued by s76 PACE 1984 which, subject to the exclusory discretions of the court under PACE 1984 and the common law, dictates the matter of admissibility. There seems to be no indication of any matter that would be likely to prevent the confession being admitted under s76(1) in spite of its apparent 'multiple hearsay' nature. The very nature of all informal confessions is that for evidence of them to be available to the court requires a general exception to the hearsay rule. For admissibility of PC Ellis's note under s24, it would have to meet the admissibility requirements of s76 PACE 1984 and s24(3) CJA 1988.

QUESTION SEVEN

Several antique shops had been burgled within a ten mile radius of Marlborough. One day in January DC Pierrepoint visited Quentin, a man with a long record of burglaries, and asked him to come down to the police station to help the police with their inquiries. Quentin agreed. When they arrived, Pierrepoint left Quentin to wait for several hours in a room without light or heating. At the end of that time Quentin asked to see a solicitor. Pierrepoint agreed to find one. Ten minutes later he falsely told Quentin that none was available. He then said that he was ready to start asking questions. Quentin was an alcoholic and had by then been without a drink for so long that he was beginning to feel sick. He wanted to get the interview over as soon as possible and so agreed to do without a solicitor. In the course of the interview he confessed to taking part in one of the burglaries but denied the rest. He told Pierrepoint that he would find the stolen property from the burglary in which he had taken part hidden under the floorboards of an empty house nearby. The police searched the house and the property was found where Quentin had said it would be.

Discuss the evidential issues arising.

University of London LLB Examination
(for External Students) Evidence June 1996 Q7

General Comment

This question requires consideration of PACE 1984 and the Codes of Practice made thereunder, the effect of breaches of the Codes upon confessions and other evidence obtained in consequence and the discretions available to the court to exclude such evidence.

Skeleton Solution

- Discussion of the circumstances of Quentin's presence at the police station.
- Quentin's treatment while at the station.
- Cautions.
- Access to legal advice.
- Section 76 PACE 1984 and the confession.

- Section 78 PACE 1984.
- The stolen property and its value as evidence.

Suggested Solution

Quentin appears to have gone to the police station voluntarily and much will depend upon the way in which he was treated and the extent to which Police and Criminal Evidence Act (PACE) 1984 Code C, for the detention, treatment and questioning of persons by the police, has been complied with. There is no mention of any caution being given to Quentin in accordance with ss10 and 16 of Code C. This should have been given, at the latest, when DC Pierrepoint said that he was ready to commence questioning, according to the guidelines in *R* v *Osbourne*; *R* v *Virtue* (1973). Assuming that Quentin had not been arrested, he should have been told at the time that he was cautioned that he was not under arrest or obliged to stay but that he could have free legal advice and the right to speak by telephone to a solicitor if he so wished: s3.15 Code C.

Leaving Quentin in a room in January without heat or light seems to indicate that Quentin was not told that he was free to leave, but insufficient information is available to know whether he had been induced by trickery to believe that he was being detained. However, Quentin has a long history of involvement with the police and is unlikely to have been mistaken as to his rights. If he was there voluntarily, the failure to provide for his comforts, while reprehensible and unsatisfactory, is not really a breach which might indicate behaviour calculated to sap the will of a person such as would constitute 'oppression' at common law so as to trigger s76(2)(a) PACE 1984 or, indeed, the exclusionary discretions in s78 or s82(3).

DC Pierrepoint's lie concerning the non-availability of a solicitor would be a very serious breach of s58 PACE 1984 and s6 Code C if Quentin was under detention. The question seems to indicate that he was not detained but that the intention was to question him before he had access to legal advice and that this was achieved by trickery. Guidance Note C: 1A describes this as an absolute right to legal advice. If it can be shown that this trickery has been practiced in association with a manipulation of the circumstances surrounding Quentin's treatment which is designed to outflank the protection offered by the Codes, the court may very well take the view that the bad faith of the police affects the fairness of the proceedings as a whole, sufficient to trigger the exclusionary discretions under s78 PACE 1984 as in *R* v *Mason* (1987) and *Matto* v *Wolverhampton Crown Court* (1987).

The effect of Quentin's alcoholic condition on his willingness to make a confession might or might not have been known to DC Pierrepoint. If this condition was known to him, the holding of an interview at such a vulnerable time could well be within 'anything said or done' which could render any confession made by Quentin on those circumstances unreliable, so as to trigger s76(2)(b) PACE 1984. This would put the burden of proving that the confession was not unreliable upon the prosecution, but *R* v *Crampton* (1991) seems to show that DC Pierrepoint would have had to know of Quentin's condition to trigger this consequence. However, the physical and mental state of Quentin at the time is part of the 'circumstances existing at the time' and will be relevant to the matter: *R* v *McGovern* (1991) and *R* v *Silcott*; *R* v *Braithwaite*; *R* v *Raghip* (1991). The confession to one burglary but denials of the rest, a 'mixed' statement, will not prevent this being a confession within s82(1) PACE 1984.

All things considered, it seems likely that there is a strong possibility that this confession will eventually be excluded, but because Quentin has enabled the police to find the stolen goods the question becomes one of what use, evidentually, the prosecution can make of this. The evidence of the finding of the stolen property at the empty house is certainly admissible by the effect of s76(4)(a) PACE 1984, reflecting the common law in *R* v *Warwickshall* (1783), but the fact that it was discovered by means of an inadmissible statement by Quentin cannot be revealed to the court because s76(5) and (6) prevents admissibility into evidence of that link: *Lam Chiming* v *R* (1991).

QUESTION EIGHT

a)   Philip was indicted for possession of cocaine with intent to supply. When the police lawfully searched his house they found, in addition to a quantity of cocaine, £5,650 in cash. The prosecution have relied on this discovery in support of their case. Philip admitted possession of the cocaine but said that it was solely for his personal use. Philip told the police that he always kept a large float of cash handy because he collected modern paintings and believed that artists were often more willing to sell their work for a lower price if they could be paid in cash. Philip repeated this explanation when giving evidence in his own defence.

How should the judge direct the jury in relation to the evidence from both prosecution and defence?

b)   Sam and Toby are indicted for robbery. Both have given evidence denying the offence. Sam's counsel has adduced evidence to show that Sam is a man of previous good character. Toby's counsel has not been able to adduce similar evidence in respect of his client because Toby has three recent convictions for burglary and receiving stolen goods. This information has not, however, emerged during the trial and the jury has heard nothing about Toby's character.

How should the judge direct the jury in the light of this situation?

University of London LLB Examination
(for External Students) Evidence June 1996 Q8

General Comment

Part (a) of the question requires consideration of the proper directions as to the significance of the large sum of money found and the incidence of the legal and evidential burdens of proof and the dangers of drawing improper inferences. Some mention of repeated explanations is called for as well as the question of willingness to be subjected to cross-examination.

Part (b) calls for some exposition of the proper direction to be given where evidence of good character is given in respect of one or more of the co-accused and the danger of drawing improper inferences therefrom, particularly where there are only two co-accused.

Skeleton Solution

a)   • Brief discussion of the incidence and nature of the legal, evidential and tactical burdens involved.

• The rule against previous consistent statements, their admissibility and permissible use in evidence.

• The money as circumstantial evidence.

• Philip's willingness to give evidence.

b) • Admissibility and purpose of evidence of good character.

    • Requirement to direct and judicial discretion.

    • Situation where two co-accused, one good character, one not.

    • Whether good character of one co-accused strengthens case against the other by illustrating relative propensities to commit the offence.

Suggested Solution

a) The judge must direct the jury very clearly here as to the incidence and nature of the legal burdens of proof on the elements of possession and intention. The obvious dangers are of the jury drawing the inferences that the large sum of money places some type of burden of explanation upon Philip that he has failed to discharge adequately or that his explanation of personal use is a lie and he must therefore be guilty. In the absence of some statutory exception or insanity, it will be for the Crown to discharge the legal burden of proof of all the elements to the criminal standard, the 'one golden thread' argument of Lord Sankey in *Woolmington* v *DPP* (1935).

There is no problem about possession as Philip admits to that. The problem lies with proving intention, where Philip has given an explanation for possessing the cocaine and the money. The evidential burden on both of these matters, the so-called 'passing the judge' to make the issue live, falls upon the Crown along with the legal burden and does not shift to Philip. The only way that this could happen would be if there were some presumption of law relating to possession of money, which there is not. There is not even a presumption of fact involved here and, at its highest, any burden placed upon Philip would be a purely tactical one which he has easily discharged by giving a plausible explanation and repeating it under cross-examination. The Crown will still have to rebut his story to the criminal standard of proof to succeed, if this is the only evidence adduced by the defence to explain the money, and the judge must direct the jury on this point.

Philip's previous statement, if admitted in evidence, would be purely narrative, unless it were introduced to rebut an allegation of recent fabrication as in *R* v *Oyesiku* (1971). The judge must direct the jury as to its significance. Inasmuch as it is an admission, it is evidence of its facts, but inasmuch as it is self-serving, it is narrow evidence of fact such as reaction to being first questioned or accused: *R* v *Pearce* (1979). Nevertheless, its main purpose is to show the consistency of Philip's evidence over time.

The judge should direct the jury as to the circumstantial evidence effect of finding the cocaine plus the money at the same place and time but, to avoid unfairness, the judge should direct the jury as to the limited weight to be attached to such evidence. Failure to do this might amount to an appealable non-direction, but the limits are by no means clear as shown in *McGreevy* v *DPP* (1973).

Although there is now a broad discretion as to the directions concerning the proper inferences to be drawn from failure by an accused to testify in his defence under ss35 and 38 Criminal Justice and Public Order Act 1994, there is no positive requirement to comment on a willingness to be subjected to cross-examination. If Philip is otherwise of good character, he will be entitled to a direction as to his credibility and also that it will be relevant to the question of guilt (*R* v *Bryant*; *R* v *Oxley* (1978); *R* v *Vye* (1993)), and this is certain to include comment on the significance of his willingness to testify and be subjected to cross-examination.

b) The danger for the judge here is of directing the jury in a way that will influence them in Sam's favour to the detriment of Toby. The situation is covered quite well by the guidelines given by the House of Lords in *R* v *Aziz* (1995) and Taylor LCJ in *R* v *Vye*. It is now well established that directions should show that evidence of good character is primarily about credibility, but may also shed light on the propensity to commit the crime, as in *R* v *Bryant*; *R* v *Oxley*. The danger to Toby of a direction as to Sam's lack of propensity is obvious. The guidelines in *Vye* indicate that Sam should be given both a limb 1 and a limb 2 direction regardless of the fact that no evidence as to Toby's character is before the court. The guidelines also indicate that the question whether the judge should comment on the lack of character evidence for Toby, or should simply say nothing, is entirely within his own discretion and ought to depend upon what has been made of character evidence within the case.

A matter that might be of significance is if the nature of the evidence is such that either Sam or Toby must have committed the robbery so that to acquit one automatically convicts the other. Some care should be taken here because *Vye* does not seem to deal with the situation where there is good character evidence for one, no character evidence for the other and a 'one or the other' situation. There may be support in *R* v *Levy* (1987) (a good character/bad character case) for an argument that the limb 2 direction on lack of propensity might need to be qualified by a warning against finding a greater likelihood of propensity in Toby, in such a situation where no character evidence, good or bad, is given for Toby.

Old Bailey Press

The Old Bailey Press integrated student library is planned and written to help you at every stage of your studies. Each of our range of Textbooks, Casebooks, Revision WorkBooks and Statutes are all designed to work together and are regularly revised and updated.

We are also able to offer you Suggested Solutions which provide you with past examination questions and solutions for most of the subject areas listed below.

You can buy Old Bailey Press books from your University Bookshop or your local Bookshop, or in case of difficulty, order direct using this form.

Here is the selection of modules covered by our series:

Administrative Law; Commercial Law; Company Law (no Single Paper 1997); Conflict of Laws (no Suggested Solutions Pack); Constitutional Law: The Machinery of Government; Obligations: Contract Law; Conveyancing (no Revision Workbook); Criminology (Sourcebook in place of a Casebook or Revision WorkBook); Criminal Law; English Legal System; Equity and Trusts; Law of The European Union; Evidence; Family Law; Jurisprudence: The Philosophy of Law (Sourcebook in place of a Casebook); Land: The Law of Real Property; Law of International Trade; Legal Skills and System (Textbook only); Public International Law; Revenue Law (no Casebook); Succession: The Law of Wills and Estates; Obligations: The Law of Tort.

Mail order prices:

Textbook £11.95

Casebook £9.95

Revision WorkBook £7.95

Statutes £9.95

Suggested Solutions Pack (1991–1995) £6.95

Single Paper 1996 £3.00

Single Paper 1997 £3.00

To complete your order, please fill in the form below:

Module	Books required	Quantity	Price	Cost
		Postage		
		TOTAL		

For Europe, add 15% postage and packing (£20 maximum).
For the rest of the world, add 40% for airmail.

ORDERING

By telephone to Mail Order at 020 7385 3377, with your credit card to hand.

By fax to 020 7381 3377 (giving your credit card details).

By post to:

Old Bailey Press, 200 Greyhound Road, London W14 9RY.

When ordering by post, please enclose full payment by cheque or banker's draft, or complete the credit card details below.

We aim to despatch your books within 3 working days of receiving your order.

Name

Address

Postcode   Telephone

Total value of order, including postage: £

I enclose a cheque/banker's draft for the above sum, or

charge my   ☐ Access/Mastercard   ☐ Visa   ☐ American Express
Card number

☐☐☐☐ ☐☐☐☐ ☐☐☐☐ ☐☐☐☐

Expiry date   ☐☐☐☐

Signature: ....Date: ....